SCOTS HERALDRY

PLATE I

✠ THE · ROYAL · ARMS ✠

As used officially in Scotland. Designed by A.G.Law Samson, ✠
Heraldic Writer to the Lyon Court, H.M.Register House, Edinburgh.

SCOTS HERALDRY

A PRACTICAL HANDBOOK ON THE HISTORICAL PRINCIPLES AND MODERN APPLICATION OF THE ART AND SCIENCE

BY

SIR THOMAS INNES OF LEARNEY

LORD LYON KING OF ARMS

K.C.V.O., ADVOCATE, F.S.A.SCOT.

SECOND EDITION
REVISED AND ENLARGED

CLEARFIELD

First Edition   1934
Second Edition, revised and enlarged   1956
Reissued   1971

American Publishers
GENEALOGICAL PUBLISHING COMPANY
Baltimore, Maryland

Published in Conjunction with
OLIVER AND BOYD
London and Edinburgh

Library of Congress Catalogue Card Number 74-152173
International Standard Book Number 0-8063-0478-2

Reprinted for
Clearfield Company, Inc. by
Genealogical Publishing Co., Inc.
Baltimore, Maryland
1994, 2000

PREFACE

HERALDRY is a living science, which still enters into our everyday life much more than people might imagine, and Scottish Heraldry particularly so, since its laws are subject to the Courts of the Realm and a growing mass of case-law keeps steadily adapting the science to individual needs and the requirements of modern life. Many requests for information show that a fresh handbook is necessary, dealing with Scottish Heraldry, on lines not attempted in any book at present available to the public and to Scots beyond the seas.

BRECHIN, LORDSHIP OF. Argent, three piles gules.

Sir W. St John Hope made the trenchant comment that—

" Most books on heraldry, in seeking to be complete, so effectively muddle up the few important points with the vast number of things unimportant, that the student is likely to give up in despair. Heraldry, which in itself is surely a gay thing, has been made to resemble grammars and dictionaries of a meaningless jargon."

In the following pages the reader will find the simple and entrancing story of how Scottish Heraldry originated, grew,

and adapted itself to Scottish requirements. The portion
" resembling a grammar or dictionary " is restricted to some
16 pages only, and contains the few essentials necessary for
those who wish to take a practical interest in this simple and
attractive decorative science. I have been at pains to tell
the reader not only about heraldry itself, but exactly how to
obtain authentic arms, or to verify those which come under
his notice, and, equally important, how to *use* heraldry, for
mere knowledge of a science is useless, unless one knows
when, where, and how to apply it. This book is also the
first to include a series of " Lyon Court styles " (form of
writs), a feature of service not only to the legal profession
but to the many Scots who desire to set their arms in order
without incurring the cost of professional assistance in simple
applications for a grant of arms or matriculation by a younger
son or near relative. Where important questions of succession
to arms or supporters arise, counsel must necessarily be
employed, but both lawyer and client will herein find important information nowhere else available.

It is difficult in these days to issue an adequately illustrated
book at a reasonable price, but thanks to the kindness of
those who have lent printers' blocks, the illustrations give
a general survey of Scottish heraldic art throughout the
centuries, and what is equally important, show actual
examples—ancient and modern—by the best architectural
and artistic exponents of the Science.

I commenced the scientific study of heraldry at the age
of fourteen, with the late A. C. Fox-Davies' *Heraldry Explained*. I hope my book may prove as useful in its own
sphere as have the works of Fox-Davies in English heraldry.
Fox-Davies did perhaps more than any other writer to
bring heraldry as a legal and scientific subject before the
modern public. As regards Scottish heraldry, however, he
unfortunately swallowed (and publicised) the " heir-male "

doctrines of Interim Lyon-Depute Tait (for the promulga-
tion of which Tait was dismissed by Lord Kinnoull) and in
the 1st edition of this book (though not subscribing to
either Tait or Davies) a measure of deference was accorded
to Fox-Davies' "simple" but misguided exposition of
armorial succession; this has now been fully corrected,
according to the doctrines of Sir George Mackenzie of
Rosehaugh and the other Scottish authorities, and the Law
of Name as now laid down.

During the many years in which I have studied Scottish
heraldry and history, I have been specially grateful for the
unceasing kindness of the late Lord Lyon Sir Francis J.
Grant, K.C.V.O., LL.D., who was ever ready to assist me
from his vast store of genealogical and heraldic knowledge—
the more invaluable since he was the doyen of all H.M.
Officers of Arms. Under his rule I spent many happy years
as Herald and Pursuivant. I am also grateful to Lord Lyons
Sir James Balfour Paul, K.C.V.O., and George Swinton,
under whom I enjoyed such opportunities for information
and guidance, not least in matters of Scottish heraldic art,
in which they both took so deep an interest. To Sheriff
Macphail, and J. H. Stevenson, K.C., Marchmont Herald,
I am indebted for much genealogical and heraldic information of a legal and historical nature, gathered during their
long experience as peerage and heraldic counsel; to the late
A. G. L. Samson, Heraldic Painter to the Lyon Court, for
the manner in which he executed a number of the illustrations; and to Graham Johnston, from whom I learnt much
regarding the technique of heraldic art, and a number of
whose book-plates I have been permitted to reproduce.
Finally, without the help of my sister, Helen C. Innes of
Cromey, who has typed and retyped for me so many heraldic
and genealogical papers, neither this work nor several others
could have attained such accuracy of detail; whilst Miss

A 2

Anne E. Simson (now Mrs. Nimmo), Lord Lyon's Secretary, has retyped and checked the revised text and many additions which make this 2nd edition a comprehensive and up-to-date work of heraldic legal reference. If there seems to be a large number of footnotes, it should be recollected that this is a comparatively short book, and though sufficient in itself for all practical purposes, it also places in the reader's hands references to an enormous amount of detailed information upon particular points which may from time to time interest him.

In short, there is more heraldry and better heraldry in use in Britain to-day than there has been at any previous period. In Scotland, under our excellent armorial legislation, our scientific national heraldry still leads the world. Nor is heraldry confined to Europe ; the need for it and the use of it is steadily extending and has spread to the modern states of both the old world and the new. As a system both of decoration and of identification which appeals to the best and deepest sentiments of human nature, heraldry is a science not of the past but of the present and of the future.

THOMAS INNES OF LEARNEY
Lord Lyon King of Arms

LEARNEY
ABERDEENSHIRE
APRIL 1955

ACKNOWLEDGMENTS

THE grateful thanks of the Author are due to those who have in various ways assisted the illustration of the book, namely :—For blocks lent : Sir William Fraser's Trustees, Initial letters from *Scots Peerage* and Figures 81, 83, and 92 ; Society of Antiquaries of Scotland, VI, VIIIa, IX, X, XI, XIIb, XXXIV, XXXV, XXXVI, XXXVIIa, XXXIX, and Figures 43-46, 48, 55, 58, 66, 73, 78, 85-87 ; Burke's *Peerage*, Figures 7, 55, 57, 62, 63, 68, 77 ; *Landed Gentry*, Figures 11, 47, 50, 56 ; Stewart of Inchmahome, Plate XVII, and Figures 13, 15, 17, 19, 39-41, 75, 100-103 ; T. C. and E. C. Jack, Figures 25, 38, 51-54, 71, 73, 74, 80 ; Colonel Balfour Paul, Marchmont Herald, Figures 22, 24, 59-61 ; *Daily Express*, Figures 64 and 105 ; H. B. Mackintosh, M.B.E., Figure 65 ; C. A. H. Franklyn and John Murray, Figure 79 ; A. G. L. Samson, Plate I ; Deeside Field Club, Plate VII ; Sir G. Macpherson-Grant of Ballindalloch, G. R. Francis and John Murray, Plate VIIIb ; The Chisholm, Plate XXIX ; J. Maclehose, LL.D., Plate XL ; The Mackintosh, Plates XXVIII and XLVI ; Reps. of R. C. Nesbitt, Plates XIX and XXX ; Macpherson of Crogga, Plate XVIII ; Jenners Ltd., Plate XLV ; H. W. Meikle, C.B.E., Plate XLIV ; a number of these having lent blocks for illustrations. For permission to copy illustrations : Debrett's *Peerage*, Figure 16 ; H. B. Coppinger, Figure 18 ; Miss Hamilton of Skene, Figure 94 ; J. H. Stevenson, K.C., Marchmont Herald, Plate II ; J. G. Mackintosh, Muchalls Castle, Plate XII ; Ex-Lord Lyon Swinton, Plate XLIII ;

Aberdeen Book Lover, D. Wyllie & Sons, Aberdeen, Plate xxxviii ; The Bank of Scotland, Figure 106 ; E. B. Livingston, Plates xxvi, xxvii, xxxi, from *The Livingston Book*.

CONTENTS

CONTENTS

CONTENTS xiii

ILLUSTRATIONS

FULL-PAGE PLATES

CONTENTS

ILLUSTRATIONS

FULL-PAGE PLATES

xv

ILLUSTRATIONS

ILLUSTRATIONS

ILLUSTRATIONS

TEXT FIGURES

B   xxi

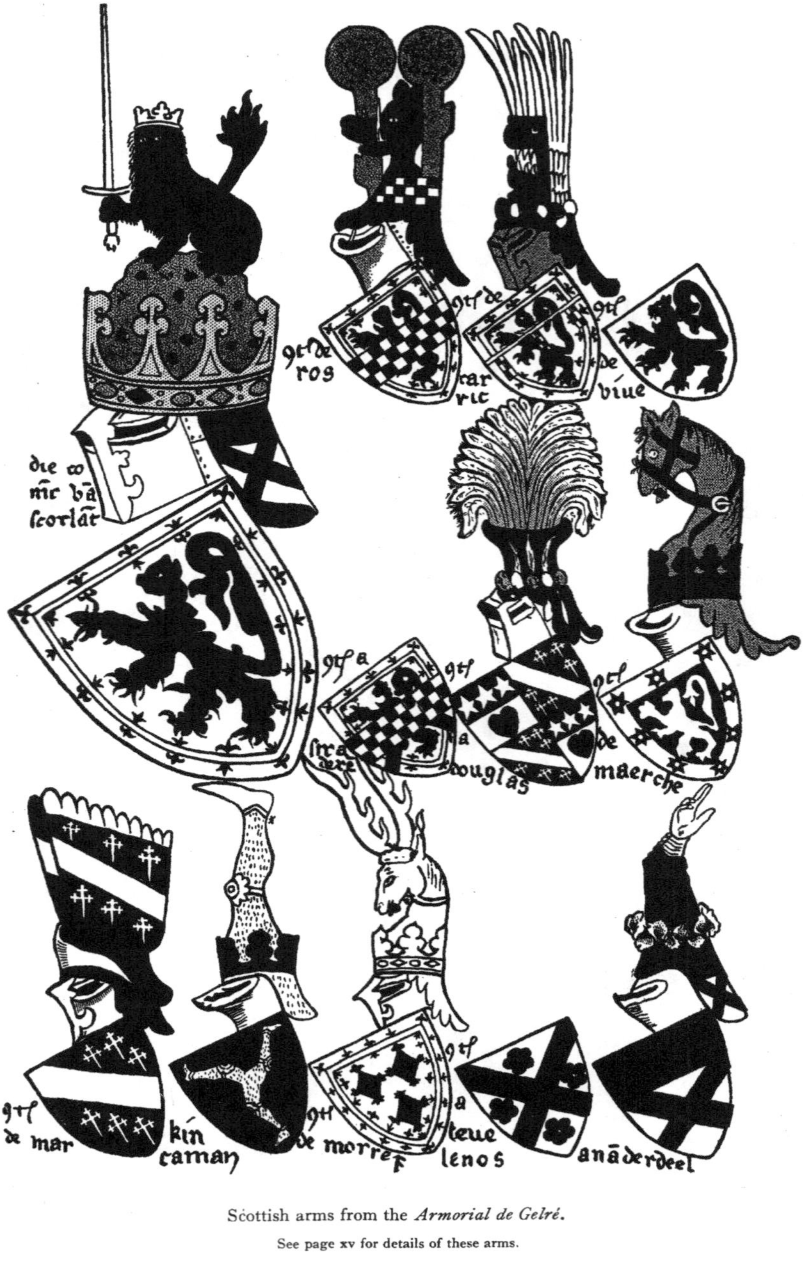

PLATE II

Scottish arms from the *Armorial de Gelré*.

See page xv for details of these arms.

CHAPTER I

SCOTTISH HERALDRY AND THE INFLUENCE OF THE CLAN SYSTEM

COTS heraldry has long been famous, on account not only of its antiquity but also of its simplicity, its scientific accuracy, and the manner in which it has preserved the high standard of mediaeval armory during periods when both the heraldic principles and the heraldic art of other countries suffered from various forms of decadence. The Scottish nation, evolving as it has from a background of Celtic culture in which clanship (with its bonds of kinship, chieftainship, chiefship, and intense local land love) forms the basis of a tribal organisation of society, was pre-eminently ground in which the Noble Science should flourish, whilst the litigious and analytical disposition of the mediaeval Scot led to the development of armory in Scotland, not merely as a feature of military or spectacular display, but also as a branch of Civil Law upon which the structure of Scots Law itself was reared, and as a highly specialised branch of the law of heritable property.

EARL OF FINDLATER. Quarterly: 1st and 4th, argent, a lion passant guardant gules, imperially crowned or (*Ogilvie*); 2nd and 3rd, argent, a cross engrailed sable (*Sinclair of Deskford*).

The Celtic social system has indeed had a vital influence upon the popularity of Scots heraldry, because, unlike any other country, Scotland, owing to its clan organisation, has enjoyed a complete absence of class distinctions or " class-consciousness ", and a corresponding popularity—indeed, whole-hearted veneration—for everything pertaining to rank and lineage, honours, dignities, and ensigns-armorial. In most countries there has been a distinct cleavage between noble and churl. Rank and heraldry were confined to the former, and often viewed with envy or contempt by the " lower classes ". In a country such as Scotland, where the fundamental theory underlying clanship (and the same principle applies to the great Lowland " houses ") is that every member springs from the founder of the clan [1] and that the chief, the chieftains, the *duine-uasal* (*i.e.* those who actually trace their descent to the chiefly line), and the body of the clan, are all of the same kin, obviously " class feeling " could not exist.[2]

In Scotland no servile peasantry cringed beneath the yoke of alien overlords,[3] nor did our burghers feel themselves despised or scorned.[4] " The good old Scots custom drew no snobbish distinction between the burgess and the country gentleman, and clannish ties of relationship ran through every rank of society, uniting its folk in a homely heartwarm way that the abstract tenets of democracy can never achieve." [5]

Chiefs and Lairds *reigned* [6] in their ancestral estates like Princes, their castle forming a little court, of which the

[1] Sir James Balfour Paul, *Heraldry in Relation to Scottish History and Art*, p. 44 ; Acts, iii, 466 ; Innes of Learney, *Tartans of the Clans and Families of Scotland*, 1938, pp. 18, 25, 26, 36.

[2] I. F. Grant, *Social and Economic Development of Scotland*, pp. 32, 190, 483, 506, 516, 559 ; E. Crawford, *Lives of the Lindsays*, i, 117 ; A. Mure Mackenzie, *Scotland in Modern Times*, p. 41.

[3] Hume Brown, *Scotland before 1700*, p. xii.   [4] *Ibid.*, pp. 178-9.

[5] I. F. Grant, *In the Tracks of Montrose*, p. 208.

[6] *Ibid.*, pp. 4, 144, 267, and cf. E. Burt's *Letters*, 1876, p. 167.

ceremonial reflected in miniature that of Falkland and Holy-roodhouse.[1] The chieftain's turreted keep with its carved escutcheons and emblazoned banner was to each surrounding cottage the embodied grandeur of that pride of race which burned as strongly beneath the ploughman's low-thatched roof as in the lofty baronial hall itself. In a similar manner the twelfth-century tribo-feudalism of olden France was very popular.[2] The " much-honoured " laird, or chief, whose armorial panoply and fluttering pennon were the emblems of ancestral fame beloved by all, was also the " traist cousin " at whose signal clansmen would gather, in family council or for defence of the *duthus*, called to his side by kinship, not gold. In the long evenings round the cottar's peat fires, the tales of Scotland's struggle, of " old unhappy far-off things ", of Earls and Knights and Laidies faire, have a different ring when those around are listening, not to legends of some unkent " high society ", but to the stirring annals of their own beloved clan.[3]

In Scotland not only heraldry and genealogy, but honours and titles, enjoyed much wider distribution than in any other country. At the time of the Union in 1707, Scotland, with a population of one and a quarter million, had 154 peers (one peer to 8000 people), whilst England, with five and a half million, had only 164 (one peer to 32,000 people). Outside its peerage, England's titled aristocracy consisted of only a few Baronets and Knights, but in Scotland the whole terri-torial " Baronage ", as well as Clan-Chiefs, and even lesser landed proprietors, all habitually used picturesque designa-tions which are founded on Scots law and which the Crown and courts recognise as " titles ". Of these there were upwards

---

[1] Lady Strachey, *Memoirs of a Highland Lady*, 1928 ed., pp. 27, 186.
[2] F. Funk Brentano, *Old Régime in France*, pp. 6, 7, 75.
[3] D. Stewart of Garth, *Sketches of the Highlanders*, 1825, pp. 50, 97-9. In old Scottish families the children were taught their genealogy on Sunday mornings.

of 10,000, who, along with their wives and heirs, used these styles, so that in Scotland approximately *one out of every forty-five people* in the country was either of, or else immediately related to, some such " house ". More than half the population considered themselves part of the Scottish aristocracy. Such an unprecedented situation goes far to explain the pride of birth and ancestry so characteristic of Scotland, and which Bishop Leslie in the sixteenth century observes was shared " by the haill people, nocht only the nobilitie ".

In these circumstances, the subject of honours and dignities, pedigrees and heraldry, which in other countries has become a source of embarrassment or ill-feeling, consequently deprecated as a subject of discussion in mixed society, is—and always has been—in Scotland the natural topic of conversation amongst all ranks, and " proud as a Scot " has become a proverb on the Continent. This love of pedigree and lineage, pageantry and colour, this " inordinate pleasure in noble birth "—shared in by all—is uniformly noticed by early commentators and historians.[1] Like the French seigneurs who " loved to read over and over again the acts and heroic deeds of [their ancestors] and to study their genealogical tree ", whereof " he boasts in his drawing-room and even in his kitchen " [2]—naturally, since the maids were regarded as part of the *familia* [3]—travellers observed of the Scottish Chieftain that " the great antiquity of his family and the heroic actions of his ancestors . . . is the inexhaustible theme of his conversation ".[4] The pinnacle of importance which the science of genealogy and heraldry

[1] Hume Brown, *Scotland before 1700*, pp. xii, 56, 167 ; E. Crawford, *Lives of the Lindsays*, p. 119 ; D. Stewart of Garth, *Sketches of the Highlanders*, 1825, pp. 50, 53, 90.
[2] F. Funk Brentano, *Old Régime in France*, pp. 84, 97.
[3] *Ibid.*, p. 5 ; *Proc. of Soc. of Antiquaries of Scot.*, lxxix, 123.
[4] E. Burt, *Letters*, No. xxv, p. 167.

occupies in Scottish history cannot be better indicated than from Scotland's principal herald—the Lord Lyon King of Arms—being accorded the rank of a Privy Councillor,[1] an Officer of State,[2] and a Minister of the Crown,[3] with a place of honour in the Parliament of Scotland.[4] Indeed, maintenance of the scientific simplicity and statutory regulation of Scottish Armory has necessarily called for a specially exacting standard of departmental administration.

[1] Great Seal, v, 1990.

[2] *Lord Lyon* v. *Usher of the White Rod* (Privy Council), 1685.

[3] *Halsbury's Laws of England* (Hailsham ed.), xxv, 69, par. 163.

[4] Stevenson, *Heraldry in Scotland*, ii, 449; *Juridical Review*, xliv (June 1932), 117.

CHAPTER II

THE HERALDIC EXECUTIVE IN SCOTLAND

HE chief of Scotland's heraldic and genealogical executive is the Lord Lyon King of Arms, who, unlike the English Kings of Arms, is not an official within the department of the Earl Marshal, but himself a great officer who, in Scotland, is responsible for many important functions which in England are shared between the Earl Marshal and other departments. The incorporation of the English College of Arms in 1483 led to the separation of the English Officers of Arms from the domestic staff of the Household [1] in such a manner

LORD LYON KING OF ARMS. Argent, a lion sejant ful-faced gules, holding in his dexter paw a thistle slipped vert and in the sinister a shield of the 2nd; on a chief azure a saltire of the 1st.

as never befell the Scottish heralds, who have remained the King's " familiar daylie servitors ",[2] and still attend as such on the Lord High Commissioner at Holyroodhouse.

In Scotland [3] the Lord Lyon King of Arms is responsible

[1] Dallaway, *Heraldic Inquiries*, p. 135.

[2] *Liber Curiarum* of Sir Robert Forman of Luthrie (H.M. Register House). A style mediaevally applied to all, even great, officers of the Crown.

[3] Lyon Court Records; Denmiln MSS. of Lord Lyon Balfour of Kinnaird, Nat. Lib.; cf. Sir Neville Wilkinson, *To All and Singular*, p. 198; *Official Programme of the Opening of the Parliament of Northern Ireland.*

THE HERALDIC EXECUTIVE IN SCOTLAND 7

for the preparation, conduct, and record of State, Royal and Public ceremonial.[1] In Scotland he is the King's " Supreme Officer of Honour ",[2] and if he had no family estate was *styled* of his official fief —Luthrie or Rathillet.

THE LORD LYON KING OF ARMS

The Lord Lyon King of Arms holds his office of " King of His Maist Excellent Majesties Armes ",[3] as an immediate fief of the Crown, and as one of the Officers of State. These were formerly classed in two categories : " Officers of the Crown " and " Officers of the Kingdom ".[4] The Lord Lyon has the specialty of being "both an Officer of the Crown and of the Kingdom",[5] and of him it has been said : "No herald in Europe exercised such powers of jurisdiction, was vested with such high dignity, or possessed so high a rank. In his armorial jurisdiction, Lyon stands in the place of the King." [6]

The Lord Lyon is one of the five high officers who are *virtute officii* the King's Lieutenants.[7] In the fifteenth and sixteenth centuries he was also *virtute officii* a Privy Councillor,[8] and as the French *Juge d'Armes* was, and Lyon still remains in matters armorial, genealogical, and ceremonial,

[1] *Encyclopaedia of the Laws of Scotland*, s.v. Lyon King of Arms, vol. ix, par. 774, Precedence, vol. xii, par. 39 ; *Royal College of Surgeons* v. *Royal College of Physicians*, 1911 Session Cases, 1054 ; Sir James Balfour of Kinnaird's *Heraldic Tracts* ; *Juridical Review*, xliv, 87.

[2] Nisbet, *System of Heraldry*, 1742, vol. ii, pt. iv, p. 172.

[3] Sir Jerome Lindsay of Annatlands Commission, 8 August 1620, *Heraldry in Scotland*, p. 452.

[4] Sir G. Mackenzie, *Works*, ii, 537.

[5] *Lord Lyon* v. *Usher*, 1685, Lyon Court Precedency Book, f. 40 ; *Privy Council*, 3rd ser., vii, 163, 167, 170.

[6] Report by Lyon-Depute Boswell (1796), Lyon Office Records.

[7] Denmiln MSS. 33-4-7, Nat. Lib.

[8] Rymour, *Foedera*, xii, 230 ; Calendar of Documents relative to Scotland, iv, 101-5 ; Great Seal, v, 1990, where the King styles the Lord Lyon " Our Councillor ".

Conseiller du Roi and this he has in appropriate circumstances continued to be.[1] From this, The Lord Lyon, like the
Lord Provost of Edinburgh, derives the prefix " Right
Honourable ", which has been borne since 1554,[2] whilst his
person is so sacred that to strike or deforce him is high
treason.[3] According to Scots custom, he was invariably
knighted on appointment, and before his State coronation.[4]
The Lord Lyon is now knighted at Holyroodhouse on appointment, when the Sovereign invests him in office by delivery
of the ancient Lyon Baton (*Court Circular*, 2 July 1946).

The title " Lord Lyon ", indicating a member of
the Scottish Government,[5] appears (as observed by Sir
Francis Grant[6]) indeed earlier than in the "*Lyndsay II*"
ms.[7] 1598–99; and such prefix has been held by all
judges with jurisdiction over all Scotland.[8] These titles[9]—
ceremoniously used in the Royal Court of Scotland, in
distinguishing the Great Officers—sometimes puzzle laymen,

[1] *Scott of Thirlestane*, 18 Dec. 1700 (*Heraldry in Scotland*, 269); *Strathmore*,
21 Dec. 1938, Lyon Reg. xxxiii, 46; in operative matters advice of the Sec. of
State follows (or of ministry, *cf.* tressure warrant of 1719, W. Fraser, *Sutherland
Book*, i, 38); *Lundin of Lundin*, 1679 (Nisbet, *Heralday*, i, 66).

[2] Burgh Court of Haddington, Riddell MSS., li, Sig. Lib. and Lyon Court
Books ; Statute 1672, cap. 74, Acts, viii, 123 ; *Juridical Review*, xliv, 206. Used
in Lyon Court writs, *e.g.* p. 70, it is the address in every extant petition prior to
1796, so not attributable to the Earls of Kinnoull.

[3] Acts, ii, 2 ; Privy Seal, ii, 1992.

[4] Green's *Encyclopaedia of the Laws of Scotland*, ix, 333, par. 770 ; Lyon
Court Precedency Book and *Arnott's History of Edinburgh*, App. X. The
knighthood, even when Lyon was a Baronet, is the seventh item in the ceremony,
coming before the actual investiture.

[5] See *Juridical Review*, September 1932, " The Style and Title of ' Lord
Lyon King of Arms ' ". The title " Lord " prefixed to the High Officers of Scot-
land is probably a rendering of the Gaelic prefix " Ard " equal to " High ", while
Messire was the sixteenth-century equivalent (Mackenzie, *Works*, ii, 541).

[6] Scot. Rec. Soc. *Court of the Lord Lyon*, p. ii (1514).

[7] MSS. Sir David Lindsay of the Mount *secundus*, Earl of Crawford's Lib.

[8] *Cf.* The Lord High Admiral.

[9] The Lord Lyon as a Great Officer uses the first person *singular*, but *Lyon
King of Arms* puts *We, Us, Our*, and has to be received " regally " (*e.g.* Scott,
Marmion, IV, 159), so except on certain special occasions it is as *Lord Lyon* that
Lyon appears and is addressed.

PLATE III

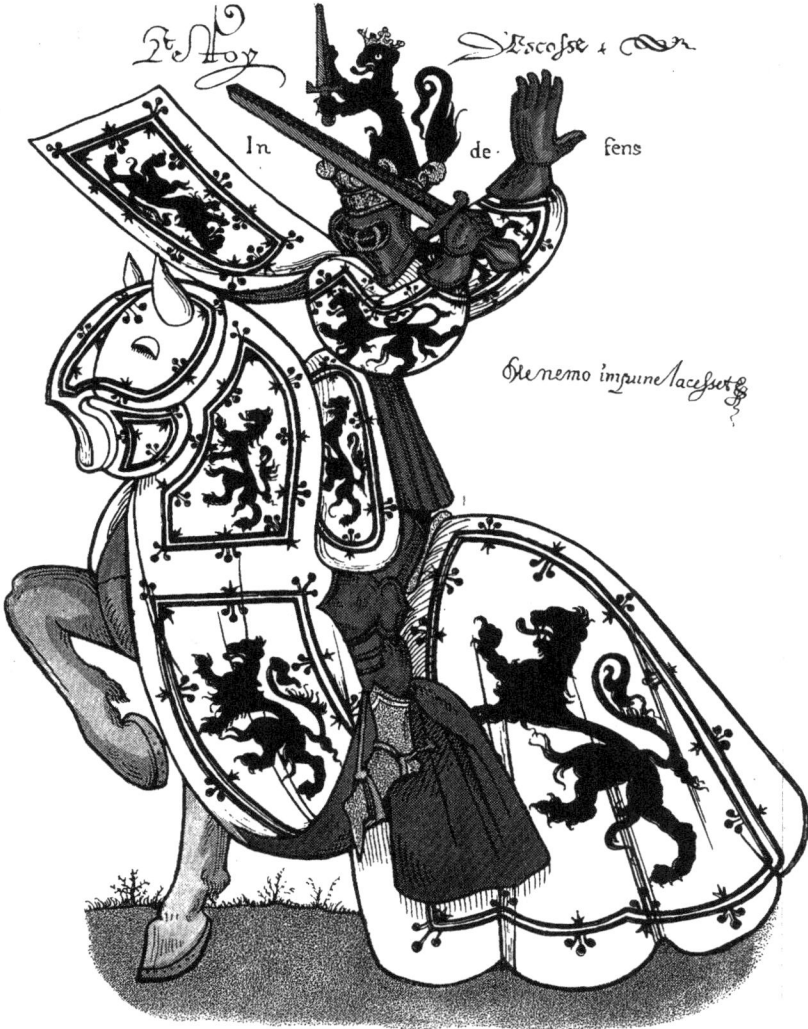

THE KING OF SCOTS.

Fifteenth-century armour, tabard and horse trappings. From the *Armorial de l' Europe de la Toison d'Or*, MSS 4790, Bibliothèque de l'Arsenal, Paris.

because the Crown, though it describes, *e.g. Nostri Domini Leonis Regis Armorum*,[1] does not address its servants [2] by these titles (which they enjoy amongst the " rights and privileges " of their offices), although everybody else is required to do so—that is, in a Royal Writ, the King addresses the Lord Advocate " Our Advocate " and the Lord Lyon " Our Lyon King of Arms ". In the case of the Lord Lyon,[3] however, the title was formally recognised in Parliament on 4 June 1663,[4] and again a few years later the " style, title, liberties, preheminencies, jurisdiction, and casualties, of old used and wont, or which did evir pertain to the said Office at any time bygone ", were ratified by the Scottish Parliament in 1672,[5] whilst the " Dignities " belonging to the Lyon were again confirmed by Statute 30 & 31 Vict., cap. 17, sec. 1. Much of the Lord Lyon's peculiar importance in Scotland is due to his incorporating the pre-heraldic Celtic office of High Sennachie of the Royal Line of Scotland,[6] and in this capacity, as guardian and preserver of the Royal Pedigree and Family Records, his certificate was requisite for the coronation of each Scottish King—whose genealogy it was his duty at each coronation as " Official Inaugurator " [7] to declaim in Gaelic [8]—latterly for seven generations, but

[1] Great Seal Commission, 26 May 1796; " Our Lord Lyon King of Arms "; K.C.V.O. Warrant, 13 June 1946.

[2] Amongst others, Lord Justice Clerk, Lord Clerk Register, Lord Advocate, etc.

[3] " The Style and Title of ' Lord Lyon King of Arms ' ", *Juridical Review*, vol. xliv (September 1932). See Act of Sed. following Court of Session Act, 1933; Act of Sed. (*Stat. Instr.*) No. 345, 3 March 1949; Secretary of State in petition *Fire Service Scotland*, 14 Dec. 1949, Lyon Register, xxxvii, 126.

[4] Acts, vii, 458.

[5] Statute 1672, cap. 74; Acts, fol. ed., viii. 123.

[6] *Sources and Literature of the Law of Scotland* (Stair Soc.), *s.v.* Heraldic Law, pp. 381-2.

[7] P. W. Joyce, *Social Life in Ancient Ireland*, pp. 47, 136, 460; *Sources and Literature of the Law of Scotland* (Stair Soc.), pp. 381-3.

[8] Nigel MacNeill, LL.D., *Literature of the Highlanders* (J. M. Campbell, Ed.), 228, gives part of the genealogy as declaimed at the coronation of Malcolm III, which the Lord Lyon claimed to do, if required, at the 1953 coronation.

originally through all the Scottish Kings back to Fergus Mor MacErc, founder of the Royal Line.[1] To Lyon has been conveyed the whole of the Crown's jurisdiction in armorial matters, as pertaining to his sphere of duty,[2] *i.e.* to his functions as High Sennachie, the Heraldic " Visitations " being analogous to the Bardic *cuairt*,[3] and in terms of the statutes, no grant of arms is effective except when made by him.[4] Since at any rate 1542, the King of Scots has never himself granted a coat of arms or augmentation, the invariable practice being a Royal Warrant ordering " Our Lyon " to " grant and give " the specified honour.[5] This ensures that all grants should go through the official channel, thereby saving the Crown from the possibility of making a grant which might conflict with some previous exercise of the prerogative. It will be noticed, however, that a Royal Warrant does not become effective until presented in Lyon Court, so that the Lord Lyon may act upon it and record the arms in terms of the statutes. Not only has the Lord Lyon jurisdiction to enforce the Laws of Arms, but if " the samine is deficient ", he may " prescryve " new heraldic rules,[6]

[1] Lindsay of Pitscottie's *Cronikilis*, ii, 126; *Privy Council*, 2nd ser., ii, 393; *Sources and Literature*, etc. (*supra*), p. 382. The late Marquis of Bute (*Four Scottish Coronations*) did not realise that the " ancient Highland bard ", clad in a crimson robe, who functioned at the coronation of Alexander III, was the Lyon, performing pre-heraldic functions, and that both the robe and many of the Celtic Sennachie's duties have continued with Lyon until modern times. (For robe see Plate V.)

[2] Official Declaration by Lord Lyon Sir Charles Erskine of Cambo, 14 December 1698; *Juridical Review*, September 1940, p. 194, n. 1.

[3] *Sources and Literature of the Law of Scotland* (Stair Soc.), p. 382; A. Wagner, *Heralds and Heraldry*, p. 3.

[4] 1672, cap. 47; *Macdonell* v. *Macdonald*, 1826, 4 Shaw & Dunlop 371.

[5] *Scott of Thirlestane*, 1542; Nisbet, *System of Heraldry*, i, 98; Mark Napier, *History of the Partition of Lennox*, p. 223; *Keith of Craig*, 10 July 1769; Lyon Register, i, 174; *Earl of Sutherland*, 24 November 1719; Sir W. Fraser, *Sutherland Book*, i, 38, 359; iii, 220; *Strathmore*, Lyon Register, xxxiii, 46.

[6] An early instance of a power which is so often conferred on other Ministers of the Crown, and, in England, by the Earl Marshal on heraldic matters.

which have the force of Law.[1] The Lord Lyon's other
official duties include jurisdiction in questions of " Name
and Change of Name " in Scotland (see p. 198) ; decisions
on questions of family representation. Disputes over Chiefship of a " noble and armigerous family " and " Chiefship
of Name and Arms " were in 1937 expressly adjudged competent before Lyon [2] and accordingly remitted to Lyon.
Moreover, Sir George Mackenzie has laid down that the
Chief of a Family and *Head of a Clan* are synonymous,[3] and
the evidence in the *Maclean of Ardgour* proof, 1938, cor-
roborated this.[4] Both Lords Shaw and Dunedin [5] identify
chiefship of a clan with right to the undifferenced arms.
Lyon Court is accordingly the judicature which can, and
does, adjudicate upon Chiefship of Clans [6]—and award the
" property " (the arms), possession of which is synonymous
with Clan-Chiefship—and upon Pedigrees and Genealogies,
conducting and executing of Royal Proclamations, Baptisms,[7]
State and public ceremonial of all descriptions in Scotland—
which it is Lyon's exclusive privilege to prepare [8]—whilst

[1] *Privy Council*, 2nd ser., iii, 594; J. H. Stevenson, *Heraldry in Scotland*,
p. 452 ; F. Adam and Innes of Learney, *Clans, Septs, and Regiments of the Scottish
Highlands*, 4th ed., 1952, p. 488.
[2] 1941 Session Cases, pp. 616, 635, 654.   [3] *Works*, ii, 618.
[4] *Clans, Septs, and Regiments of the Scottish Highlands*, 4th ed., Appx. xxxix.
[5] *Ibid.*, p. 190; 1922 Session Cases (H.L.), pp. 42, 47.
[6] *Chiefship of Clan Chattan*, Burnett's MSS., p. 24; *Chiefship of Clan Allan*,
1777 ; Register of Genealogies, i, 229; Lyon Register, i, 575; *Macgregor of
Macgregor*, 1795, Lyon Register, i, 529; Register of Genealogies, iii, 2 ; *Chiefship
of Maclachlan*, 3 July 1946, Lyon Register, xxxv, 72; *Chiefship of Clan Rose*,
10 November 1946, *ibid.*, xxxvi, 9; *Chiefship of Clan Chattan*, 9 April 1947,
ibid., xxxvi, 36; *Chiefship of Clan Mackintosh*, 9 April 1947, *ibid.*, xxxvi, 46;
Chiefship of Clan Donald, 7 May 1947, *ibid.*, xxxvi, 44.
[7] *Clans, Septs, and Regiments of the Scottish Highlands*, 4th ed. 1952, p. 190 ;
Tartans of the Clans and Families of Scotland, 3rd ed., W. & A. K. Johnston,
pp. 28, 50.
[8] Lyon Office Precedency Book, 10 August 1822, when on the occasion of
George IV's visit, a programme submitted by Usher of the White Rod was rescinded
on a complaint by Lord Lyon the Earl of Kinnoull. Order for state progress on
24 June 1953, *Edinburgh Gazette*, 23 June 1953.

to him is committed the marshalling of State processions and
public solemnities of all descriptions.[1] He is, in numerous
matters relating to Scottish Honours and ceremonial, the
Official Adviser of the Secretary of State for Scotland,[2] and
" the only official connected with the law who can trace his
descent from the patriarchal and tribal form of Society " of
Celtic Scotland.[3] Finally, as Controller of Her Majesty's
Messengers at Arms, the Lord Lyon is the head of the whole
Executive Department of the Law of Scotland.[4]

THE HERALDS AND PURSUIVANTS OF SCOTLAND

There are six of His Majesty's Officers of Arms under
the Lord Lyon [5]—three heralds, Albany, Marchmont, and
Rothesay, and three pursuivants, Carrick, Kintyre, and
Unicorn. They are members of the Scottish Royal Household, formerly in daily attendance at the Palace,[6] and in that
capacity performed many ceremonial duties in Scotland, as
they still do on various State occasions and in connection
with Scottish public life. The heralds and pursuivants have
also many statutory duties in connection with Scottish
heraldry,[7] and may act as judges of first instance in Genealogy

  [1] *Royal College of Surgeons* v. *Royal College of Physicians*, 1911 Session Cases,
1059; *Juridical Review*, xliv, 96. In Scotland the Lord Lyon (not the Earl
Marshal) issues any general mourning order (*Precedency Book*, p. 272).
  [2] Green's *Encyclopaedia of the Laws of Scotland*, s.v. Precedency, vol. xii,
par. 40.
  [3] J. Cameron, *Celtic Law*, p. 197 ; *Encyclopaedia of the Laws of Scotland*, s.v.
Precedency, vol. xii, par. 40 ; *Sources and Literature of the Law of Scotland*, p. 353.
  [4] G. Seton, *Law and Practice of Heraldry in Scotland*, p. 41.
  [5] Prior to the Statute 16 & 17 Vict., cap. 17, there were twelve established
officers. Two Pursuivants Extraordinary (Falkland and Linlithgow) are put in
commission when required, under Sec. I of the Act, per Privy Council 1569, vol. i,
p. 655 ; *Edinburgh Gazette*, 23 June 1953.
  [6] *Liber Curiarum et processus* of Sir Robert Forman of Luthrie, and *Lord
High Treasurer's Accounts* at large.
  [7] Statute 1592, cap. 125 ; *Acts*, iii, 554 ; *Heraldry in Scotland*, pp. 46, 52, 421.

PLATE IV

Scottish Heralds on horseback : from the plates of the Riding of Parliament of Scotland, 1685. (*Juridical Review*, June 1932, p. 87.)

PLATE V

Lord Lyon King of Arms, Sir Alexander Erskine of Cambo, Baronet, riding in his robe of state—crimson velvet, bordered of gold lace, and ermine cape—(from the plates of the Riding of the Parliament of Scotland, 1685). (*Juridical Review*, June 1932, p. 87; and *Proc. Soc. of Antiquaries of Scotland*, s.v. Robes of the Feudal Baronage, &c., Vol. 79, p. 111, Plate XIII.)

(Narrative of Evidence by Lord Lyon Sir Charles Erskine of Cambo, in Lyon Office). They may be consulted about heraldry and genealogy in a professional capacity like an advocate or law agent, by members of the public, and may appear for their clients before the Lyon Court,[1] or other nobiliary Courts, and before the English Court of Chivalry.[2] Usually some of them are members of the Scots Bar. Cumming of Inverallochy, Marchmont Herald at the commencement of the sixteenth century, was frequently procurator before the Lords.[3] They wear a special variety of the uniform of the Royal Household, and over it His Majesty's tabard, like the Lord Lyon's, which differs, however, in being of velvet and gold. They have also a blue service uniform, worn on service occasions, and in 1746 Lord Lyon Brodie rode throughout the campaign which ended at Culloden, in attendance, as Lord Lyon, on the G.O.C.-in-C. the Duke of Cumberland.

THE COURT OF THE LORD LYON

The Lord Lyon is not only a Minister of the Crown[4] but also a Judge of the Realm; nowadays it is perhaps in this capacity that he comes most in contact with the public, for almost all Scottish heraldic business is conducted on judicial lines, through the machinery of the Court of the Lord Lyon, which exercises both a civil and a penal jurisdiction under the old Common Law of Scotland[5] as well as sundry Acts of

[1] 1941 Session Cases, p. 613.
[2] Letter from Garter Howard, *Juridical Review*, 1943, p. 32.
[3] Illustrated in *Scottish Field*, January 1950, p. 39. It existed from before 30 & 31 Vict., cap. 17.
[4] Green's *Encyclopaedia of the Laws of Scotland*, s.v. Lyon King of Arms, pars. 768, 774; *Halsbury's Laws of England* (Hailsham ed.), xxv, 63, par. 163.
[5] *Macrae's Trustees* v. *Lord Lyon King of Arms*, 4 June 1926, 1927, Scots Law Times, 285; Parl. Debates (Lords), 28 June 1927, 5th ser., vol. 67, col. 1094.

C

Parliament. Scotland and Spain are probably the only
countries where a court of heraldry and genealogy still exists
in daily operation, before which lawyers plead in wig and
gown, though, thanks to the courtesy and interest shown by
the Lord Lyon and his officers, most of the business of the
ordinary applicant is settled without even the need for legal
assistance. The Court of the Lord Lyon indeed reflects, not
the curt severity of the Police Court or the Magisterial
Bench, but rather the stately benevolence of distant days
when our ancient Scottish laws were administered upon the
" moot hill " of some old barony or thaneage. The statutes
drawn up by the skilful Scottish statesmen of the sixteenth and
seventeenth centuries function as smoothly and efficiently
to-day—and serve the lieges as effectively—as they did in
the Middle Ages. The Court of the Lord Lyon is situated
in H.M. Register House, Edinburgh, opposite the North
British Station Hotel, its records (part of the National
Records of Scotland) being entrusted to the Lyon Clerk.
When sitting in full Court the Lord Lyon wears, as he did
in Parliament before the Union, a robe of crimson velvet
and ermine,[1] somewhat like the coronation robe of a British
peer, but with cords and tassels and no hood.

The duties of the Court[2] are divided into two broad
categories : (a) Establishing rights to arms and pedigrees,
which, when satisfactory evidence is produced, results in a
judicial " Interlocutor " granting warrant to the Lyon Clerk
to record in the *Public Register of All Arms and Bearings
in Scotland*, or in the *Public Register of All Genealogies*

[1] National Library MSS. 34-3-22 ; *Heraldry in Scotland*, p. 449 ; see also
Plate of Sir Alexander Erskine of Cambo, Bart., *Juridical Review*, September
1932 ; Nisbet, *System of Heraldry*, iv, 171. In ordinary clothes, the Lyon-badge
is worn on the right hip from a purple riband across the left shoulder (cf. Lord
Lyon Balfour of Denmiln's portrait) ; in uniform, from the triple-chains of gold.

[2] The more important judgments of Lyon Court are now (since 1950) reported
(*in abbreviated form, so in important matters the original record must still be
consulted*) in the Scots Law Times.

and Birthbrieves in Scotland, the particular coat of arms and genealogy which have been established to his Lordship's satisfaction. (*b*) The penal and semi-penal (State Revenue) jurisdiction is concerned with protecting the rights both of private individuals and of the Crown in Scottish armorial bearings, and over H.M. Messengers at Arms. This is regarded as a matter of signal importance, for where persons or corporations have paid fees to the Crown in return for the exclusive right to armorial bearings, and a Scots coat of arms can belong to only one person at a time, it is only proper that these rights should be protected. Without such protection arms are indeed useless to anybody or for anything. The misappropriation or unauthorised display of a man's coat of arms is a " real injury " under the Common Law of Scotland.[1] Accordingly the registered owner of a Scots coat of arms may obtain judicial interdict in Lyon Court[2] against any person depicting his arms against his wishes or to his prejudice. The Crown and the public have also an interest,[3] the former because in Scotland the fees on registration of armorial bearings and pedigrees are payable to H.M. Treasury, and the latter for prevention of fraud through improper assumption of coats of arms—because armorial bearings are legal evidence which may be used in cases of succession and identity.

The Lyon Court, like other Courts in Scotland, has a public Prosecutor, styled, like those of Scots Sheriff Courts, a " Procurator-Fiscal ". He raises proceedings, when neces-

---

[1] Sir G. Mackenzie, *Works,* ii, 174.

[2] *Roy. Warrantholders* v. *Alexander & Co.,* 21 March 1933 (Lyon Court), *Scotsman,* 22 March.

[3] *Lord Fraser* v. *Laird of Philorth, Privy Council,* 2nd ser., vi, 392. But where any question regarding right to arms arises, Lyon Court alone has jurisdiction (*Macdonell* v. *Macdonald,* 4 Shaw & Dunlop 371), and the Lord Lyon is entitled to " replegiate " (recall) to Lyon Court all cases in any way connected with armorial bearings (*Privy Seal,* xxxvii, 44 ; *Privy Council,* 2nd ser., iii, 156 ; Statutes 1672, cap. 47, and 1672, cap. 74).

sary, against those who improperly usurp armorial bearings, and in view of the financial interest of the Treasury, the Scots Courts of Appeal regard the Fiscal's intervention as analogous to an Inland Revenue prosecution.[1] The armorial offender in Scotland is accordingly viewed with the same stern and unromantic outlook which meets any other culprit caught evading national taxation. Lyon Court has by Statute 1592, cap. 125, and 1672, cap. 47, full powers of fine and imprisonment, and by 1669, cap. 95, Letters of Horning as well as, at common law, power to erase unwarrantable arms,[2] and to " dash them furth of " stained-glass windows, break unwarrantable seals, and, where the Fiscal or complainer moves for forfeiture, to grant warrant for seizing movable goods and gear upon which arms are unwarrantably represented.[3] He may also interdict usurpers of arms.[4]

The granting or regranting of Arms by Letters Patent and various Birthbrieves, e.g. Diplomas of Nobility or of Chiefship (*Diploma Stemmatis*), is not judicial but the exercise by Lyon of the Sovereign's Armorial Prerogative,[5] and with this the Courts of Appeal " cannot interfere ".[6] In this branch of Armorial jurisdiction Lyon, after considering

[1] *Macrae's Trustees* v. *Lord Lyon*, 4 June 1926, 1927, Scots Law Times, 285, per Lord Constable, but actually comprehends a further element, since it is not a mere question of fees, but of inhibiting and erasing to maintain the purity and accuracy of the family organisation of the Realm, cf. Statute 1592, cap. 125.

[2] 1927, S.L.T., 292.

[3] *Campbell of Shawfield*, 1732 Lyon Court, and *Warrantholders* v. *Alexander & Company*, 1933, where the Fiscal arranged to defer moving for forfeiture pending removal of the arms ; where necessary he grants warrant for incarceration. The bogus Burgh Seal of *Blairgowrie* was surrendered on complaint, 1929, and the 11th *Lord Reay's* stall-plate, surreptitiously erected in the Thistle Chapel, 1911, was removed by Lyon's Warrant, 1948. The 13th Lord matriculated 19 July 1951 (Lyon Register, xxxviii, 99), after which it was replaced.

[4] 1592, cap. 125 ; *Warrantholders* v. *Alexander & Co.*, 1933 ; cf. also *Fiscal of Lyon Court* v. *Kirkwood (Western General Hospital)*, 11 Jan. 1954 ; and *Scottish Watchmakers' and Jewellers' Association*, 18 Jan. 1954.

[5] *Macdonell* v. *Macdonald*, 1826, 4 Shaw 371.

[6] And see *Heraldry in Scotland*, p. 79.

the Petition, issues a Warrant, which is the heraldic equivalent of the Queen's " Signature " for a Crown Charter, " authorising " the Lyon Clerk to prepare the Letters Patent. On all these proceedings fees are payable to H.M. Exchequer.[1] It is not often realised that the Lyon Office is a revenue-earning Government Department as well as being custodian of the pageantry and romance of Scotland's mediaeval grandeur.

[1] The statutes are still strictly enforced, and two offenders have been fined for using unwarrantable arms as recently as 1954 (*Western General Hospital*, 11 Jan. 1954; *Scottish Watchmakers' and Jewellers' Association*, 13 Jan. 1954). Those who themselves take the initiative to get illegally used arms rectified are not prosecuted. In the two foregoing cases there had been publicisation of the unlawful assumptions. The value of Scottish heraldry depends on this enforcement of the law. Both registration dues and penalties go in relief of the general taxpayer.

CHAPTER III

THEORY OF HERALDRY IN SCOTLAND

T is now accepted by most historians that whilst conventional designs were used on shields in and prior to the eleventh century, heraldry in the sense of scientific hereditary armorial symbols had not then begun to exist. The designs which we can affirm to have subsequently become hereditary are found in the first half of the twelfth century — say 1138–57 — and are repeated in the following generation, so that by 1189 heraldry had automatically evolved, and by the end of the century was a recognised science of identification.[1] The earliest known Scottish armorial bearings are those on the seals of Allan, High Steward of Scotland, about 1177, and Patrick, Earl of Dunbar, about 1182.[2] Early armorial seals show the owner of the seal on horseback, with the device by which

DOUGLAS. Argent, a heart gules, imperially crowned proper; on a chief azure three mullets of the 1st.

[1] J. R. Planché, *The Pursuivant of Arms*, 1873, p. 283; J. H. Stevenson, *Heraldry in Scotland*, p. 16; C. A. H. Franklyn (*The Bearing of Coat Armour by Ladies*), summarising Fox-Davies, also states the latest evidence succinctly, pp. 2-7.

[2] *Heraldry in Scotland*, p. 17.

he was distinguished from other men emblazoned on his shield, surcoat, and horse-trappings. There is, however, good reason to suppose that use of " ensigns armorial " was first made on leaders' flags, from which the devices soon came to be re-peated on their shields and sur-coats.[1]

" The idea of hereditary arm-orial symbols was conceived by kings and nobles, without any necessary connection with fighting, and the convenience ex-perienced from the use of seals on deeds, charters, and leases had more to do with the recognition of the advantages of armory, than the use to be made of it in war." [2]

FIG. I.—Great Seal of David II, showing armorial shield, tabard, ailette and horse-trappings of the King of Scots.

Identification and therefore heraldry were for practical purposes necessary for prelates, military leaders, chiefs of clans, landowners, and public officials, the categories who were, either by descent or from office, " nobles ". Con-

---

[1] Nisbet, *System of Heraldry*, 1722. This view has lately been further expounded by J. Storer Clouston of Smoogro, a careful student of North European Heraldry ; " Our Wardhills and Ensigns ", *Proc. of Orkney Antiquarian Society*, vol. x. Cf. *Art of Heraldry*, p. 11 ; A. R. Wagner, *Heraldry in England*, p. 7.

[2] F. E. Whitton, *Nineteenth Century and After*, ci, 454 ; see also *Heraldry in Scotland*, p. 31.

sequently, heraldry became necessarily an indication of nobility.[1]

Nevertheless, the instant popularity of the new science came because it supplied the people of an illiterate age with a means for the immediate identification of local and national leaders. Heraldry is therefore not, as some people have supposed, an idle amusement, but is essentially a practical science for the service of the general public. Its use has been rendered even more popular by the artistic and architectural appreciation of its decorative advantages.

In these modern days when the public has no time to read more than headlines, as in the twelfth century when few people could read at all, heraldry remains *par excellence* the decorative shorthand for identification of our clan houses, national leaders, and public institutions.

A coat of arms is the outward indication of nobility,[2] and arms are officially described as " Ensigns of Nobility ".[3] A patent of arms is—and I say this with full official weight— a Diploma of Nobility,[4] and as such both the Scottish and English Kings of Arms have treated their patents, issued by them as Royal Commissioners. Since the power to ennoble is vested in the Crown,[5] armorial bearings very soon became subject to strict regulations. There were also practical

[1] 1592, cap. 125 ; E. Crawford, *Lives of the Lindsays*, i, 227 ; Seton, *Law and Practice of Heraldry*, p. 84 ; *Juridical Review*, September 1940, pp. 195, 198. 205 n. 2, 218 n. 1 ; T. Innes of Learney, *Law of Succession in Ensigns Armorial.*

[2] Edmondson, *Complete Body of Heraldry*, p. 154 ; Statute 1592, cap. 125 ; Acts, iii, 554 ; A. C. Fox-Davies, *Right to Bear Arms*, p. 34 ; *Privy Council*, 2nd ser., iii, 594 ; Sir J. Balfour, *Heraldic Tracts*, " On Nobility ", p. 9, No. 37 ; Nisbet, *System of Heraldry*, iii, ii, 68, " insigne verum nobilitatis ".

[3] Nisbet's *Heraldry*, iii, ii, 65 ; *Juridical Review*, September 1940, p. 198.

[4] *Ibid.* p. 218, n. 2 ; J. Woodand and Burnett, *Heraldry British and Foreign*, 1896 ed. pp. 11-15.

[5] The old Earls of Scotland who were *Righ* or provincial Kings " by the Grace of God " (*Scots Peerage*, iv, 6) had provincial nobles and baronages of their own (W. C. Dickinson, *Court Book of Carnwath*, xvi, li ; *Proc. of Soc. of Antiquaries of Scot.*, lxxix, 156).

reasons for this, namely, to prevent disputes in civil life and confusion in the field of battle ; to these we should add fraud in connection with legal sealing of documents, and proofs of pedigree in succession to estates and dignities. A coat of arms, like a peerage, baronetcy, or right of salmon-fishing, became a recognised form of " incorporeal heritable property ",[1] the power of granting which is " a part of the Royal Prerogative ",[2] and the Court of Session has laid down, per Lord Robertson,[3] that infringement of a right to arms " involves a question of property, which a right to bear particular ensigns armorial undoubtedly is ", and that the Scottish Courts must in such cases give redress.[4] Nowadays this may seem strange, but in Scotland a right of any sort, be it of " nobility " only, or be it of a peerage or other " honour ", has always been considered a " right " to which one must have proper " title deeds ", and over which one can have a " guid gangin' plea " before a Court of Justice, should there be any cause for dispute.[5]

The same principle reconciles an apparent anomaly, viz. : if all clansmen are " noble ", how comes it that anybody requires to be ennobled ? The juridical Scottish mind instantly answers that " nobility "—like any other right—must be proved,[6] and if for any reason a descent from some armigerous ancestor cannot be judicially proved, then the Crown must " intervene by some formal act ", such as a

[1] *Right to Bear Arms*, p. 26 ; Mr Justice Chitty in *Austen* v. *Collins* (*The Times*, 6 May 1886), but cf. *Juridical Review*, September 1940, lii, pp. 184-6, 195-6 ; and Lord Aitchison in *Maclean of Ardgour*, 1941 S.C., p. 683.
[2] *Macdonell* v. *Macdonald*, 1826, 4 Shaw & Dunlop 371 ; Edmondson, *Complete Body of Heraldry*, i, 155.
[3] *Macdonell* v. *Macdonald*, *supra.*
[4] Commented on and approved in House of Lords by Lord Shaw of Dunfermline, *Stewart-Mackenzie* v. *Fraser-Mackenzie*, 1922 S.C. (H.L.), 39, at pp. 46 and 47.
[5] Green's *Encyclopaedia*, xi, par. 417, 434 ; Innes of Learney, *Law of Succession in Ensigns Armorial*, p. 3 n.
[6] Balfour's *Heraldic Tracts*, " On Nobility ", No. 116.

patent from Lyon, usually granted unless the applicant be
" undeserving ", *e.g.* publican, bookmaker. Arms once
validly acquired, like other property " held of " the Crown,
" become as much a person's property as anything else he
possessed ",[1] though indeed they are a very " strictly en-
tailed estate ", which he cannot assign or dispose of, except
under the strictest procedure.[2] In Scotland this exclusive
" right of property " in armorial bearings is a serious legal
fact. So recently as 1922, two litigants carried such a dispute
through the Courts of Appeal to the House of Lords, where
it was finally decided,[3] and the total expenses of the
litigation are understood to have been about £7000.

When we say that arms are " property " yet " tokens of
nobility ", it is necessary to point out that in most ancient
realms the concept of nobility has been related to the tenure
of *noble terre* and that arms themselves are regarded as
incorporeal *fiefs annoblissants*. Much of the interest of
Scottish heraldry lies in the fact that the law and practice
of arms in Scotland are living and functioning survivals of
old feudo-tribal laws of honour as applied to " Earldoms,
Baronies and other impartible tenures " as these existed in
the eleventh to seventeenth centuries. Lyon Court and the
Armorial Noblesse of Scotland are thus a living survival of the
old mediaeval realm, and accordingly of immense legal and
social interest, perpetuating as they do the organisation and
concepts of the old clan or family organisation of the kingdom.

In Scotland the development of heraldry has indeed
differed from that in most other countries, owing to the small
number of clans or families in our nation, each with numerous

---

[1] Per Lyon-Depute Boswell, Lyon Office Record Book, p. 183.

[2] *Grant of Auchernack*, 31 December 1777, Lyon Register, i, 515 ; Register
of Genealogies, i, 229 ; *Steuart of Allanton*, 1813, Lyon Register, ii, 101 ; *Macneil
of Barra*, 1915, *ibid.*, xxii, 160 ; *Scottish Notes & Queries*, 1933, p. 187 ; *Rintoul*,
1950, Scots Law Times, 12 ; Haig, *ibid.*, 26.

[3] *Stewart-Mackenzie* v. *Fraser Mackenzie*, 1922, S.C. (H.L.), 39.

members, all virtually claiming to be of noble descent.   In
consequence of this, the salient feature of Scottish heraldry
is that, as compared with England and other countries, the
basic coats of arms are relatively few in number,[1] but numerous

Fig. 2.—Achievement of Sir Alan Colquhoun of Luss, 6th Bt.,
impaling the arms of his wife, Dame Anna Helena MacRae of
Conchra, Lady Colquhoun of Luss.

differenced versions of each basic shield exist.   The basic, or
simple undifferenced arms and crest, are the property, not
of the " family ", but of the " Chief " of each clan or house,
so that, as Sir George Mackenzie points out, the Scottish and
French systems of armorial differencing distinguish chief,
chieftains, and cadets of each such noble and organised name.
The whole bent of Scottish heraldry has been to develop this

[1] *Heraldry in Relation to Scots History and Art*, p. 47.

system of differencing on scientific lines in order to give practical identification to the numerous chieftains and *duine-uasal,* and to prevent cadets from assuming arms inconsistent with their actual position in the family tree. In no other country has heraldry even approached the splendid scientific system of individual differencing which in Scotland has been carried on from the Middle Ages to the present time.

Some confusion has in recent times been caused by the phrases " personal arms " and " personal flag " of the Sovereign, and of Chiefs or Lairds, and is leading to a delusion that they are " private " devices, which is not so. The distinction is truly from " badge/identity " flags and devices, usable by the whole lieges, or clan/following, to show themselves " dependers " on such Sovereign or Chief.

The Royal Arms are Ensigns of Authority over the realm and all the lieges thereof. Similarly, the Chief's arms are his *ensigns of patriarchal authority* over the whole Family/Clan/Name, *i.e.* those belonging to *his* community " be pretence of blude or place of their duelling " (A.P.S. (1587), iv, p. 40), and those of a Chief of a branch (S.C., 11 D., 1149, 1151) or Laird-Baron, of the " hail dependers " of his branch, or to whom he is *in loco parentis.*

The " house " (*mansionata*) comprehends not only the affiliated relatives, even remote cousins, but also the tenantry, servants and workmen supporting and supported by " the house ", who are " united like a corporation " (Funk Brentano, *Old Régime in France,* p. 5). The " corporation " is indeed that " erected " or " recognised " under the *caput toties progenii* (R.M.S., vol. i, No. 509), or a branch-chieftain, in a patent or initial confirmation of arms. In these arms the *whole community* has a pride and interest, for they are those of and indicative of the *authority of* their hereditary *Representer,* the Chief or Chieftain, Baron or Laird, and are " personal " only in the sense that they denote him or her (and the relative honourable authority), whereas the plant-badge or strap-and-buckle cap and sash badge is the device indicating *membership* of the *mansionata* or clan, as distinct from position of authority within it.

Armorial bearings are thus essential machinery for the governing of a clan or family, and are of the widest popular interest.

CHAPTER IV

THE SCIENCE OF HERALDRY

ERALDRY is a simple and practical science, invented and used for the convenience of everybody, in days when few could write, and education was of an elementary standard. The science is, indeed, so simple and straightforward that anyone can grasp it in the course of an afternoon, though a few days may elapse before some of the terms are fixed in the mind.

French was the international language of the Middle Ages, so a number of heraldic terms are of Old French origin. Most of these are already well known in ordinary literature. Their use has made heraldry of international convenience, because from a blazon or written prescription, any European herald can draw any coat of arms.

HOPE, MARQUESS OF LINLITHGOW.
Azure, on a chevron or, between three bezants, a laurel leaf vert.

The term " coat of arms " is derived from the armorial jacket or " tabard " worn by knights over their armour. This coat still survives in the heraldic tabard, the significance of which originated in the theory that the herald, when arrayed in his master's coat, actually represented him. In the High-lands, the saffron-dyed *leine croich* interfered with the general adoption of the armorial surcoat, except in cases such as

Strathearn, Drummond, and Cameron, where the charges
were easily depicted on the yellow surface of the *leine croich*
itself. The shield, however, was made heraldic, as soon as

the science of armory came to Scotland,
as evidenced by a number of Celtic
sepulchral slabs, such as that of Maclean
of Ross of Mull (Fig. 4). In the late
fifteenth and early sixteenth centuries, when
the armorial surcoat had become a close-
fitting *jupon*, it became the practice to
depict the arms upon an escutcheon
embroidered on the middle of the back
and breast, instead of over the whole surcoat as in the tabard. In Britain this
fashion was peculiar to Scotland. It may
have come from the Continent, and no
coloured effigies survive to establish the
prevailing colour of the surcoat. This

Fig. 3.—Effigy of Stewart
of Lorn, at Culross;
jupon-surcoat fully em-
blazoned with arms.
15th century.

may have been of the owner's livery
colour, but possibly it remained saffron
yellow, as a survival of the *leine croich*.
Amongst the baronage the normal loose
tabard and neat close-fitting *jupon*-surcoats were of course the
fashion and survive on numerous carved effigies, now, alas,
through the actions of vandal " Reformers ", usually broken.
The effigies of Gilbert de Greenlaw, 1411 (Plate vi), and
Stewart of Lorn (Fig. 3) are good examples.

" Coat of Arms " is now a generic term loosely applied
to the entire armorial device (including helmet, crest, motto,
etc.), technically called an " Achievement ". This normally
consists of the following parts : [1]

---

[1] The order and manner of explanation in the following pages, though specially
adapted to Scottish heraldry, are based to some extent on the late A. C. Fox-
Davies's excellent system in *Heraldry Explained*.

FIG. 4.—Effigy of Maclean of Ross of Mull, showing *leine croich*, or saffron shirt, and armorial shield, which bears : a galley in chief, a lion rampant contourné in base, a bordure per fess, invected in chief and embattled in base. (Monument at Iona.)

FIG. 5.—Effigy of Stewart of Bute, at Rothesay, 15th century, showing close-fitting surcoat (probably saffron-yellow), charged with escutcheon of arms.

(This has been supposed to represent either Walter, 6th Lord High Steward, or Robert II, but the arms can belong to neither, and the monument is evidently that of the first, or even a subsequent, Sheriff of Bute. In Scotland, armour-fashions were often half a century or more behind England.)

(*a*) " The Arms ", *i.e.* Shield and devices thereon—which were exactly the same as those on the tabard itself, and those on the square flag called a banner ; (*b*) Helmet ; (*c*) Mantling ; (*d*) Wreath or Torse ; (*e*) Crest ; (*f*) Motto.

In addition to these, there may in certain cases (viz. Chiefs and those specially favoured or of higher rank) also be :

(*g*) Supporters ; (*h*) Compartment ; (*i*) Slughorn, or Cri-de-guerre—as often as not, simply the motto of the Chief ; (*j*) Badge ; (*k*) Pinsel ; (*l*) Guidon.

In other cases there may also be one or more of the following :

(*m*) Augmentation ; (*n*) Insignia or decoration of some of the Orders of the Knighthood, etc.,

whilst a Knight will have (in addition to supporters in the case of Knights Grand Cross and Knights of the Thistle) the (*o*) Collar of the Order.

A Peer will also have his appropriate (*p*) Coronet of Rank, and may have (*q*) a special coat granted to descend along with the dignity.

And a feudal Baron will, if he applies for them, receive : (*r*) Cap of Estate ; (*s*) Standard.

THE PARTS OF THE " ACHIEVEMENT "

THE SHIELD

The shield is the foundation of everything. Some people only have right to a shield alone, but without the shield neither crest nor anything else can exist.

The shield may be of any shape. The fourteenth-century " heater " type (Fig. 6) is neatest, but every variety of outline, from a plain circle to rectangular cartouches, and elaborately

PLATE VI

Incised slab commemorating Gilbert de Greenlaw, Armiger, killed at
Harlaw, 1411, wearing heraldic *jupon* over his armour.—*Proc. Soc.
of Antiquaries of Scotland*, vol. 80, p. 44.

PLATE VII

Arms of ALEXANDER IRVINE OF DRUM, d. 1457.

Arg., three sheaves of as many holly-leaves vert, banded gules. *Crest*—a sheaf of holly-leaves
vert, banded gules. (Splendid example of fifteenth-century carved stone at Drum Castle,
showing badge, a holly-bush eradicated, at either side, also true proportions of shield and
helmet.)—*Deeside Field*, iii. 81.

scalloped escutcheons, has been the fashion at different periods.

A few ancient families still have shields devoid of " charges " and merely divided in two or more colours, but practically all coats of arms consist of the shield as a background (technically termed the " field ") and some device drawn thereon, which is termed the "charge", or charges if there be more than one.

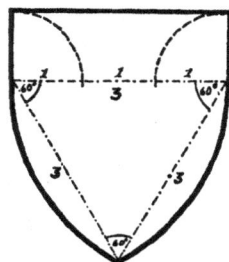

FIG. 6.—Heater-shaped Shield.

THE HELMET

So long as armour was worn, everyone who had a shield wore a helmet of some description. Specific forms have been assigned to the following ranks :

(1) *Royal helmet.*—Gold, always shown *affronté*, *i.e.* full face, the facial opening guarded by grills or bars.

(2) *Peers.*—Silver, with gold grill (usually 5 grills) and gold-garnished.

(3) *Knights and Baronets.*—Steel, open visor, no grill, *or* great tilting-helm (they being of " tournament rank "), steel garnished with gold, where the normal open-visored helmet is incongruous.

(4) *Feudal Barons.*—The great tilting-helm garnished with gold (they being of " tournament rank "), *or* a steel helmet with grill of one or three grills, garnished with gold, but the tilting-helm is most used.

(5) *Esquires.*—Steel " pot " helm, or helmet with closed visor garnished with gold.

(6) *Gentlemen.*[1]—Steel, pot, closed visor, ungarnished.

The great " tilting-helm ", being index of tournament rank, ought *not* (as by many artists in recent years) to be

[1] Prior to 1672, Scots gentlemen were allowed shields only (Lord Lyon Sir James Balfour of Denmiln's MSS., 34-4-16 (Addenda), Nat. Lib.).

D

depicted for Esquires and Gentlemen. For those below the rank of Knight and feudal-Baron it is not now allowed, or used, in official or officially approved achievements.

When helmets are shown in profile[1] they always face *dexter*, except when there are two helmets above a shield. In that case they may either both face dexter, or may both face the centre. The latter is the practice usual in Scotland and on the Continent.[2] The dexter helmet, of course, reverts to face dexter on any occasion when it is shown alone.[3]

Subject to these rules, the period and style of helmet may be selected at pleasure, but should conform to the same period as the shield. Heraldic stationers usually make helmets ridiculously small. The real mediaeval helmet was almost as big as the shield, which when suspended by its strap, naturally hangs below it in a *couché* position, *i.e.* tilted sideways. Stall plates of Knights of the Thistle are always thus engraved.

MANTLING, OR LAMBREQUIN

The mantling is the cloth cape, suspended from the top of the helmet and hanging down the wearer's back to absorb the heat of the sun, which in warm weather would have made the helmet and armour intolerable ; in early examples usually a plain or scalloped cloth. This was liable to get jagged in battle, so artists seized on this as an opportunity to elaborate on the well-known flowing designs. The original simple form is shown in the *Armorial de Gelré* (Plate II).

COLOUR RULES.—*The Crown* : gold, lined ermine.

[1] The seventeenth-century English rule, which artists have long ridiculed, that helmets of Peers and Esquires *must* be shown in profile, which one writer (O. Barón, *Ancester*, i, 43) said " has made foolscaps of all our crests ", is no longer observed in Scotland.

[2] Nisbet, *System of Heraldry*, iv, ii, 6.

[3] In church, helmets and crests were often made to face towards the altar (Nisbet, iv, ii, 26), so that those on the *north* side of a pre-Reformation church seem *contourné*.

Peers and certain of the Officers of State: outside—crimson ; lining (technically " doubling ")—ermine. *All others since 9 July 1891*:[1] outside—principal " colour " of arms ; lining—principal metal. A fur doubling, *e.g Noble of Ardmore*,[2] is occasionally found.

The technical description for a red mantling lined white is : " a mantling gules, doubled argent " (see page 51 for particulars of " tinctures ").

WREATH, OR TORSE

A skein of silk, with gold or silver cord twisted round it, is placed as a fillet upon the helmet to cover the joint between the crest and mantling. It is conventionally depicted by showing six alternate twists of the principal " metal " and " colour " of the shield, and technically described as " a wreath of the liveries ". Sometimes these differ from the tinctures of the arms ;[3] moreover, when there is no wreath, the " colours " may as such be defined in the matriculation [4] which illustrates Lyon's jurisdiction over " liveries ".

CAP OF MAINTENANCE, OR CHAPEAU

Sometimes in place of a wreath the crest is set upon a chapeau, consisting of a velvet cap, lined with ermine, the edge being turned up and split at the back. It first appears in the *Armorial de Gelré*, where the Earl of Mar bears a chapeau gules, but examination of *Gelré* shows the chapeau was used by many entitled *Sire*, and that it was not confined to Earls. Such a cap is the privilege of the feudal Baronage [5]

---

[1] *Stewart of Southwick*, Lyon Register, xii, 52, marked the change.
[2] *Ibid.*, xvii, 30, 27 December 1902, doubled contre-ermine.
[3] Nisbet, *System of Heraldry*, iv, ii, 10.
[4] *Elgin*, 9 October 1678, Lyon Register, i, 461.
[5] *Proc. of Soc. of Antiquaries of Scot.*, lxxix, 149.

and seems technically to have indicated ownership of jurisdiction. In England anciently even some holders of knights-
fees bore it,[1] but it is now confined to Peerage houses. In
Scotland the chapeau has been definitely assigned [2] to the
" minor barons ", for whom it is constitutionally appropriate,
and being now more freely applied for in rematriculations, it
serves a useful purpose in distinguishing the arms of such of
them as are not entitled to supporters. By varying the
colour of the cap the varying categories of minor barons are
distinguished, viz. *Gules doubled Ermine*, Barons hereto-
fore in possession of their fief or jurisdiction ; *Azure doubled
Ermine*, Barons in respect of being Chiefs of Baronial
Houses who no longer possess the baronial fief or jurisdiction.
The ermine doubling is altered to *contre-ermine* in the case of
Barons of " Argyll and the Isles " or in any of the old
Earldoms,[3] and Representatives of such no longer in possession of the fief or jurisdiction at the time of applying for
the chapeau receive the cap azure, cf. the analogy of those
on the (*c.* 1461) stall plates of Beaumont, titular " Earl of
Buchan " and " Comte James de Douglas ".[4] The chapeau,
like supporters, is indivisible, and passes to the successive
Barons, or Representatives, of the Baronial house only, *i.e.*
it will not be rematriculated for cadets.

CREST-CORONET (SHOWING THREE STRAWBERRY LEAVES)

This circlet, consisting of four strawberry leaves, of which
three are visible, and which is sometimes termed a Ducal
Coronet, though it never indicated a dukedom, or indeed any

---

[1] St J. Hope, *Heraldry for Craftsmen*, p. 55.

[2] *Ainslie of Pilton*, 28 January 1836, Lyon Register, iv, 2 ; petition, *Gordon
of Hallhead*, 4 September 1934, *ibid.*, xxxi, 20 ; *Chisholm of Chisholm*, 29 March
1938, *ibid.*, xxxiii, 12 ; *Douglas of Brigton*, 21 May 1941, *ibid.*, xxxiv, 33 ;
Carnegy of Lour, 28 February 1945, *ibid.*, xxxv, 24.

[3] *Campbell of Dunstaffnage*, 1942, Lyon Register, xxxiv, 71.

[4] St J. Hope, *Garter Stall Plates*, xv, lxxii.

peerage rank,[1] is comparatively rare in Britain, but is
nowadays lavishly assumed
on the Continent. Of this
coronet,[2] Nisbet states that
it pertains to " Gentlemen
of Name and Arms " [3] and,
in Scotland, to " Knights
and lesser Barons ",[4] presumably " of Name and
Arms ", *i.e.* " of that Ilk ",
holders of a baronial estate
of the same style as their
name. This seems the
Scottish equivalent of the
description in *L'Estat et
Comportement*. Lairds
" of that Ilk " with non-
baronial holdings might be
entitled to the coloured ones,
of which there are many
examples in *Gelré*. Jehan
Scohier [5] (1551–93) says the
qualification for a crest-
coronet was descent from
some ancestor in personal
attendance on a Sovereign at
his coronation. These, and
cadets of the Royal House,
were entitled to golden
crest-coronets, and coronets

FIG. 7.—DUKE OF HAMILTON. Quarterly:
1st and 4th grand quarters counterquartered; 1st and 4th, gules, three cinquefoils ermine (*Hamilton*); 2nd and 3rd,
argent, a lymphad with sails furled proper,
flagged gules (*Earldom of Arran*). 2nd
and 3rd grand quarters, argent, a man's
heart gules, ensigned with an imperial
crown proper; on a chief azure, three
mullets of the first (*Douglas*). Above the
shield is placed the coronet of a duke, and
thereon two helmets befitting his degree,
having mantlings gules doubled ermine,
and for *crests*—dexter, on a ducal coronet,
an oak tree fructed, and penetrated trans-
versely in the main stem by a frame-saw
proper, the frame or, and over the same
this *motto*: "Through" (*Hamilton*); sinister, on a chapeau gules, lined ermine, a
salamander in flames proper, and over
same this *motto*: " Jamais Arrière " (for
Douglas). *Supporters*—Two antelopes
argent, armed, unguled, ducally gorged,
and having chains reflexed over their
backs or. (1903, Lyon Register.)

[1] Nisbet, *System of Heraldry*, iv, ii, 39.
[2] Stevenson, *Heraldry in Scotland*, p. 196.
[3] *System of Heraldry*, iv, 39.
[4] *Ibid.*, p. 40.
[5] *L'Estat et Comportement des Armes* (Brussels, 1597), cap. xii.

D 2

of red, green, or black were assigned to those *de la suite de celui qui porte la couronne d'or*. Such coloured coronets are seen in the *Armorial de Gelré* (Plate II). Scohier's statements might account for the golden crest-coronet of the Keiths and others, though many of them probably originated in *Chef du Nom et d'Armes*,[1] and it has now been adjudged that the gold crest-coronet indicates a *Chef du Nom et d'Armes* (" of that Ilk ").[2] As with chapeaux, such coronets are not rematriculated for cadets, but reserved for the representatives alone.

Mural Crown.—A coronet of embattled masonry [3] which, in the case of individuals, is usually granted only to distinguished soldiers. The " Chieftain's Cap ", a chequered and embattled circlet, seems another version of this.[4]

Naval Crown.—Alternate representations of stern and sail of a ship ; now exclusive to admirals.

Antique Crown.—Metal circlet with tall spikes,[5] which becomes a *Celestial Crown* when each spike is surmounted of a star ; no settled significance ;[6] by some associated with high service in India or the East and by others with " Pictish " chiefship. Now it is not being granted, until its precise heraldic import has been fixed.

Under Sir James Balfour Paul a few such crest-coronets, mural crowns, and chapeaux were granted on no heraldic ground whatever, but under Sir Francis J. Grant each has become limited to an ancient and express heraldic purpose.

---

[1] The coronet confirmed to the heir of line of the House of Douglas ; *Archibald Douglas of Douglas*, 28 May 1771, Lyon Register, i, 143, is an instance.

[2] *Maclachlan of Maclachlan*, 2 May 1946, Lyon Register, xxxv, 72.

[3] This is the coronet assigned to all Scottish Burghs (see Figs. 64 and 105).

[4] *Tartans of the Clans and Families of Scotland*, p. 34.

[5] See Plate XVI, Fraser of Reelig, 2nd quarter, argent, three antique crowns, gules.

[6] A somewhat similar coronet of five pales vert, alternated with four garbs or, has been assigned as a " County Council coronet " as complementary to the burghal coronets. *Kirkcudbright*, May 1951, Lyon Register, xxxviii, 139.

THE CREST

Crests developed both from the plume and from the fan-shaped ridge along the top of the helmet which was designed to temper a blow. This ridging came to be cut either in the form of an animal or other object, or in a fan-shaped design, later conventionalised as a " wing " upon which the arms or part of them was painted. Large crests formed of moulded leather were worn at tournaments. Although originally confined to the higher nobility, or those of " tournament rank "—which [1] is identified in early times with " chevalerie/ knighthood ", probably in the sense of Knight-service (the next rank below feudal Baron) and accordingly in later times [2] with " Esquire/Ecuyer ", crests are nowadays granted or recorded along with the arms of those who wish them, except the following :

(a) Ladies, other than such as have become " Representative " of their house, clan, or family—who succeed to the complete armorial insignia of their house, including the crest.[3]

(b) Clergymen, whose shields are usually ensigned with an ecclesiastical hat and tassels, or mitre if a bishop. The ecclesiastical hat assigned to a clergyman in Scotland is black and with one tassel on either side.[4] Chaplains to the King get the cord and tassels gules.[5] The title Bishop was

[1] See the Articles for Tournament of 1508, Juridical Review, 1944, p. 30.
[2] See Nisbet, Heraldry, iv, ii, 3, and Lord Lyon Balfour in Denmiln MSS. 34-4-16 ; Playfair, 4 June 1917, Lyon Register, xxiii, 28 ; Fortune of Bangairn, 30 August 1910, ibid., xx, 74.
[3] Graden of Earnslaw, 1672, Lyon Register, i, 314 ; Farquharson of Inver-cauld, 11 November 1815, ibid., ii, 130 ; 3 December 1936, ibid., xxxii, 34 ; Gibsone of Pentland, 5 October 1810, ibid., ii, 52 ; Macleod of Macleod, 28 November 1935, ibid., xxxi, 74 ; Douglas of Brigton, 21 May 1941, ibid., xxxiv, 33 ; Maclean of Ardgour, 10 October 1941, ibid., xxxiv, 42.
[4] Cooper, 20 February 1917, ibid., xxiii, 16 (see Fig. 9).
[5] Very Rev. J. H. Cockburn, 5 July 1948, ibid., xxxvi, 145.

abolished by the Presbyterians [1] but is again recognised in law,[2] and bishops of the Episcopal and the Roman Catholic Churches are now allowed to use the title again as descriptive of their ecclesiastical office. When an ecclesiastical hat is assigned to a bishop in Scotland, it is green and has six *fiocci*, or tassels, on either side,[3] whilst an archbishop's hat is green and has ten tassels on either side.[4] The Dean of the Chapel-Royal has a black hat with three red

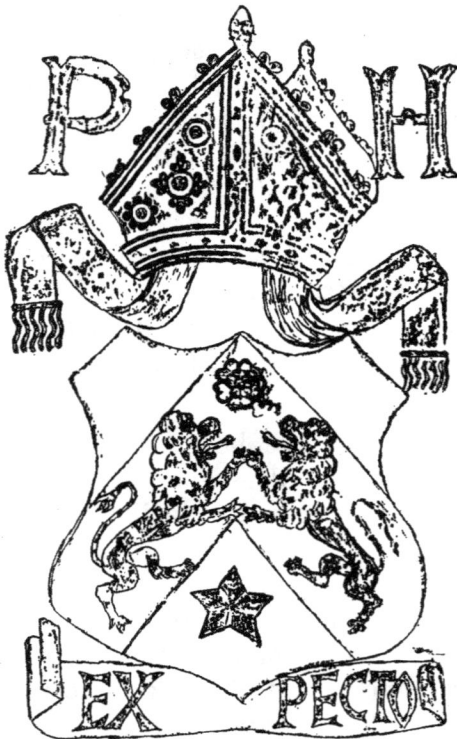

FIG. 8.—PATRICK HEPBURN, BISHOP OF MORAY. Gules, on a chevron argent, two lions passant, pulling at a rose of the first. A mullet of the second in base, for difference. Above the shield is set a bishop's mitre, and in an escrol beneath this *motto* : " Expecto ".

[1] *Drummond* v. *Farquhar*, 6 July 1809, Faculty Collections. The titles *Abbot* and *Prior* were not abolished at the Reformation, and the holders of such churches are still legally entitled to these titles and the relative insignia (*Abbacy of Crossragual*, Lyon Register, xxxviii, 119).

[2] Walker Trust Act, 1877; *Walker Trustees*, 31 October 1877, Lyon Register, x, 34. A bishop gets a gold, jewelled, mitre-*pretiosa*, when such is shown, and a gold pastoral staff. Abbots get a white mitre with gold-embroidered cross, unjewelled (*Lady Kinloss*, supporter, 18 July 1947, *ibid.*, xxxvi, 61), and a silver pastoral staff, or a *quigrich*. A prior (*Pluscarden Priory*) gets a silver pastoral staff but no mitre (6 April 1950, *ibid.*, xxxvii, 151). A Scots Abbot gets, by the ancient rule, a black hat with three tassels (*Nunraw*, 9 November 1954, *ibid.*, xl, 45).

[3] *Mellon*, 26 January 1946, Lyon Register, xxxv, 59; *Chisholm*, 6 March 1902, *ibid.*, xvi, 78.   [4] *Macdonald*, 1 May 1922, *ibid.*, xxv, 39.

tassels on each side.[1] A Kirk Session may get arms, but is given no hat,[2] though the minister could use its arms with the hat proper to his own ecclesiastical rank.

(c) Corporations, which have no head upon which to wear a crest, and therefore should not be granted crests. As Mr Stevenson points out, the crest and badge are virtually (though not altogether) synonymous in Scotland.[3]

The crest cannot exist without a concurrent right to a shield, and people who assert a right to a crest whilst admitting no right to arms, are assuming a position which is untenable and ridiculous.[4]

Crests, like all other heraldic objects, invariably face *dexter*, unless they are stated to be *affronté* (full face) or *contourné* (facing sinister). If, however, two helmets are shown "respecting" each other—a common practice where an achievement has

FIG. 9.—REVEREND PROFESSOR COOPER, D.D., Lyon Register, xxiii, 16; argent, a chevron gules between two laurel branches in chief, and in base a man's heart proper pierced with a Greek cross sable; above the shield is placed a clerical hat befitting his degree.

---

[1] *Dean of the Chapel-Royal and the Thistle*, 30 November 1951, *ibid.*, xxxviii, 119, and cf. *A. C. Don, Dean of Westminster*, 20 July 1946, *ibid.*, xxxv, 76.

[2] *Kirk Session of Dunblane*, 23 June 1948, *ibid.*, xxxvi, 142; *Canongate*, March 1952, *ibid.*, xxxviii.

[3] *Heraldry in Scotland*, p. 222; Mackenzie, *Science of Herauldrie*, cap. xxix; Nisbet, *System of Heraldry*, 1742, iv, ii, 16; see also p. 177 below.

[4] A. C. Fox-Davies, *Heraldry Explained*, p. 47, but see *Boutell's Heraldry*, 1891 ed., p. 349.

two crests—then the dexter crest turns to face the centre along with its helmet, and no statement is required, as such an arrangement is merely a matter of drawing, and the dexter crest, if shown by itself, would instantly revert to face dexter again. (In pre-Reformation churches, helmets carved on the north side are sometimes turned to " respect " the altar.)

THE MOTTO

Mottoes originated upon the standard and seal but now form part of the achievement, and in Scotland are invariably registered. The matriculation specifies whether the position is above the crest or below the shield, the latter position being normally assigned only when two mottoes are registered. A corporation escutcheon with no crest often, however, has the motto below. Cadets' mottoes should "answer" the chief's.

SUPPORTERS

FIG. 10.—Seal of Robert, Duke of Albany, Earl of Fife and Menteith, 1403.

These originated on the seal, apparently as badges, filling up the blank space on either side of the shield and helmet (Fig. 10). They are in practice confined to (*a*) Peers ; (*b*) Knights Grand Cross, or of the Thistle ; (*c*) Heirs, male or female, of the minor barons of Scotland ; (*d*) Chiefs of old families and clans; (*e*) Certain high officials ; (*f*) Persons upon whom the Lord Lyon in the exercise of his prerogative confers them, a power which the Lord Lyon has enjoyed from the Middle Ages, but which he never exercises without some excellent reason for granting these distinguished ornaments.

THE COMPARTMENT

In Scotland, supporters are always depicted on a suitable mount, rocks or maybe seashore, but occasionally the grant lays down some special feature; thus the Earl of Perth's supporters are set on "a compartment strewn with caltraps", and those of Dundas of that Ilk set on "a salamander in flames of fire". Nisbet restricts compartments to the Baronage,[1] but they are occasionally granted as a distinction or for special services.[2] They represent the bearer's territories, and are thus feudal honours,[3] now only assigned to historic territorial houses, and in the case of clan-chiefs, now usually incorporate the plant-badge.[4]

FIG. 11.—DUNDAS OF THAT ILK. Argent, a lion rampant gules. *Crest*—On a wreath of the liveries, a lion's head, full - faced, looking through a bush of oak, proper. *Supporters* —Two lions gules, and below the shield for a compartment, a salamander in flames of fire, proper. *Motto* above the crest— "Essayez".

THE SLOGAN, OR SLUGHORN

The "Slughorn", Slogan, or *Cri-de-guerre*, is confined to the Chief of a clan or house.[5] Some are identical with the motto; others differ. In many cases the slogan appears as a second motto, in which case the "crest" will often be found

[1] Nisbet, *Heraldry*, iv, ii, 137.

[2] *White of Milton*, 16 November 1762, Lyon Register, 444; *Leslie*, 6 March 1935, *ibid.*, xxxi, 39.

[3] Nisbet, *Heraldry*, iv, ii, 138; Mackenzie, *Works*, i, 631; *Maclean of Ardgour*, 10 October 1941, Lyon Register, xxxiv, 42.

[4] *Maclachlan of Maclachlan*, 2 May 1946, *ibid.*, xxxv, 72.

[5] Mackenzie, *Works*, ii, 633; *Chief of Clan Chattan*, 9 April 1947, Lyon Register, xxxvi, 36; *Chief of Mackintosh*, 9 April 1947, *ibid.*, xxxvi, 40.

to be a representation of the gathering-place.[1]   This has, from the Middle Ages, been a matter of heraldic record.[2]

THE BANNER

This is a square flag, showing the same arms as the shield, or, of course, the surcoat (Katherine of Aragon is said

FIG. 12.—Seal of James, ninth Earl of Douglas, showing armorial banners. 1452–1488.

to have " made a banner out of the King of Scots' coat ",[3] being that of James IV captured at Flodden. Similarly the Master of Forbes displayed the "bloody shirt" of James III after his murder. If this was the Royal surcoat (see p. 19) it would have been virtually a ready-made banner), and covering the whole surface of the flag. The earliest banners, how-ever, were not square but rectangular, the width being only one-half or two-thirds of the height. This shape was more effective for heraldic display.[4] The crest, motto, and supporters should *not* appear on the banner.[5] Technically

---

[1] *Macleod of Lewis*, 28 October 1674, Lyon Register, i, 184; W. Fraser, *Earls of Cromartie*, 2, cclxiii; *Grant of Grant*, Nisbet, *Heraldry*, iv, ii, 24; *Macfarlane of that Ilk*, Lyon Register, i, 377. The slogan is sometimes recorded as issuing from the mouth of an armed retainer. (*Gowrie*, J. R. Stodart, *Scottish Arms*, i, pl. 29; Nisbet, *Heraldry*, iv, ii, pl. 3, p. 1.)

[2] A. R. Wagner, *Heralds and Heraldry*, p. 57.   [3] *The Times*, January 1936.

[4] *Heraldry for Craftsmen and Designers*, p. 221.

[5] Hope aptly says : " Let a banner be regarded in the light of a rectangular shield " (*ibid.*, p. 199) ; cf. *Heraldry in Scotland*, pp. 13, 30, 31.

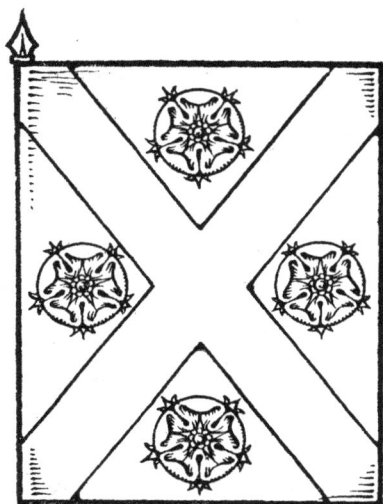

Earl of Lennox   ❖   Lord of Annandale.

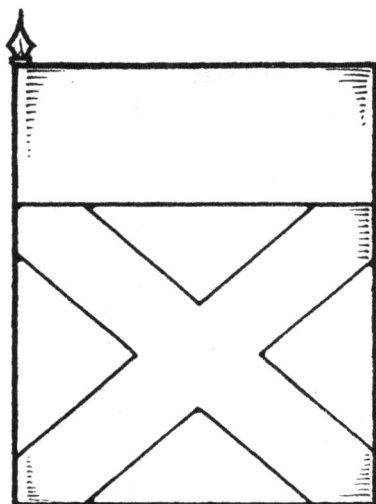

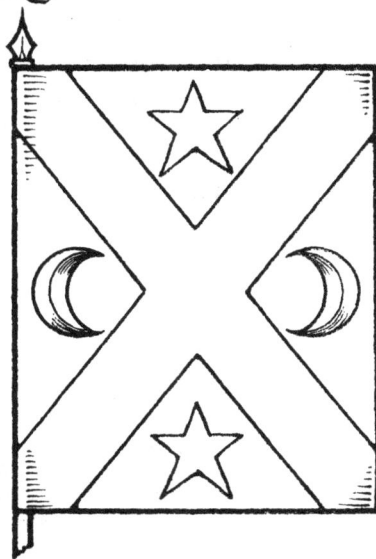

Lord Maxwell   ❖   Haig of Bemersyde.

Fig. 13.—Armorial Banners.

the correct sizes are : Sovereign, 5 feet square ; Duke, 4 feet square ; Earls, 3 feet 6 inches square ; Baronets and feudal barons, 3 feet square.[1] In actual mediaeval warfare none below knights-banneret and (feudal) barons displayed the *square* banner. Other nobles used, and can still only use, the " upright " banners as in Fig. 13. A rectangular banner always had been, and still is, recognised as the proper form of displaying arms on a " house flag " *where the occupant is armigerous* and aspires to more personal display than the St Andrew's Cross (Scottish National Flag) or Union Jack. The best-known examples of the banner are " the ruddy lion ramping in his field of tressured gold " (banner of the King of Scots), and the quartered flag popularly called the " Royal Standard " of the King of Great Britain. These are banners, not standards at all. Most peers, chiefs, and lairds display their own heraldic banners on their castles as house-flags, and many corporations (Edinburgh, Glasgow, Aberdeen, Inverurie) and companies (Bank of Scotland, Commercial Bank of Scotland, Scottish Life Assurance Co.) use their arms in this way.[2] In St George's Chapel the banners of the Knights of the Garter are hung above their stalls. As the Thistle Chapel was too small to accommodate the banners of the Knights of the Thistle, these are in St Giles'.

THE ENSIGN

The " Ensygnye " is a small and highly decorated rectangular flag, fringed with bullion, and with a ground of

---

[1] The correct size of banners for carrying in gatherings and processions has by Lyon Court been laid down as : Peers, 4 ft. by 5 ft.; Feudal Barons, 3 ft. by 3 ft. 9 in. ; Other Chiefs, 33 in. by 42 in. ; Chieftains, 30 in. by 3 ft. Special sizes, 5 ft. by 4 ft. or 3 ft. 9 in. by 3 ft., were, however, appointed by order of the Lord Lyon for the Murrayfield Clan Gathering, 18 August 1951. See *Coat of Arms*, January 1952, p. 9.

[2] 5 ft. by 4 is the best *proportion* for a house-flag. *Size* depends on the height of the building. No non-armigerous person or corporation can display any banner except St Andrew's Cross or the Union Jack.

the livery colours. On this is embroidered the full achievement, including helmet, crest, mantling, and supporters.
Examples of such flags were reproduced on stall plates, *e.g.*
of the Garter,[1] and as flags for identification in a crowd at a
reception are still beautiful and useful.[2] These small-size
heraldic banners were made up on a stiff foundation so as
to display the arms effectively and prevent flapping.

THE STANDARD

The Standard is a long, narrow flag with split ends.[3]
Guidons, which are one-third shorter than standards, display
the crest (or formerly arms, without supporters (see Fig. 14))
or badge, now rounded at the end. Pennons are half the
size of guidons,[4] whose ground-colour was usually either the
livery colours of the owner, or green, the colour of the Scots
national badge, the Thistle. At the end of the standard,
next the staff, was displayed St Andrew's Cross, the Scottish
national flag, so that people could instantly recognise the
owner's nationality. Since the Union, however, it has
become more usual to display the owner's arms in the hoist,
which indeed is more useful. Then follows the badge, crest,
or " beast ", *i.e.* crest, or one of the supporters, whilst the
motto, or slughorn, is inscribed on two or three ribands

[1] St J. Hope, *Heraldry for Craftsmen*, p. 229; figs. 136-8.
[2] *Proc. of Soc. of Antiquaries of Scot.*, lvii, 169. In the seventeenth century
these were loosely, and incorrectly, called (rectangular) " standards ".
[3] Length of standards: King, 8 yds.; Duke, 7 yds.; Marquis, 6½ yds.; Earl,
6 yds.; Viscount, 5½ yds.; Lord, 5 yds.; Baronet, 4½ yds.; Knight and Baron,
4 yds. In the case of chiefs of clans or of families, the standard is now parted in
two per fess, in the case of very major branch-chieftains, tierced per fess, and in the
case of other cadets, even if peers or barons, in four tracts. Those of peers and
barons are split at the ends, those of non-baronial chiefs or others who from special
(governorship or such-like) reasons get standards, have round unsplit ends. (*The
Coat of Arms*, April 1951, p. 193). Only persons who *have* supporters may have
their standard, banners, etc., held up by a single supporter.
[4] *Kinghorn of Auchinhove*, 30 January 1943, Lyon Register, 64; *Maclean of
Ardgour*, 11 July 1944, *ibid.*, xxxv, 15. These are "special" pennons.

drawn bendways across the standard.[1] In a guidon it runs
along into the tail of the flag. Standards, guidons, and
pennons are assigned by Lyon in grants or matriculations
to those who are peers, baronets, knights, barons, or chieftains, *i.e.* those who from their position or feudal tenure
may be presumed to have a " following ". Lairds of non-
baronial tenure are only allowed guidons. Standards and
guidons are legally regarded as an " addition to " the

FIG. 14.—Guidon of David Boswell of Balmuto. " This guidon was captured by Sir William Norris "—at Pinkie, 1547 (Harleian MSS. 1997/86/B). For coloured facsimile see G. Seton, *Family of Seton*, p. 111.

armorial achievement.[2] Pennons, and *pavons* (high diagonal),
charged of the arms, were, strictly, the *only* flags for those
below the rank of baron and banneret.

When a badge or standard is recorded in Lyon Register
it is painted into the script, and if there be supporters in the
arms one of these is drawn holding up the staff,[3] which in
the case of peers is ensigned with the coronet.[4] A standard is
" sette before the pavilion or tente "—nowadays, *e.g.* at High-

---

[1] *Fraser of Reelig*, Lyon Register, xxx, 22, and Plate XVI, p. 79.

[2] *Stewart of Inchmahome*, 27 July 1935, Lyon Register, xxi, 74 ; *Kinghorn of Auchinhove*, 30 January 1943, *ibid.*, xxxiv, 64.

[3] *Fraser of Reelig*, *ibid.*, xxx, 22 ; Plate XVI, p. 79. Only persons *with* supporters are allowed to have one hold their standard or banner-pole.

[4] *Earl of Caithness*, 6 January 1673, *ibid.*, i, 54.

PLATE VIII

(a) The Marchmont standard of Sir Patrick Home of Polwarth, Lord Warden of the Marches
circa 1592.

(b) Arms of Mary Queen of Scots and the Confederate Lords at Carberry Hill.

Shows (1) use by Lords of square heraldic banners; (2) only tressured lion rampant is Royal Banner of Mary Queen of Scots as Sovereign; (3) several St. Andrew's Crosses (national flags) are seen.

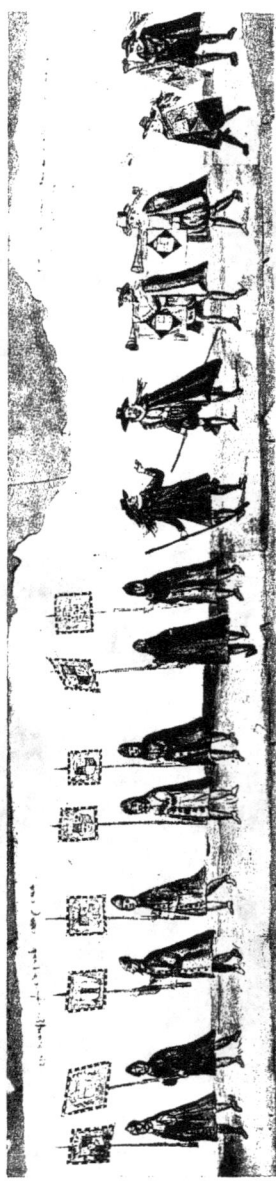

— Armorial Ensigns in seventeenth-century Heraldic Funeral Procession. (*Proc. Society of Antiquaries of Scotland*, vol. 77, Pl. 18.)

land Gatherings—and was "not to be borne in battaile ".[1]
The standard denoting the chieftain's headquarters is set in
the morning. His banner is raised on his personal arrival,
with a fanfare and *failte* on bagpipes. This ceremonial
is observed at, *e.g.*, the Aboyne Highland Gathering.

In flags the charges always face the staff. This is a
practical necessity, since a banner or standard is seen from
both sides. Pennoncels and certain pennons are an exception.

THE PINSEL

This is a triangular flag, 4 ft. 6 in. long by 2 ft. high,
containing the crest within a strap (of the principal charge)
and buckle (gold for full chiefs), bearing the motto, and
within a gold circlet (if necessary fimbriated vert) inscribed
with the chief or baron's title, and ensigned with coronet or
cap. In the fly is the plant badge and a scroll of the slogan
or motto.[2] This flag is used by a Chief's *Tosheadeor* or
local Commander exercising his authority in his Chief's
absence. Given only to Chiefs or very special Chieftain-
barons for practical use.

THE BADGE

The " Badge " in Scotland is often synonymous with
the chief's crest, being so termed when depicted within a
" belt and buckle "[3] on which the motto is displayed (see
p. 178).[4] There are, however, a number of Scottish families
with badges distinct from the crest, and the Scottish national
badges are St Andrew's Cross and the Thistle (see p. 218).

---

[1] Nat. Lib., 25-15, p. 35.
[2] *Mackay, Lord Reay*, Lyon Register, xxxviii, 99; *Chisholm of Chisholm*,
ibid., xxxiii, 12. Murrayfield Flag Order, 1951 (*Coat of Arms*, January 1952, p. 9).
[3] *Faculty of Advocates*, 6 February 1856, Lyon Register, 81 ; Mackenzie,
Works, ii, 628.
[4] It is illegal for clansmen and followers to " use " their chief's crest. It is
worn only to " badge " them as " his " (see pp. 178, 180).

E

The badge was often inherited along with a feudal fief, and indeed had been the " crest "/badge of the original vassal. Its purpose was to be worn by the whole following and displayed on the rallying-flag, whereas the arms and banner denoted the leader himself, *i.e.* the system was practical and related to the organisation of a numerous following.[1]

The recording of badges and standards has become more frequent, but awards of such are restricted, in general, to Peers, Baronage, Chiefs, Chieftains, and the older landed houses ; in fact, where Lyon is satisfied that it is required on practical grounds.[2]

FIG. 15.—STEWART, EARL OF GALLO-WAY. Or, a fess chequy azure and argent, surmounted of a bend engrailed gules, within a double tressure flory counterflory of the last.

AUGMENTATIONS

These are special grants conferred by an order of the Sovereign directed to the Lord Lyon King of Arms. Numbers of such augmentations have been granted for distinguished services in the course of our national history.[3] Perhaps the most usual has been a grant of the Royal Tressure to Scottish nobles in some way connected with the Royal House,[4] or occasionally for distinguished

---

[1] The " plant badges " used by clans are not identificationary but mystic or " totem " plants related to the race. They are heraldically represented on the compartment of the Chief's arms and on his pavilion-pennon, 2 ft. 6 in.

[2] *Maclean of Ardgour*, 10 October 1941, Lyon Register, xxxiv, 42, and *Synopsis of Argument*, p. 77 ; cf. badges on background, *Heraldic Exhibition Catalogue, Edinburgh*, pl. xvi (Crawford), xxxv (Erroll).

[3] Nisbet, *Heraldry*, iii, ii, 73.

[4] *E.g.* Randolph, Earl of Moray ; Duke of Sutherland ; Earl of Strathmore, 1938, Lyon Register, xxxiii. 46 ; Earl of Galloway, etc.

services.[1] Sometimes a King of Arms has himself given an augmentation for distinguished services.[2]

ORDERS OF KNIGHTHOOD

Knights may surround their shields with the *circlet* and motto of any Order to which they belong (Fig. 41, p. 66), the star or badge being pendant beneath. Knights Grand Cross and Knights of the Thistle also surround their shields with the *collar* of their Order (Plates XXI, XXII). So does the Lord Lyon King of Arms, whose arms are surrounded with the collars of the Thistle,[3] and (recently) of S.S. When more than one collar is displayed round the shield, the inner one ranks highest. In recent years *Companions* of Orders have also been allowed to display the circlet of the Order, but the option to do so has not yet been much exercised, and is not encouraged, in Scotland. The inclusion of insignia of knighthood in matrimonial achievements is discussed on pp. 147-8.

BARONETS

Baronets of Nova Scotia are entitled to bear a canton of the arms of Nova Scotia, which is accordingly—being arms—a " property "[4] incident to, and indication of, the holder being a Baronet.[5] It cannot be used as a mark of cadency.[6]

---

[1] *Scott of Thirlestane*, 1542; Nisbet, *Heraldry*, i, 98; *Dundas of Fingask*, 31 March 1769, Lyon Register, 12 December 1770, i, 448; *Wingate*, 14 February 1930, *ibid.*, xxiv, 23.

[2] *Misc. Geneal. et Heraldica*, 1st ser., vol. i, *Bennet*, p. 49; *Innes of Chelsea*, 24 June 1722, Lyon Register, i, 338, and Lord Lyon Erskine's " journal " (L.O.), p. 20.

[3] *Earl of Kinnoull*, *ibid.*, iii, 1a; portrait of Lord Lyon Brodie of Brodie; *Edinburgh Heraldic Exhibition Cat.* 1892, pl. xcviii; *Juridical Review*, xliv, 94, 99.

[4] *Macdonell* v. *Macdonald*, 4 Shaw 374.

[5] *Cuningham*, 11 Dunlop, pp. 1149, 1151. [6] *Heraldry in Scotland*, p. 349.

Fig. 16—Achievements of the Scottish Peerage and Baronetage
(By courtesy of *Debrett's Peerage*)

(*a*) **Duke of Atholl.** Quarterly: 1st grand quarter counterquartered; 1st and 4th, paly of six or and sable (*Atholl*); 2nd and 3rd, or, a fess chequy azure and argent (*Stewart*). 2nd grand quarter azure, three mullets argent, a double tressure flory counterflory or (*Murray*). 3rd grand quarter counterquartered; 1st, argent, on a bend azure three bucks' heads cabossed or (*Stanley*); 2nd, gules, three legs in armour proper, garnished and spurred or, flexed and conjoined in triangle at the upper part of the thigh (*Isle of Man*); 3rd, or, on a chief indented azure, three plates (*Latham*); 4th, gules, two lions passant in pale argent, armed and langued azure (*Strange*). 4th grand quarter counterquartered; 1st and 4th, or, a lion rampant azure, armed and langued gules; 2nd and 3rd, azure, five fusils in fess or (*Percy*). *Crest*—A demi-savage, wreathed about the temples and waist, his arms extended and holding in the right hand a dagger and in the left a key, all proper. *Supporters*—Dexter, a savage proper, wreathed about the temples and loins, his feet in fetters, the chain held in his right hand, proper. Sinister, a lion rampant gules, armed and langued azure, gorged with a plain collar of the last, charged with three mullets argent.

(*b*) **Marquis of Breadalbane** Quarterly: 1st and 4th, gyronny of eight or and sable (*Campbell*); 2nd, argent, a lymphad with the sails furled and oars in action sable (*Lorne*); 3rd, or, a fess chequy azure and argent (*Stewart*). *Crest*—A boar's head erased proper. *Supporters*—Two stags proper, attired and unguled or.

(*c*) **Earl of Dalhousie.** Argent, an eagle displayed, beaked and membered gules. *Crest*—A unicorn's head, couped at the neck argent, armed, maned and tufted or. *Supporters*—Dexter, a griffin argent; sinister, a greyhound argent, gorged with a collar gules, charged with three escallops of the first.

(*d*) **Viscount of Arbuthnott.** Azure, a crescent between three mullets argent. *Crest*—A peacock's head couped at the neck, proper. *Supporters*—Two wyverns, wings elevated, tails nowed vert, vomiting flames, proper.

(*e*) **Lord Elphinstone.** Quarterly: 1st grand quarter, argent, a chevron sable, between three boars' heads erased gules, armed of the field and langued azure (*Elphinstone*). 2nd grand quarter counterquartered; 1st, gules, a chevron within a double tressure flory counterflory argent (*Fleming*); 2nd, azure, three fraises argent (*Fraser*); 3rd, argent, on a chief gules, three pallets or (*Keith*); 4th, or, three bars wavy gules (*Drummond*). 3rd grand quarter, argent, a chevron between three otters' heads erased gules, within a bordure of the last (*Fullerton*). 4th grand quarter, sable, on a cross argent, square pierced of the field, four eagles displayed, of the first; in the dexter canton, an arm embowed proper, issuing out of a naval crown, the hand holding a trident or (*Buller*). *Crest*—A lady from the waist upwards, richly habited in red, her arms extended, the right hand supporting a tower, and the left holding a branch of laurel, all proper. *Supporters*—Two wild men, wreathed about the temples and loins with laurel, and holding on their exterior shoulders clubs, proper.

(*f*) **Burnett of Leys,** Baronet. Argent, three holly-leaves in chief vert, and a hunting-horn in base sable, stringed and garnished gules. *Crest*—A hand with a knife, pruning a vinetree proper. *Supporters*—Dexter, a Highlander in hunting garb; sinister, a greyhound, proper. *Baronet's badge* pendant below shield.

(a) DUKE OF ATHOLL.

(b) MARQUIS OF BREADALBANE.

(c) EARL OF DALHOUSIE.

(d) VISCOUNT OF ARBUTHNOTT.

(e) LORD ELPHINSTONE.

(f) BURNETT OF LEYS, Bart.

E 2

A claim to this " property " (or the equivalent " red hand " canton conferred on British Baronets by the terms of their patents) involves a judicial decision determining the claimant's right before a competent Court, and in relation to " heritage " inseparably related to the Baronetcy.[1] Such a judicial decision on the descent of property descending like the

FIG. 17.—Badge of Baronets of Nova Scotia.

Baronetcy the Keeper of the Roll of Baronets is bound to follow,[2] and illustrates the practical effect of the recognition of the King of Arms' jurisdiction in the Baronetage Warrant, 1911, sec. 13—arms in Scotland being an estate, *i.e.* " feudal heritage ", per Lord Justice Clerk in *Maclean of Ardgour* v. *Maclean*, p. 683.[3]

In addition to the canton, the badge of the Baronets of Nova Scotia[4] is suspended beneath the shield from an orange tawny ribbon (see Fig. 16 (*f*)). Other baronets have recently obtained the right to a badge likewise suspended beneath the shield. Their ribbon is orange tawny, edged with blue. The Nova Scotia Baronet's badge (minus circlet) was originally conferred as a canton or inescutcheon, within the shield, a privilege which continues to be matriculated by

[1] *Grant of Grant* (Lord Strathspey), 27 January 1950, Lyon Register, xxxvii, 143; 1950, Scots Law Times, 17 (and equally in *pereduct* form).

[2] *Baronetage Report*, Home Office, 1907, sec. 20; Treaty of Union, Acts 18 and 19.

[3] Cf. F. W. Pixley, *History of the Baronetage*, p. 184; *A.P.S.*, v, 223.

[4] Originally granted (without circlet) as a canton, and still frequently matriculated thus, *Stirling-Maxwell of Pollock*, Lyon Register, xxviii, 56; *Castlestewart*, 25 June 1945, *ibid.*, xxxv, 44; *Strathspey*, 27 January 1950, *ibid.*, xxxvii, 143, 1950, S.L.T., p. 17; *Mackay of Farr* (Lord Reay), 19 July 1951, *ibid.*, xxxviii, 99.

Baronets, whose arms are not obscured by the addition. It accordingly appears in various, indeed quite recent, arms.[1] An inescutcheon argent charged with a hand gules is similarly a right of British Baronets.

CORONETS OF RANK

Coronets consisting of the Cap of Maintenance within a circlet of gold of varying patterns (see Fig. 16) have been assigned to the five ranks of the peerage : Duke, Marquis, Earl, Viscount, and Lord (Baron) of Parliament. Until the seventeenth century, Lords of Parliament, like the other feudal Barons, wore the Cap of Maintenance alone.[2] The circlet of a Lord-baron's coronet has six silver balls ; a Viscount's has sixteen ; an Earl's coronet has eight balls on long spikes, alternated with eight strawberry leaves ; a Marquis's, four balls on short spikes, alternated with four strawberry leaves ; [3] a Duke's coronet has eight strawberry leaves only.

THE SHIELD AND ITS CONTENTS

The Shield consists for practical purposes of a background called the *field*, and of objects upon this, technically called *charges*. Both field and charges are depicted in certain bright and simple colourings.

THE HERALDIC TINCTURES

To secure the instant recognition for which armory exists, heralds soon discovered the simple rule (to which there are only a few exceptions), that if the field is of colour, the charges

---

[1] *Stirling-Maxwell of Pollok*, 1929, Lyon Register, xxviii, 56 ; *Earl of Castlestewart*, 25 June 1945, *ibid.*, xxxv, 44.

[2] *Art of Heraldry*, pp. 279, 288 ; Barons' chapeaux were lined with miniver (heraldically depicted " ermine ").

[3] See coronet of Earl of Linlithgow, coloured in Plate XXXI, p. 141.

DIVISIONS OF THE SHIELD

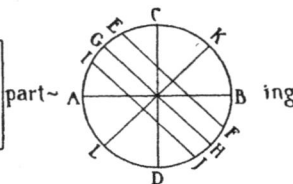

A B the Horizon ⎤
C D the Vertical ⎥ part~
G.H the Zodiac ⎥
K L the Axis ⎦

ing ⎡ Per Fess
⎢ Per Pale
⎢ Per Bend Dexter
⎣ Per Bend Sinister

Per Bend   Per B.Sinistr   Per Chevron   P.Cross or Quarterly   Per Fess   Per Pale

Per Pale & Base   P.Pale & P.Chev   Per Saltier   Angled P Fess, acute   A P Fess, rectangled

POINTS OF THE ESCVTCHEON

SHIELD

Points of the Shield Explained		The Dexter		The Sinister	E	The centre or fesse point
The dexter chief point	A	or	A B C	or	F	The navel or nombril point
The middle chief	B	Righthand side	D E	Lefthand side	G	The dexter base
The sinister chief	C	of the	F	of the	H	The middle base
The honour or collar point	D	SHIELD	G H I	SHIELD	I	The sinister base

LINES

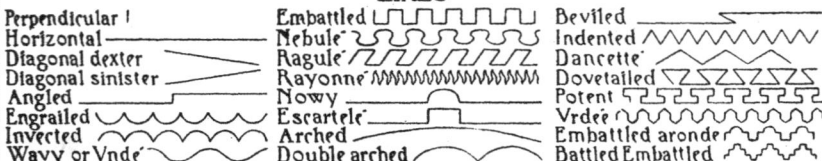

Perpendicular ǀ
Horizontal ───
Diagonal dexter
Diagonal sinister
Angled
Engrailed
Invected
Wavy or Vnde

Embattled
Nebule
Ragule
Rayonne
Nowy
Escartele
Arched
Double arched

Beviled
Indented
Dancette
Dovetailed
Potent
Vrdee
Embattled aronde
Battled Embattled

METALS, COLOVRS OR TINCTVRES

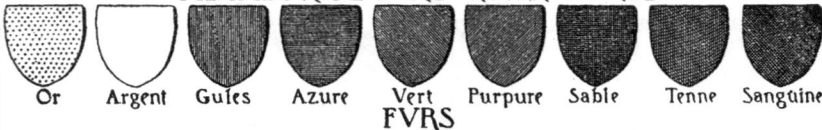

Or   Argent   Gules   Azure   Vert   Purpure   Sable   Tenne   Sanguine

FVRS

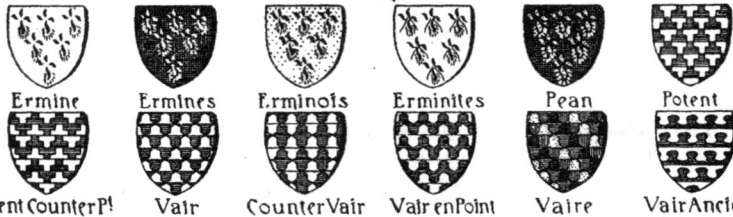

Ermine   Ermines   Erminois   Erminites   Pean   Potent

Potent Counter Pt   Vair   Counter Vair   Vair en Point   Vaire   Vair Ancient

FIG. 18.—Lines, Partitions, and Tinctures.
(From Professor Coppinger's *Heraldry Simplified*.)

must be metal, and *vice versa.* Hence the well-known heraldic rule, that one must not put " colour upon colour ", or " metal upon metal ", simply because the result will lack contrast, and be difficult to recognise readily. Where, however, the field is divided, the rule is to a certain extent modified. The heraldic tinctures are as follows : [1]

Heraldic Term	Abbreviation	Description	Conventional Hatching, etc.
Metals—			
Or . .	Or	Gold or Yellow	Small dots
Argent . .	Arg.	Silver or White	Plain
Colours—			
Gules . .	Gu.	Red	Vertical lines
Azure . .	Az.	Blue	Horizontal lines
Sable . .	Sa.	Black	Cross hatching
Vert . .	Vert	Green	Lines in bend
Purpure .	Purp.	Purple	Lines in bend sinister
Tenny . .	Ten.	Orange	Hatchings in Fig. 18
Sanguine .	Sang.	Blood colour	ditto
Furs—			
Ermine .	..	White fur, black spots	
Contre-ermine	Ermines	Black fur, white spots	
Erminois * .	..	Gold fur, black spots	
Pean . .	..	Black fur, gold spots	
Vair † . .	..	Alternate rows of shield-shaped pieces (actually squirrel skins) in blue and white	
Vairy . .	..	Of any two tinctures (metal and colour) specified, ditto	
Potent . .	..	A fur made of alternate crutchhead-shaped pieces	

* This fur presumably represents brown marten, the municipal and professional fur, as instanced by the most ancient Lord Provosts' robes, *e.g.* Aberdeen. (Robes of the Feudal Baronage, *Soc. of Antiquaries of Scot.,* lxxix, p. 130 *et seq.*)

† This fur, worn by the baronage (as distinct from the Earls) under 1455 cap. (*A.P.S.,* ii, 43), seems in origin to have been the fur of the allodial *uradel, e.g.* the arms and mantle of the celebrated *Sire de Coucy.* (Mackenzie, *Works,* ii, 590 ; *Soc. of Antiquaries of Scot.,* lxxix, 133.)

There are a few other colours and furs, too seldom met with to be worth mentioning. The colours may be of any shade most suitable for the work in hand, but bright colours usually look best in heraldry. Until recently, it has been

[1] The conventional hatching-lines are shown in Fig. 18.

difficult to get silver paint guaranteed not to tarnish, but some manufacturers now supply satisfactory silver-coloured paint of the sort used for hot-water radiators.

· The field may consist of a single metal, a single colour, or a single fur, but it may consist of two or more of these, parted in the various divisions I shall mention presently. The two tinctures may both be colours, both be metals, or both be furs, for neither is imposed on the other ; or they may be of metal and colour, metal and fur, or colour and fur.

THE LINES OF PARTITION

Many coats consist merely of a field of two or more tinctures, divided by " lines of partition ", the terms and nature of which will be most easily grasped from studying Fig. 18, page 52. Briefly, shields of more than one tincture are divided by lines. When the line is perpendicular, it is termed " per pale "; when horizontal, " per fess "; diagonal from the dexter chief, " per bend " ; diagonal from sinister chief, " per bend sinister ". When a line is not simple and straight, it has a heraldic name expressive of its form. These are best understood from studying Fig. 18 on page 52.

FIG. 19.—CAMPBELL, DUKE OF ARGYLL. Quarterly: 1st and 4th, gyronny of eight or and sable (*Campbell*); 2nd and 3rd, argent, a lymphad, sails furled, pennons flying, and oars in action sable (*Lorne*).

When the field is divided into several strips according to any of the above lines of partition, the shield is said to be " paly ", " bendy ", " chevronny ", or (if the divisions are fess-ways) " barry ", and if the divisions are less than ten in number the qualification " of four ", " of six " (the most usual, *e.g. Atholl*, Fig. 16 (*a*)), or " of eight " is added.

Similarly when the shield is parted per gyron (Fig. 23, No. 11) it is blazoned " gyronny of " the precise number of divisions (see Fig. 19, which is " gyronny of eight ").

If the shield is divided into four equal parts it is "quartered", and the details of each quarter must be separately expressed. If any of the quarters are subdivided,[1] the first or main four quarters are termed " grand quarters ", and those which are subdivided will be referred to as " grand quarters counter-quartered ", and then each quarter of this " grand quarter " individually described (see pp. 138, 149).

FIG. 20.—Per pale dexter and sinister.

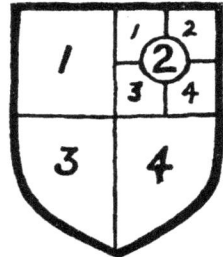

FIG. 21. — Quarters and grand quarters —how numbered.

Heralds distinguish nine positions in the shield, which are simply described in a figure in Fig. 18.

When a man holds his shield in front of him, the *dexter* is at *his* right hand, the *sinister* at *his* left. Consequently the dexter side of the shield is to the left, and the sinister to the right, of persons *looking at a shield* from the front.

CHARGES ON THE SHIELD

THE ORDINARIES

The simplest and earliest charges are certain stripes and patterns known as " The Ordinaries ", which are of a standard size, and most of them have one or more diminutive.[2]

[1] See Fig. 16 (a), *Duke of Atholl*, and (e), *Lord Elphinstone*.

[2] The classification of the Ordinaries varies (see *Art of Heraldry*, p. 63). I have here given a list of those concerning which there is no question, and which may usefully be memorised.

The pale is a stripe from top to bottom, a little less than
one-third the width of the shield ; the bend is similar, but
crosses the shield either from dexter, or sinister, chief ; the

Ordinary	Diminutive	Further Diminutives
1. The chief . . .	Comble	..
2. The fess . . .	Bar	Barrulet
3. The pale . . .	Pallet	..
4. The chevron . .	Chevronel	..
5. The bend . . .	Bendlet	Riband
6. The saltire . .	*None* *	..
7. The cross . . .	*None*, but over 100 varieties	..
8. The pile . . .	*None* *	..
9. The pairle . . .	*None*, but when couped is termed a shakefork (Fig. 23, No. 17)	..
10. The quarter . .	Canton (Fig. 23, No. 10 shows the diminutive, *i.e.* the canton)	..

* A cross or saltire *formée* is one in which the edges are straight and the ends broader than
the centre. (*Campbell of Craignish*, 1948, Lyon Register, xxxvi, 48.)

cross is that known as St George's ; the saltire, our Scottish
national device, St Andrew's Cross ; the chevron is like the
couples of a house.

There cannot normally be more than one of the same
ordinary in any single shield [1] (or quartering—if the shield
itself comprises quarterings). When more than one of these
basic devices is shown, it is always in the diminutive—*i.e.*
you can only have one pale but two or three pallets ; one
fess but two or more bars or barrulets. A cotise is a very
narrow repetition of the charge, following its outline, and
with the field showing through a narrow intervening space.
There are numerous minor variations of the ordinaries ; *e.g.*
the cross is subject to many variations, some of which are
seldom met with. In case of difficulty one should consult
a heraldic dictionary.

English heralds call the bordure (Fig. 22, No. 9) an

[1] The pile is an exception ; three are often found.

ordinary, and such it is in the sense that not more than one
bordure can be displayed on a single shield.   In Scotland,

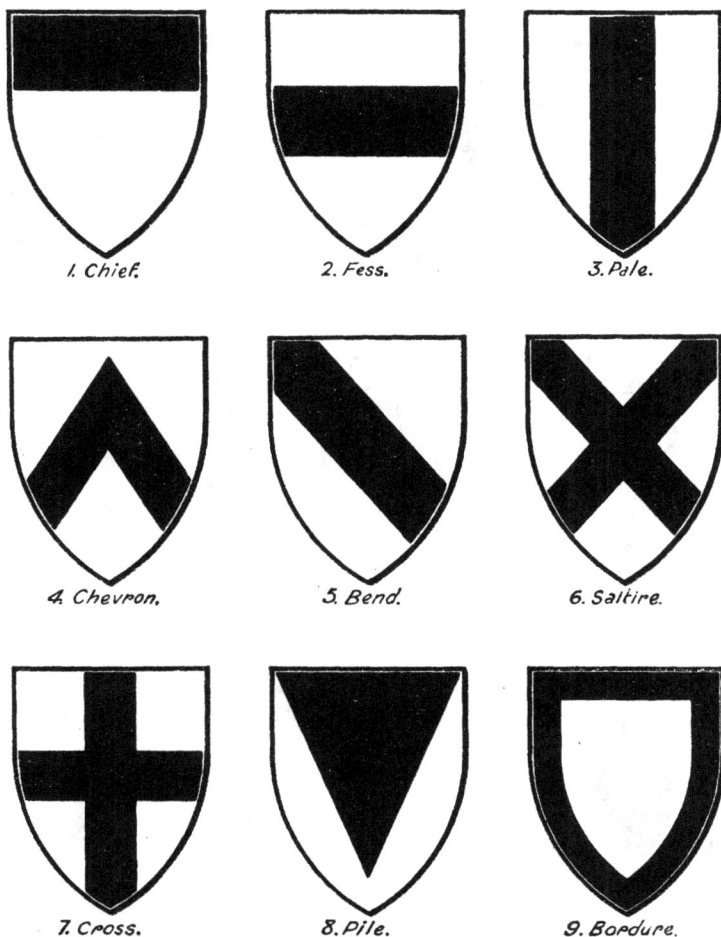

FIG. 22.—The Honourable Ordinaries.

however, the bordure is never a charge, and when it appears
it is invariably as a mark of cadency.

THE SUB-ORDINARIES

There are several other conventional patterns, so usual in heraldry that they may here be mentioned. They differ from

10. Canton.

11. Gyron.

12. Inescutcheon.

13. Lozenge.

14. Rustre.

15. Mascle.

16. Fusil.

17. Pairle.

18. Fret.

FIG. 23.—The Sub-Ordinaries.

the " ordinaries ", in that more than one " sub-ordinary " may appear in a single coat of arms. The number of sub-

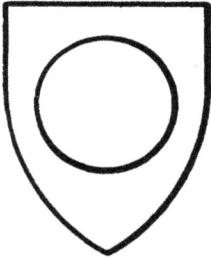

FIG. 24.—Roundel.

ordinaries has been variously stated, but the most usual are the gyron, the inescutcheon, the lozenge, the rustre, the mascle, the fusil, the fret, and the roundel. The name of this last differs according to its tincture, viz. : a roundel or is a " bezant " ; argent, a " plate " ; gules, a " torteau " ; azure, a " hurt " ; vert, a " pomeis " ; and sable, a " pellet ". It is unnecessary to memorise these, but it is useful to know that a roundel barry-wavy azure and argent is termed a " fountain ". The pairle (Fig. 23, No. 17) is an ordinary.

HERALDIC ANIMALS

It has to be said that heraldic charges include everything in the world, the heavens, and beneath, as well as other objects such as the griffon and the unicorn, which appertain to neither. To enumerate even a portion of the charges would be impossible, and the simple course is, when you meet a term you do not understand, look up the dictionary in Grant's *Manual of Heraldry, Debrett's Heraldry,* Fox-Davies' *The Art of Heraldry,* or Nisbet's compendious *System,* and verify the details. No one can carry these innumerable objects in their memory, and many of them are but seldom met with. Even when charges are described as " proper ", *i.e.* in their natural colours, the herald—like the caricaturist—seizes the striking

FIG. 25.—Lion statant.

FIG. 26.—Lion passant.

features of every creature, and emphasises these. Thus it is rather the *leoninity* of the lion, or the *oakishness* of the

FIG. 27.—Lion passant guardant.

FIG. 28.—Lion passant regardant.

FIG. 29.—Lion rampant.

oak-tree, which the heraldic artist emphasises, consequently making the shield instantly recognisable.

It is the rule in heraldry that every object which is not *affronté* is shown facing dexter. If it is not, that is if it is facing sinister, then it is termed *contourné*, and that *must* be stated. If two creatures are facing each other, they will be *combatant*—if they are of a fierce nature—otherwise they will be said to be *respecting* each other.

FIG. 30.—Lion rampant guardant.

FIG. 31.—Lion rampant regardant.

FIG. 32.—Lion couchant.

The most usual positions occupied by the bodies of heraldic animals are best demonstrated by the lion, viz. rampant, passant, statant, sejant, sejant-erect, couchant, dormant (sleeping), and salient. The head requires special attention, unless it is facing forward, for if the lion be full-

FIG. 33.—Lion sejant.   FIG. 34.—Lion sejant erect.   FIG. 35.—Lion sejant guardant erect.

faced he is *guardant*, and if his head be turned backwards, *regardant*. These terms apply to all animals, with a few exceptions, *e.g.* a griffon rampant is termed *segreant* ; a stag passant is *trippant* ; whilst a stag, horse, or dog at full speed is *courant*.

Whenever part of an animal appears, the description must state how much of it is shown ; and whether couped, *i.e.* cut with a clean line ; or erased, *i.e.* torn or jagged. If an

FIG. 36.—Two lions rampant combatant.   FIG. 37.—Lion coward.   FIG. 38.—Lion tricorporate.

animal's head be shown " affronté ", *i.e.* cut off close behind the ears,[1] it is termed " cabossed " ; but a lion's or leopard's

[1] See Plate XVI, *Fraser of Reelig*, 3rd quartering for *Moniack*.

F

head in that position is merely termed his "face", or where it is a fox, his "mask". An eagle with wings expanded [1] is said to be "displayed"; a fish is "naiant" when swimming across the shield,[2] but "hauriant" if placed vertically, viz., "in pale".

All animals and birds of prey are said to be "armed" if their beaks and claws are some special colour. The term

FIG. 39.—MACKAY, LORD REAY. Azure, on a chevron or, between three bears' heads couped argent, muzzled gules, a roebuck's head erased, between two hands grasping daggers, the points turned towards the buck's head, all proper. (Lyon Register, xxxviii, 99.)

FIG. 40.—MACGREGOR OF MAC-GREGOR. Argent, a sword in bend azure, an oak tree in bend sinister proper, on the dexter canton an antique crown gules, in centre chief the inescutcheon of a baronet of Great Britain. (Lyon Register, i, 584.)

applies to the tusks of a boar, and the horns of a bull, goat, or ram. A stag,[3] however, is "attired of" his antlers, and creatures with hoofs are "unguled"; the term "langued" refers to the tongue.

Amongst a few common heraldic objects, one may observe that an uprooted tree is "eradicated", a sheaf is always a "garb", a star of five points and straight edges [4] is nowadays

[1] See Fig. 16 (c), p. 49, *Earl of Dalhousie*.   [2] See Fig. 41, p. 66.
[3] For examples of stags "attired and unguled", see Plate XVI, p. 79.
[4] See Plate XLIII, *Innes of Learney*, 1st and 4th quarters; Lyon Register, xxii, 73.

called a "mullet ",[1] a star with wavy rays an "estoile ", and an oyster shell an "escallop ". A rose is usually "barbed and seeded ", and a castle or tower "masoned ", *i.e.* the masonry outlined, in some contrasting tincture.

THE RULES OF BLAZON

To *blazon* a coat of arms is to describe it scientifically, in words which cannot be misunderstood, just as a doctor writes a prescription, or an architect a specification. From a correct blazon, anyone versed in heraldry can instantly picture what the arms look like, and draw a reproduction of a shield he has never seen. To *emblazon* is to depict a coat of arms in colour. The rules of blazon, or verbal description, are few and simple :

1. If the shield is impaled, or quartered, or both, these facts must first be stated, and then each several quartering and both sides of the coat must severally be described by itself—such description commencing with a statement as to whether it is *dexter* or *sinister*, or in a quartered shield, the number of the quartering, 1st, 2nd, 3rd, or 4th ; but if—as often happens—the fourth quartering is a repetition of the first, the blazon will commence, " Quarterly, 1st and 4th ".

2. First describe the field, simply by mentioning its tincture. If it be composite, say in what form, *e.g.* " parted per fess [or whatever it may be] or and gules ". The colour to be first mentioned is that applicable to the portion of the shield which is either " in chief ", or " in dexter ".

[1] In Scots heraldry the term " star " is properly applied to what is now—following English practice—usually termed a " mullet ", hence cases of confusion over old " celestial " blazons, where " star " does *not* mean " estoile ". (Nisbet's *Heraldry*, 1722, p. 252.) Legally, therefore, " star " and " mullet " are similar.

3. Name the principal charge or ordinary, qualified by any particular outline, and specify its tincture.

4. Describe any other charges on the field, naming their situation, metal, or colour.

5. Thereafter describe any charges situated on the ordinary, stating their outline, position, and tinctures.

6. The position of a charge need not be stated, when there can be no mistake about its natural position—otherwise it must be explicitly described.

7. If there be no ordinary on a shield the principal charge is mentioned first, then its colour, then the subsidiary charges, unless these are of the same colour.

8. When an ordinary, or any one figure, is placed on another it is always named after the ordinary, or figure, over which it is placed, with the words " over all ". The charge underneath is mentioned first.

9. When an ordinary surmounts a single object, the latter is said to be *debruised* by the ordinary.

10. When the situation of the principal charge is not expressed, it is understood to occupy the centre of the field.

11. When any single figure is borne in any other part of the shield than the centre, or issuant from any border of the shield, the point of issue must be named.

12. If a mullet, or similar figure, has more than five points, they must be specified, and if pierced, it must be mentioned. Similarly, if any object has special features, or an animal is " armed " or " langued " of a special colour, say so.

13. If any natural object be displayed in its natural colours, it is termed *proper*, and that term follows after the

PLATE X

(*a*)

(*b*)

(*c*)

(*a*) The Lerags Cross ; arms of Archibald Campbell of Leraig (1516), incorporated with
Celtic tracery and design. (*Proc. Soc. of Antiquaries of Scotland*, lxi. 145.)

(*b*) Carved stone from Fornett House ; arms of Master Robert Irvine of Fornett, surmounted by those of his feudal superior, the Earl Marischal.

(*c*) Carved wooden panel, *circa* 1473 ; Arms of Thomas Spens, Bishop of Aberdeen.
(*Proc. Soc. of Antiquaries of Scotland*, lxiv. 337.)

PLATE XI

(a) Tympanum of dormer window at Edzell Castle ; Lindsay arms. (*Proc. Soc. of Antiquaries of Scotland*, lxv. 169.)

(b) Carved stone fireplace-lintel, painted in colour, Cromarty Castle ($60\frac{1}{2}'' \times 33''$), displaying arms of Sir Thomas Urquhart of Cromarty (1651).

Arms—Or, three boars' heads erased gules, armed and langued azure. *Crest*—A female figure from the waist upwards, arms extended, holding in her dexter hand a sword, and in her sinister hand a tree eradicated. *Supporters*—Two greyhounds argent, having collars and leashes reflexed over the back, gules. *Motto*—"Meane weil, speak weil, and doe weil." This is an excellent example of seventeenth-century design. (*Proc. Soc. of Antiquaries of Scotland*, lxi. 182.)

PLATE X

(*b*)

(*a*)   (*c*)

(*a*) The Lerags Cross ; arms of Archibald Campbell of Leraig (1516), incorporated with
   Celtic tracery and design. (*Proc. Soc. of Antiquaries of Scotland*, lxi. 145.)

(*b*) Carved stone from Fornett House ; arms of Master Robert Irvine of Fornett, surmounted by those of his feudal superior, the Earl Marischal.

(*c*) Carved wooden panel, *circa* 1473 ; Arms of Thomas Spens, Bishop of Aberdeen.
   (*Proc. Soc. of Antiquaries of Scotland*, lxiv. 337.)

PLATE XI

(a) Tympanum of dormer window at Edzell Castle; Lindsay arms. (*Proc. Soc. of Antiquaries of Scotland*, lxv. 169.)

(b) Carved stone fireplace-lintel, painted in colour, Cromarty Castle (60½″ × 33″), displaying arms of Sir Thomas Urquhart of Cromarty (1651).

Arms—Or, three boars' heads erased gules, armed and langued azure. *Crest*—A female figure from the waist upwards, arms extended, holding in her dexter hand a sword, and in her sinister hand a tree eradicated. *Supporters*—Two greyhounds argent, having collars and leashes reflexed over the back, gules. *Motto*—"Meane weil, speak weil, and doe weil." This is an excellent example of seventeenth-century design. (*Proc. Soc. of Antiquaries of Scotland*, lxi. 182.)

description of the object, its bodily position, etc., and situation.

14. When several similar figures appear in the arms, their individual attitude and their position in the shield must both be expressed. *Example* : Azure, three swords in fess paleways ; and Azure, three swords paleways in fess— indicate in the first case that the three swords are lying across the shield, and in the latter that they are standing vertically.

15. When a specified number of charges is immediately followed by the same number of charges elsewhere, the number of charges is not repeated, the words " as many " being substituted.

16. When a coat of arms is parti-coloured in its field, and the charges are alternatively of the same colours transposed, the term *countercharged* expresses the description.

It is the practice, in blazoning, never to mention the same colour more than once, subsequent references being " of the first ", " of the second ", or " of the third ", according to whichever colour was first mentioned in the description. With expert heralds, this causes no confusion, indeed prevents mistakes, but the beginner need not hesitate to repeat each colour if he finds it easier to do so, until he becomes more expert.

The simplest and quickest way to learn the art of blazon is to spend an afternoon examining Burke's or Debrett's *Peerage and Baronetage*, successively comparing the blazons of each coat of arms with the adjoining illustration. Very little practice will enable anyone to describe a coat of arms intelligibly, to carry it in his mind or to reproduce a drawing of any coat of arms of which he receives a written description.

As an example, the arms of *Kaid* Sir Harry Maclean, K.C.M.G., are blazoned :

F 2

Quarterly, 1st, argent, a rock gules; 2nd, argent, a dexter hand fesswise couped, gules, holding a cross crosslet fitchée, azure; 3rd, or, a lymphad, oars in saltire, sails furled, sable, flagged gules; 4th, argent, a salmon naiant proper, in chief two eagles' heads respectant gules; all within a bordure engrailed gules for difference; around the shield is placed the circlet, and pendant therefrom the badge of a K.C.M.G., and above the shield is placed a helmet befitting his degree with a mantling gules doubled argent, and on a wreath of his liveries is set for crest, a branch of laurel and another of cypress in saltire surmounted of a battle-axe erect in pale all proper, and in an escrol over the same this motto, " Altera Merces ".

FIG. 41.—*Kaid* SIR HARRY A. DE V. MACLEAN, K.C.M.G. (Lyon Register, xx, 27). This shows the knight's helmet and the circlet of his order with pendant badge.

CHAPTER V

RECORDS OF SCOTTISH MEDIAEVAL HERALDIC PRACTICE

THERE are few countries in which the use of heraldry was more extensive than in Scotland, but the repeated invasions, domestic feuds, and finally the vulgar craze for Anglo - classical architecture, involved the destruction of much of the characteristic Scottish work in both architecture and furnishings. Military trappings, surcoats, shields, and banners are necessarily perishable, and few examples of these, upon which heraldry was so freely displayed, now survive. These must now be traced principally from inventories of the furniture which formerly existed in castles and abbeys, and upon those monumental effigies originally painted in heraldic colours, of which a number still survive, usually in a multilated condition, amongst the ruins of our cathedrals and churches. Several ancient banners and

EARL OF CRAWFORD. Quarterly: 1st and 4th, gules, a fess chequy argent and azure (*Lindsay*): 2nd and 3rd, or, a lion rampant gules, debruised by a riband sable (*Abernethy*).

pennons are still extant,[1] but the faded tinctures and perished silk necessarily cannot now display the brilliant colours as they were in far-off days. Of our pre-Reformation Scottish stained glass, only a few panes still exist. The earliest and most ample surviving sources of practical heraldry are the armorial seals, of which thousands still hang from documents in Scottish charter-chests, though all too many have perished from careless handling or neglect. A collection of some 3000 seal-casts is preserved in the Lyon Office, and descriptions are in the extant

FIG. 42.—Seal of William Graham, Earl of Airth, Menteith and Strathearn, 1622.

works of Henry Laing and W. Rae Macdonald.[2]

Scottish mediaeval buildings teemed with heraldic decoration. Some splendid examples of this still survive, such as the ceilings at the Castles of Collairnie) Plate XXXVIII, Muchalls, Balbegno, Crathes, and Delgaty, and the galleries of Earlshall [3] and Pinkie, though others, such as the glorious halls at Seton and Huntly, have been destroyed. Our Scottish churches also, deprived at the Reformation of the religious

---

[1] *Heraldry in Relation to Scots History and Art*, p. 133, but see A. Ross, *Old Scottish Regimental Colours*, p. 64.

[2] *Scottish Armorial Seals*, 1904 (new edition 1939, a very limited one).

[3] Plate VII ; and *Heraldry in Relation to Scots History and Art*, pl. 69.

PLATE XII

(a)

(b)

Heraldic ceiling in modelled plaster at Muchalls Castle.

(a) Arms of Burnett of Leys. (The achievements are coloured.)
(b) Arms of Maitland, Earl of Lauderdale, impaling Seton of Dunfermline.

PLATE XIII

(a) Sixteenth-century Armorial Embroidery showing the arms and supporters of Campbell of Glenorchy. (The embroiderer has, however, made certain heraldic errors—the gyrons are disposed with sable "ist" and the fess chequy has four instead of three tracts.)

(b) Carved effigy of the Earl and Countess of Menteith at Inchmahome Priory; showing fine example of early heater-shaped shield, with finely proportioned seven-point label for difference. (*Proc. Soc. of Antiquaries of Scotland*, vol. 84, Pl. 28.)

motif usual in ecclesiastical architecture, expanded into splendid schemes of heraldic decoration, many of which have unfortunately been destroyed by nineteenth-century modernisation. Galleries such as that at Kilbirnie still remain, and there is now a tendency amongst Scottish architects to revert to the national love of heraldry in archi-

FIG. 43.—Armorial panel from seat in the old church of Prestonpans (date 1626), showing the arms of the two Lairds of the family of Hamilton of Preston and their wives, on separate shields, viz.—George Hamilton of Preston and Barbara Cockburn, his wife; Sir John Hamilton of Preston and Dame Katharine Howieson, Lady Preston, his wife.

tecture, both ecclesiastical and secular. Buildings such as the Thistle Chapel, the Highlanders' Memorial Church in Glasgow, St Leonard's Church, Dunfermline, the heraldic gallery at Echt in Aberdeenshire, and greatest of all, the Scottish National War Memorial, carry on the traditions of Scottish ecclesiastical heraldry. It is only to be regretted that some modern church architects decorate Communion tables and church furniture with banal, meaningless, or far-fetched " symbols ", whereas the Inventories of the Scots Chapel-Royal, the magnificent ceiling of St Machar Cathedral in Aberdeen,[1] and the luxuriant traceries at Roslin Chapel, for example, as well as numbers of ancient Scottish Communion vessels, *e.g.* the Duirinish Communion cups, decorated with the arms of the celebrated Sir Rory Mor Macleod of Macleod (Fig. 44), show how Scottish architects made our northern fanes and their furnishings literally blaze with heraldic decoration throughout their whole fabric—including the very reredos and altars. The castellated and domestic architecture of Scotland, which, like our national ecclesiastical style, embodied the combination of square and round, lofty lines, turrets, and crow-stepped gables, naturally lent itself to a lavish use of heraldry. There is hardly an ancient building in Scotland which does not display many heraldic carvings. To single out any would be almost invidious, but the façade of Glamis, the staircase towers at Huntly and Druminnor, and the varied heraldic display at Fyvie, are perhaps the most splendid of all.

FIG. 44.—The Duirinish Communion Cup engraved with the arms of Sir Rory Mor Macleod of Macleod.

The works of Billings and M'Gibbon and Ross contain innumerable examples. Modern architects are sometimes nervous of heraldry, because they do not understand its details, and fear they may go wrong. No science is more adaptable to the modern taste for simple straightforward decorative art, and no architect or designer need experience difficulty. If doubts arise on any point, a call at the Lyon Office (opposite the North British Station

[1] " Heraldic Ceiling of St Machar Cathedral ", New Spalding Club Publication.

Hotel, Edinburgh), or letter to the Lyon Clerk, will ensure helpful advice, and prevent any mistakes. In most cases the requisite information will be obtained gratuitously, or, at most, for a Government search fee of 5s. Before expending time and money on heraldic decoration, it is often wise, if any doubt is felt, to suggest that a client should send the designs to the Lyon Office for opinion. All heraldry for buildings under H.M. Office of Works has to be revised in this way.

Great architects, such as the late Sir Robert Lorimer, are continually in touch with the Lyon Office, and so are all our prominent craftsmen and designers, most of whom are personally known to H.M. Officers of Arms.

FIG. 45.—Archery Medal of James Bethune of Balfour (697). Quarterly: 1st and 4th, azure, a fess between three lozenges or (*Bethune*); 2nd and 3rd, argent, on a chevron sable, an otter's head erased argent (*Balfour of that Ilk*). *Crest*—An otter's head argent. *Motto* above —" Debonnaire". *Supporters*—Two otters proper.

In heraldic gold and silver plate, Scotland is not so poor as might be supposed, and indeed may be considered rich, when we realise how little of our ancient Scottish plate survives. The Archery medals attached to the arrows and bowls of the King's Bodyguard, and those at St Andrews, preserve examples of contemporary heraldic engraving from the sixteenth century onwards (see Figs. 45, 55, 89, 97). Unfortunately neither our Universities nor our Trade Incorporations have had the wealth with which to build up collections such as those of the Colleges and Livery Companies of England, but they carved on tables and chairs [1] what, had means permitted, they would have certainly engraved upon plate of silver and gold, and the Universities of St Andrews and Glasgow still possess splendid examples of ancient silver maces adorned with heraldic shields.

Of private plate, the most ancient, as well as the most beautiful, example is the Bannatyne or Bute Mazer (flat cup) which graced the table of the High Steward of Scotland at Rothesay Castle in the reign of Robert the Bruce.[2] This piece might well form an inspiration for many modern family or presentation pieces, for it illustrates, by workmanship of one of the best heraldic periods, how armorial bearings can and should be used. Marchmont Herald has fascinatingly shown how these enamelled shields—whose beautiful proportions are shown in Plate xxxix, p. 173—tell the whole story of the dish, the castle, its guests, and its seneschal. This was no " royal " dish, and it is therefore of interest to note the designer's delicate yet strictly unexceptionable allusion to the Regal Lion. No vulgar misuse of the royal shield mars a heraldic composition where the " ruddy lion ramping in his field of tressured gold " would have been historically and heraldically out of place, but in the central culminating point of the boss, round which the arms of the Steward and his vassals revolve, appears quite naturally a natural lion, sprawling amidst natural foliage, which recalls, yet does not pretend to

[1] James Paton, *Scottish History and Life*, Figs. 230-32 ; J. Gillespie, *Details of Scottish Domestic Architecture*, Plates 91, 95, 96.
[2] *Proc. of Soc. of Antiquaries of Scot.*, lxv, 217.

imitate, the Royal Tressure.   Here there is no attempt to mislead or to misuse the sacred " ensigns of public authority ", for the central lion is as unheraldic as the surrounding shields are magnificently armorial.[1]   Yet, when we look at this mazer, still more had it been passed to us at the festive board, with the lion's blazing eyes and its surrounding heraldry shimmering through the white wine which came from France to Scotland, we could scarcely think of a more inspiring vessel from which to pledge the ancient toast—" Gentlemen, the Queen ! "

OLD SCOTTISH ARMORIAL MANUSCRIPTS

The earliest armorial manuscript illustrating Scottish heraldry is the *Armorial de Gelré*, 1369–88, preserved in the Bibliothèque Royale, Brussels.   There are several reproductions.[2]   Next comes the armorial manuscript of *Berry, Roi d'Armes de France* ;[3] and third, the *Armorial de l'Europe*, compiled for the Duke of Burgundy by *Charolais, Roi d'Armes du Toison d'Or*.   The Scottish section of this manuscript not only includes the equestrian figure of the King of Scots,[4] but a valuable collection of fifteenth-century Scottish coats of arms.   This important manuscript, a transcript of which was printed at Paris in 1897, dates from the first half of the fifteenth century, and has been entirely overlooked by Scottish heraldic writers.

The fourth manuscript, and earliest Scottish armorial,[5]

---

[1] At this period, so soon after the competition for the Crown, any subject who dared to decorate the centre of his plate with the royal shield, would assuredly have paid with his head for his impertinence.

[2] *Proc. of Soc. of Antiquaries of Scot.*, xxv, 9 ; Stevenson, *Heraldry in Scotland*, Plates 12, 13, and 14.   Plate II at p. 1 of this book shows a facsimile page.

[3] Stoddart, *Scottish Arms*, Plates i-xi.

[4] *Scots Magazine*, xix, 55 (1933), and see Plate III, p. 8.

[5] A Scottish Armorial MS, apparently anterior to Flodden, was found in the Newcastle—Wriothesley—collections, but has not yet been examined.

consists of certain portions of the bulky Register of Lord Lyon Sir Robert Forman of Luthrie. It is known as the *Forman-Workman* Manuscript,[1] and is made up of several armorial registers bound together. The earliest portion dates, in the view of Lord Lyon Burnett, from the reign of Lord Lyon Sir William Cumming of Inverallochy, 1508–19.

Fig. 46.—Shield from Sir David Lindsay of the Mount's Manuscript (1542)—Logan of Restalrig. Quarterly: 1st and 4th, or, three piles sable (*Logan*); 2nd and 3rd, sable, an eagle displayed argent (*Restalrig of that Ilk*, per Lord Lyon Forman). Lindsay gives: argent, an eagle displayed sable, which suggests that the *De Restalrigs* were Ramsays.

Our next armorial is the celebrated *Register of Sir David Lindsay of The Mount*, the poet Lord Lyon King of Arms, dated 1542.[2] This celebrated manuscript was, at the instance of Lord Lyon Sir James Balfour of Kinnaird, " approven by the Privy Council ", 9 December 1630, and, although an official record belonging to the Lyon Office, lay in obscurity at Denmiln Castle after Balfour's death until it passed by purchase, along with Sir James's collections, to the Faculty of Advocates, and is now in the National Library of Scotland. Perhaps the best known examples of work from this manuscript are the arms of the two Scottish Queens, Magdalene of France and Mary of Lorraine.

Then comes the *Hamilton Armorial*, apparently made for the 2nd Earl of Arran in 1561–64, of which a copy exists in the Lyon Office. It is supposed to be of English workmanship.

The Armorial compiled by Lord Lyon Sir Robert Forman of Luthrie and presented by him to Mary Queen

---

[1] An inaccurate verbal description of all the arms in the *Forman-Workman MS.* is given in Stoddart's *Scottish Arms*, ii, 95.

[2] Reproduced in facsimile, 1822 and 1878, ex. Fig. 46.

of Scots in 1562,[1] just after her return, is now also in the National Library. It is beautifully executed, and a somewhat similar one, probably a copy, is in the British Museum (Harleian MSS. 115). Of Forman's Office Register, the *Forman-Workman* MS., we have already spoken. The last compilation of this active Lyon was " Kings' and Nobility's Arms, Vol. I "—now in the Lyon Office—which dates from between the birth of James VI and Queen Mary's marriage with Bothwell.[2] It is executed in a style somewhat suggesting " poster art ", the effects being obtained with a few touches of paint, in a striking manner.

With the death or removal of Sir Robert Forman, and the execution, for " witchcraft "—or maybe darker political reasons—of his successor, Sir William Stewart of Luthrie, close the armorial manuscripts of Queen Mary's reign, and to the Reformation Lord Lyon, Sir David Lindsay of Rathillet, we owe a good, though less voluminous armorial, now also in the National Library.

Two other manuscripts—the " Le Breton ", originally the property of the *Sieur de La Doinaterie, Roi d'Armes de France* (now in the Heralds' College, London), and the *Dunvegan Armorial* (Plate IV), which passed, through the daughter of Lord Lyon Brodie of Brodie, to the Macleods of Macleod—are derived from Rathillet's manuscript. It appears from an inscription by *Du Bartas*, the French poet-ambassador who died in 1590, that the *Dunvegan Armorial*— now one of the treasures preserved in Macleod's celebrated West Highland fortress—was the property of William Shaw, Master-Mason to the King of Scots. Sir James Balfour Paul considered it, from an artistic point of view, one of the finest we have. Next comes the *Seton Armorial*, made in 1591 for George, 5th Lord Seton. This is a very beautiful

---

[1] 1532 (*sic*), probably 1562 (see Plate XV (*a*)).
[2] Stoddart, *Scottish Arms*, ii, 6.

piece of work. One interesting point—hardly indeed heraldic —is that Malcolm Canmore is depicted in trews of tartan cut on the cross—much like the supporters of Skene of Skene in the carving of 1692,[1] which shows how little Highland dress had changed, at any rate since the painting of this manuscript.

Next comes the *Armorial Register of Sir David Lindsay of The Mount* (*secundus*) (Plate xv (*b*)), whose arms and title, *Sir David Lindsay of The Mount, Lord Lyon King of Armes*, are inscribed upon its frontispiece. It is a beautifully executed manuscript, dated from internal evidence between 17 April 1598 and 16 November 1600.[2] Several copious manuscripts, made in the reign of Sir David Balfour of Kinnaird, are preserved in the National Library, but although exceedingly useful, they are not of artistic importance. With this, and the Cromwellian Civil War, closed the period of our Scottish mediaeval heraldic manuscripts. The Lord Protector was a far-sighted man, and unlike some modern revolutionaries of lesser mental calibre, he appreciated the business value of heraldry. He appointed Sir James Campbell of Lawers as successor to Lord Lyon Sir James Balfour of Kinnaird, but unfortunately none of the Commonwealth heraldic registers have been preserved. They may still exist, but when in 1660 the clouds of usurpation rolled back, the Knight of Lawers discreetly retired, Sir Alexander Durham of Largo received the Lyon's Crown from Charles II, and in the reign of Durham's successor, Sir Charles Erskine of Cambo, we approach the foundation of the celebrated Lyon Register.

---

[1] W. Forbes Skene, *Memorials of the Family of Skene of Skene*, p. 48.
[2] W. Rae Macdonald's preface to Lyon Office copy of the MS.

PLATE XIV

(*a*) Arms of MACLEOD OF MACLEOD, from Dunvegan Armorial, *circa* 1590.
(*Proc. Soc. of Antiquaries of Scotland*, xlvii. 128.)

(*b*) Three modern Scottish book-plates.

PLATE XV

(b) Armorial Manuscript of Lord Lyon Sir David Lindsay
of the Mount (*secundus*), 1592–99, folio 112.

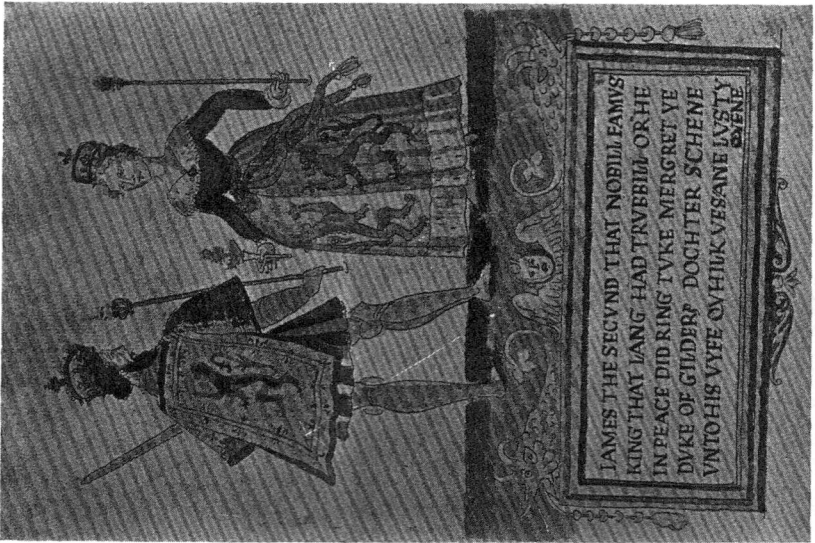

(a) Page from the Armorial Register (*circa* 1567) of Lord
Lyon Sir Robert Forman of Luthrie. (National Library
MSS. 31.4.2, folio 13.)

CHAPTER VI

THE PUBLIC REGISTER OF ALL ARMS AND BEARINGS IN SCOTLAND

Y Statute [1] 1592, cap. 125, " the usurpation of arms by any of His Majesty's lieges, without the authority of Lyon King of Arms ", is expressly forbidden. Statutory power is given for Lyon and his heralds to " visit the whole arms used in Scotland, and to matriculate the same in their Registers, to fine in £100 all who have unjustly usurped arms,[2] to escheat[3] all such goods and geir as shall have the unwarrantable arms engraven on them ". The celebrated Statute,[4] 1672, cap. 47, not only reiterated that of 1592, but in order to render it more effectual, provided for the establishment of a single

ELPHINSTONE, LORD BALMERINO, Argent on a chevron between three boars' heads erased gules, as many hearts argent.

---

[1] Acts, iii, 554. This Statute refers to previous Acts not now extant.

[2] *Fiscal of Lyon Court* v. *Scottish Watchmakers' and Jewellers' Association*, 18 Jan. 1954.

[3] This term simply means " confiscate ", not being one of the two specific " escheats " (*Erskine*, ii, v. 23-6), and does not fall automatically but arises only when craved, and ordered by the Lord Lyon (*Warrantholders* v. *Alexander & Co.*, 1933), like the confiscation of poachers' apparatus.

[4] Acts, viii, 95 ; also, 1672, cap. 74, *ib.*, p. 123 ; 1669, cap. 95, *ib.*, vii, 633.

Public Register of All Arms and Bearings, analogous to the then recently instituted *Register of Sasines* (1617) for landed property, which had proved so successful. The Statute [1] enacted :

1. That whosoever made use of any arms or signs armorial should bring or send an account of these, along with: (*a*) a statement whether they were descended from the family whose arms they bore ; (*b*) of what brother of the family they were descended ; (*c*) a certificate, both of their arms and descent, from " persons of honour, noblemen, or gentlemen of quality ", in the case of cadets, usually from the Chief.[2]

2. Those who obtempered the Act were to receive " statutory receipts " which, in the case of any omission in the Register, were to be statutory evidence that the Act had been obtempered.[3]

3. The Lord Lyon was to correct, or difference, the arms given in, where that was necessary, and, if satisfied of the claim, to matriculate them in the new Public Register.

4. This new Register was declared to be " The True and Unrepealable Rule of All Arms and Bearings in Scotland ", and " one of the Public Registers of the Kingdom " from which extracts might be obtained by anyone.

5. " Whosoever [4] shall use any other arms any manner of

---

[1] 1941 Session Cases, pp. 671-2. The Summary of heraldic law given there on pp. 670-79 may be regarded as an informal but authoritative expression of the Law of Arms, and is that officially and judicially applied in Lyon Court.

[2] *Macleod*, 16 April 1948, Lyon Register, xxxvi, 124.

[3] *Burgh of Elgin*, 9 October 1678, recorded 21 November 1888, Lyon Register, i, 461 ; *Earl of Caithness*, 6 January 1673, recorded 7 April 1931, *ibid.*, i, 54; *Scott of Harden*, 29 November 1700, recorded 5 February 1820, *ibid.*, ii, 189; *Bank of Scotland*, 1 March 1701, recorded 20 February 1849, *ibid.*, v, 1.

[4] A term which, from the first, included corporations : *Burgh of Jedburgh*, 13 March 1680, see p. 164.

PLATE XVI

way ", after expiry of the year and day, was rendered liable to fine and imprisonment, and confiscation of movables whereon the arms were represented.   The only evidence that the Act had been obtempered was to be (*a*) an entry in the Register, (*b*) an extract therefrom, or (*c*) one of the statutory " Receipts " issued between 1672 and 1677.

The statutory power of " visitation " empowered the Lord Lyon and heralds to enter premises throughout Scotland and inspect and " reform " arms, a duty which was assiduously executed,[1] and Lyon has been held to have a Common Law right to deface and remove " unwarrantable arms " wherever he finds them.[2]   The Statute not only worked smoothly, but proved amazingly successful, though it took five years instead of one to deal with the great mass of material " given in ", whilst the heralds scoured Scotland, rectifying heraldic errors and " casting down " unwarrantable arms.

In 1677 Lord Lyon Sir Charles Erskine of Cambo died, the period of gratuitous registration closed, and the " Public Register of All Arms and Bearings in Scotland " was then engrossed and the initial volume bound up in the sight of Robert Innes of Blairton, the Lyon-Depute.   Since then, all future grants and matriculations of arms have been chronologically registered on payment of the statutory fees, and the Register has continued to grow uninterruptedly.

The Register now extends to thirty-nine great volumes of parchment, ever steadily expanding.   Its pages have been illuminated by a succession of our greatest heraldic artists, and the " True and Unrepealable Rule of All Arms and Bearings in Scotland " has, under the fostering care of

---

[1] Narrative of Commission to James Skene, Lyon Office Records, 10 November 1677, E. D. Dunbar, *Docs. rel. to Province of Moray*, p. 143.

[2] Mackenzie, *Works*, ii, 582 ; *Macrae's Trustees* v. *Lord Lyon King of Arms*, 6 June 1926, 1927 Scots Law Times, p. 285.

successive Lord Lyons, become the most magnificent heraldic manuscript in Europe.[1]

A few people inevitably neglected to take advantage of the Statute, and thus lost the opportunity of enrolling their arms free of charge; but considering the difficulties of communication and registration in seventeenth-century Scotland, the manner in which the Act was enforced can only be described as an astonishing piece of legislative and administrative efficiency. Sir Alexander Erskine, 2nd Baronet of Cambo, succeeded his father as Lord Lyon under a patent for two lives, when only fourteen years old. In 1681 he was " crowned " at the regal age of eighteen. Thenceforth, and throughout the eighteenth century, the Lyon Court functioned with vigorous activity. All classes—from earls to excisemen[2] —suffered with judicial impartiality the penalties which Scotland's Parliament had imposed for the vulgar offence of displaying bogus heraldry.

The only drawback to the 1672 Act was that, as in other contemporary legislation, the officers were paid from the " profits of their office ", i.e. the fees and penalties exigible. Under modern conditions of public life such arrangements proved a drawback to official activity. In accordance with the recommendation of a Royal Commission, 1822, this was therefore remedied by the statute 30 & 31 Vict., cap. 17, which placed the Lord Lyon upon a salaried basis. Henceforth fees on registrations of arms in Scotland and penalties for use of " unwarrantable " arms became payable to H.M. Treasury,[3] since when there has been no difficulty in

[1] Plate XVI, in the 1st ed. of this work *Loch of Drylaw*, 1674, showed the style of heraldic art employed at the time of the institution of the Lyon Register. In this edition, Plate XV (p. 76), *Balfour of Pittendriech*, shows the sixteenth-century style. Plates XVI, XVII, XVIII, XXVIII, XXIX and XLVI show modern official emblazonments.

[2] *E.g. Fiscal* v. *Earl and Countess of Wemyss*, 7 August 1732 (arms pulled down); *Fiscal* v. *Wood*, 8 June 1773 (chariot confiscated).

[3] The fees payable to H.M. Treasury under 30 & 31 Vict., cap. 17, fall under

enforcing the law with the same wholesome vigour shown in the seventeenth and eighteenth centuries. Not only has Lyon Court prosecution been sustained in the Supreme three categories : (1) Court Fees under Schedule B ; (2) Preparation and Illumination of Parchment and Registers under Sec. 9 ; (3) Stamp Duties, where such are exigible. The Schedule B scale * is :

	£	s	d	
Patent † of arms with supporters ‡ .	49	12	0	
Patent † of arms without supporters §	29	18	0	
Matriculation of arms with supporters	15	16	6	
Matriculation of arms without supporters .	12	0	6	
Matriculation of arms with patent of supporters	34	13	6	
On every genealogy recorded ‖ .	10	10	0	
Additional for every member of pedigree .	0	5	0	
Certificate regarding change of surname .	0	15	0	
Search in register of arms . .	0	5	0	*These fees are not exacted in case of searches for purely literary or historical purposes.*
Search in register of genealogies .	0	5	0	
General search in heraldic MSS. .	1	1	0	
General search in genealogical MSS. .	1	1	0	
On every extract from a register . .	0	10	6	*Plus engrossing*
On entering a caveat ¶ . .	0	5	0	
On affixing seal of office to warrant, decree, or precept . . .	0	5	0	

The stamp duty previous to 1949 was £10 on each *grant* of arms, but is now under reconsideration, and will probably be fixed *ad valorem* as upon a grant of feudal heritage. The costs of illumination (in duplicate) of registers and parchments (fixed by the Lord Lyon as judge) under Sec. 9 vary according to the nature of the armorial bearings, being (since the War) about 6 to 8 guineas for arms without supporters, and 15 to 16 guineas for supporter coats ; orders and decorations, or standards and badges, may involve slightly extra costs. (*Chisholm of Chisholm*, 30 March 1944, Lyon Register, xxxiii, 12. Award of a pinsel was included ** in the reinvestiture, cost £8. *Ogston*, 21 March 1888, *ibid.*, x, 10.)

The total charges, including the matriculation of patent (the " feudal infeft-

* The scale is not exhaustive and there are a number of documents not covered, and for which the costs are judicially assessed according to the circumstances.

† These Exchequer-dues of Honour, upon Letters Patent, being *discretionary* (whilst those upon matriculations, being a matter of heritable right, are fixed), it is probable that under 30 & 31 Vict., cap. 17, Sec. i, the Patent-dues will shortly be increased to cover the decreased stamp duty and depreciated value of money.

‡ A special compartment, or a compartment apart from supporters, is £6 : 10s. (*White*, 16 Nov. 1762, Lyon Register, i, 444.)

§ Grant of a crest is chargeable as an additional award of arms (as if, in a separate patent or destination) or in certain circumstances at 50 per cent of the supporter-badge.

‖ Certain special varieties of short birthbrieves are issued at 3 guineas and 5 guineas.

¶ A caveat remains in force for one month only unless renewed and further 5s. paid.

** The matriculation of the Patent in Lyon Register (the " feudal infeftment " of the arms) is the taking of sasine on the armorial heritage (cf. p. 83).

Court of Scotland so recently as 1926,[1] but there are many buildings in Scotland where arms surreptitiously erected have, on official discovery, been removed or amended at the Lord Lyon's command, perhaps the most spectacular instances being when, in 1862,[2] a number of heraldic stained-glass windows were removed from Glasgow Cathedral, and when in 1927 the Government approved in Parliament [3] the orders of the Lord Lyon, by which a number of bogus County and Burgh arms were razed off the walls of the Scottish National War Memorial.[4]

ment " of the arms) in Lyon Register, and stamp duty, are therefore *approximately* as follows :

Patent of arms with supporters	.	.	.	£91 0 0
Patent of arms without supporters		.	.	60 0 0
Matriculation of arms with supporters	.		.	32 0 0
Matriculation of arms without supporters		.		19 0 0
Matriculation of arms with patent of supporters			.	52 0 0
Patent of crest in addition to arms	.	.	.	29 18 0
Grant of special compartment	.	.	.	6 10 0

In some cases very elaborate patents have been prepared, and the cost of genealogies and birthbrieves naturally varies according to the number of ancestors recorded and the amount of armorial illumination desired.

[1] *Procurator-Fiscal of the Lyon Court* v. *Sir Colin Macrae, Session Notes,* 1926, p. 91 ; 1927 Scots Law Times, p. 285.

[2] *Blackwood's Magazine,* June 1865.

[3] Report; 28 June 1927, Duke of Sutherland's (Paymaster-General) reply to Duke of Buccleuch ; *Parliamentary Debates* (House of Lords), vol. 67, col. 1094.

[4] Since that incident, steps have been taken to make all defaulting Burghs obey the law, and 98 per cent have since conformed. A firm of manufacturers was recently fined for using the Royal Arms as a trade-mark, and interdicted by Lyon Court from using these or any other arms (*Royal Warrantholders Association* v. *R. F. & J. Alexander & Co.*), 21 March 1933 ; *Scotsman* report, 22 March.

CHAPTER VII

A SCOTTISH GRANT OF ARMS

HE granting of Arms is part of the Royal Prerogative committed to the Kings of Arms,[1] who issue Letters Patent, in exercise of the Royal Authority, wherein they " devise [2] and do by These Presents Assign, Ratify and Confirm " the arms brought into existence by the Warrant and Patent—which is a grant of them as an incorporeal *fief noble* and of which the Grantee takes " peisible seisin " [3] by recording the

LORD ELIBANK. Quarterly, 1st and 4th (*Murray of Blackbarony*), 2nd (*Oliphant of Bachilton*), 3rd (*Murray of Elibank*).

[1] *Macdonell* v. *Macdonald*, 1826, 4 Shaw, 374. A person cannot create arms unto himself (cf. *Austen* v. *Collins*, 5 May 1886, per Mr Justice Chitty), and it is illegal and a statutory offence to " adopt " arms.

[2] Whilst the applicant's wishes are carefully considered, the design of the arms to be granted (*if* he be pleased to make a grant at all) is entirely for the King of Arms. The phraseology occasionally used by minor corporations, that they have " adopted " and " registered with the Lyon Office ", is erroneous, and when one recently issued such an announcement to the press between interlocutor and issue of the Patent, this was held up until the Petitioner had made due apology for contempt of Court and of the Crown.

[3] 1941 S.C., p. 672, nn. 36 and 37 ; *Law of Succession in Ensigns Armorial*, pp. 27-9, n. ; *Lyachou* v. *Fishiar* cited in *Albany's Observations on Armorial Conveyancing*, pp. 67-8 (ex. *Notes & Queries*, 1939–41).

Patent in the Public Register of All Arms and Bearings, just as a grant of land is recorded in the Register of Sasines, and until so matriculated in Lyon Register the Patent is of no effect,[1] conform to the maxim *nulla sasina nulla terra*.

There is nothing in the Statute 1672, cap. 47, to forfeit a then existing right to arms, if, of course, the use was " of right " and not a usurpation,[2] though penalties are imposed for using these until they are " ascertained " by Lyon Court *and* recorded in Lyon Register, and every coat of arms proved to have been justly borne or used anterior to 1672 is deemed to have been brought into existence by a grant from the Crown or its King of Arms.[3] Arms " are presumed to be the creation of the Crown", but since a title to heritable property must be proved " by writ " unless an earlier patent or confirmation is proved or produced for registration under the 1672 Act, what happens is that Lyon, after judicial inquiry regarding the pre-statutory " possession ", issues and records a " Confirmation " of the arms (if necessary with any technical corrections), which then becomes the foundation of the feudal title to such coat of arms.[4] It is consequently still possible for anyone to prove that he or she is the legal representative of some person who used arms before 1672, and to get these recorded with any "difference" which the Lord Lyon may consider necessary, upon payment of the statutory fees under 30 & 31 Vict., cap. 17, Secs. 11 and 13, and Schedule B.[5]

The ordinary application is either for (*a*) a new grant of

---

[1] *Cameron of Lochiel* v. *Cameron of Erracht*, 24 February 1792, Lyon Register, i, 567-8. [2] *Law of Succession in Ensigns Armorial*, p. 28 n.

[3] *Heraldry in Scotland*, p. 333, n. 1, and *Cuninghame* v. *Cunyngham*.

[4] The doctrine of *uradel*, " original nobility ", however, involves a modified view in regard to certain very old arms borne by allodial and analogous houses ; in effect, however, they became " feudalised " heritage (11 D. at 1150 quoted by Lord Shaw in 1922 S.C. (H.L.), 45) under 1672, cap. 47.

[5] Innes of Learney, *Law of Succession in Ensigns Armorial*, p. 28 ; Lord Lyon Grant's judgment (cf. " on record ") in *Maclean of Ardgour* v. *Maclean*, 1941 S.C., p. 662, and see Respondent's Argument on Appeal, pp. 671-3.

PLATE XVII

Book-plate of JOHN ALEXANDER STEWART OF INCHMAHOME.

Facsimile of painting in the Public Register of All Arms and Bearings. (*Lyon Register*, xxi. 74.)

PLATE XVIII

Arms of Michael R. de la Valée Macpherson, son of Major Roderick W.
Macpherson, at Crogga, Isle of Man, a matriculation containing a par-
ticular destination for special family arrangements, as matriculated 16th
December 1941 in Lyon Register, xxxiv. 45.

Per fess invected or and azure, a galley of the first, mast, oars and tackling proper, sails
furled, flagged gules, below a dexter hand couped fessways holding a dagger in pale in dexter
chief point gules and in sinister a cross crosslet futchee of the last, and a label of five points or
charged with azure, charged with three fusils and two fleurs-de-lys alternately, or.

arms ; (b) a rematriculation of some existing coat, either with or without what the old Statute calls " a congruent difference ".

Our old Scots laws required every landowner to possess a coat of arms.[1] Those who had none applied to the Lord Lyon, who, exercising *virtute officii* the armorial prerogative of the Crown, assigned such arms as the applicant " might leifullie bear ", and an ancient manuscript says that the Lyon " refuses arms to none who are able to maintain a horse with furniture " (armour and trappings) for the service of the Sovereign.[2] Both the Lord Lyon's Commissions and the Statute 1672 expressly authorise him to grant arms to " virtuous and well deserving persons " who are " in all places of honour and worshipe among other noblemen to be renouned reputed taken and accepted by shewing certayn ensignes and demonstrations of honour and noblesse ",[3] *i.e.* persons deserving of being raised to the nobility and who, in virtue of the grant of arms, become the root of a " noble stok " as described in 1592, cap. 125, established as a family organised in " stem " and " branches " as a *noble* community.[4]

In Scotland, not only peers and lairds, but professors, lawyers, merchants, and business men, have continually registered arms as a matter of course, by descent if proved, otherwise under new grants. Our Scottish burgesses did not hesitate to decorate the picturesque old houses in which they both lived and carried on their trades with their armorial symbols,[5] and at long last were not ashamed to inscribe both

[1] 21 February 1400, Acts, i, 575 ; 1430, cap. 21, Acts, ii, 19 ; *Heraldry in Scotland*, p. 103 ; A. Agnew, *Hereditary Sheriffs of Galloway*, p. 111.

[2] Nisbet, *Heraldry*, ii, iv, cap. 16 ; Account of the Office of Heraulds, Nat. Lib. MSS. 34-3-22.

[3] Bell, 26 June 1542, J. Dallaway, *Heraldic Inquiries*, p. 172.

[4] *Kinghorn of Auchinhove*, 30 January 1941, Lyon Register, xxxiv, 64 ; *Proc. of Soc. of Antiquaries of Scot.*, 1942-3, p. 169.

[5] The arms of Mossman, the goldsmith, upon " John Knox's House " in Edinburgh, gave the clue to the history of this celebrated house.

their *arms and trade description* together upon their tombstones, and would have scorned to conceal the latter under the title of " esquire ".[1] Any man who says he is a " gentleman " may just as well have the courage of his convictions, and affirm it with heraldry, which establishes that the Crown has accepted him as such. Whether his coat of arms, once registered, becomes romantic, famous, or historic, depends entirely upon himself and his successors. The aim of every clansman is, as Bishop Leslie says, to " shawe thameselfes worthie of the hous they are cum off ", and " to decore their hous " by a worthy and distinguished career.[2] With that aim, the first step more often than not has been to obtain a suitably cadenced version of their chief or chieftain's arms. Upon this honourable ambition to sustain the credit of the clan much of the picturesque romance and strength of Scottish character depends.

Everyone who has worked his way to a position of public responsibility owes it to his neighbours, to posterity, and to his own family, to obtemper the spirit of our old Scottish Statutes, and to obtain, by registration, heraldic " tokens " by which he and his may thereafter be known and recognised. The high official, or the public man, who churlishly spoils the heraldic series on the walls or gilded roof of some public building, by failing to register armorial bearings, merely proves, first, that he has degenerated from the Scotsman's native pride ; second, that *he was non-armigerous because he was, in very truth, undeserving*, for had he applied for arms he would have obtained them as a matter of ordinary course incidental to a public career. No one need be afraid of approaching the Scottish Officers of Arms, who, like all good Scotsmen, are very human and tactful people, and even the humblest pedigree can be made exceedingly interesting.

---

[1] Green's *Encyclopaedia*, xi, 445 ; xii, 31, 32 ; inferred from crested helm, see p. 29.　　　[2] Hume Brown, *Scotland before 1700*, p. 179.

LYON COURT PROCEDURE

So far, no book has told the inquirer exactly how to proceed about registration of arms and pedigree. It is quite easy, and the same to-day as it has been for centuries.

Of our ancient Confirmations or Patents of Arms, two excellent examples are those granted to Sir James Balfour of Pittendreich and Sir James Maxwell of Terregles, Lord Herries,[1] both issued in 1567 under the seal of Queen Mary's Lord Lyon, Sir Robert Forman of Luthrie. They show that in the sixteenth century, just as to-day, the proceedings in connection with a Scottish registration of arms were of a judicial nature.[2] Whilst a grant of arms is actually issued by Lyon in his capacity as the Queen's representative, the issue of the Letters Patent is preceded by an inquiry, sometimes judicial, sometimes merely Departmental and " Ministerial ",[3] as to the claims and merits of the applicant—a historic principle of which no " virtuous and well-deserving " Scot need be afraid.

The procedure is as follows : the applicant, either through himself, a law agent such as the family solicitor, or a herald or pursuivant, draws up a Petition somewhat in the form shown on pages 89–90. Care should be taken that : (a) the petitioner is carefully named and designed ; if he holds or claims a territorial designation (see pp. 201-4) that this is inserted before the affix " Knight ", " Esquire ", or other " letters ", and that a corresponding signature is used ; (b) if he holds an estate (or *caput baroniae*) *in liberam baroniam*,

---

[1] *Heraldic Exhibition Catalogue*, Plates i and ii, Items No. 48 and 49.

[2] Also Katharine Forbes, in *Liber Curiarum et Processus Dni Roberti Forman de Luthrie Leonis Regis Armorum*, fol. 27 ; *Antiquities of Aberdeen and Banff*, iii, 502. See Plate XXIV, p. 108.

[3] Whether an " application " for a patent involves judicial or Ministerial approach depends largely on whether the claim is " of right " or " of grace " ; most grants fall under the latter category.

or represents it, he is designated " Baron of X . . ." and may apply for a chapeau, or crest-coronet if he be *Chef du Nom et d'Armes* (see p. 34), and if he be the representative of an ancient baronial house, also for supporters.[1] The Register was accordingly divided into sections for (1) Peers, (2) Knights and Barons (who are frequently put together, Barony and Knights-fee being closely, though not completely, analogous), (3) Gentlemen. In vol. i those entered in sec. 2 did not require to be specifically intituled Baron, but in the subsequent volumes of consecutive (and unsectional) matriculations insertion of the title became appropriate and, indeed, necessary, and accordingly is duly inserted, where the Petitioner is " of baronial race ".[2]

The Petition is lodged, personally or by post, with the Lyon Clerk. Some discussion usually follows regarding petitioner's wishes as to the nature of the coat of arms, and the Lord Lyon (who has an absolute discretion as to (*a*) whether he will grant arms at all ; (*b*) what the arms granted shall be) is usually disposed to meet the petitioner's wishes as far as heraldically possible. The destination desired in a grant or regrant must be carefully set forth.[3]

Soon after these details are settled, and any doubtful

[1] The Act 1672, cap. 47, specially qualifies the degrees thus : Nobles (*i.e.* peers, the term being here used in a restricted seventeenth-century English sense), Barons (*i.e.* Lairds of baronial fiefs and their "heirs", who, even if fiefless, are equivalent to *heads* of Continental baronial houses) and Gentlemen (apperently all the other *armigeri*).

[2] *Proc. of Soc. of Antiquaries of Scot.*, lxxix, 157, 160.

[3] If the applicant is dissatisfied with Lyon's Ministerial Act, his only remedy is to apply through the Scottish Office for a Royal Warrant ordering " Our Lyon to grant " as desired. Obviously, even apart from the soundness of the principle laid down in *Macdonell* v. *Macdonald* (that with Lyon's Ministerial discretion the Court of Session *cannot* interfere), attempts to force a King of Arms to make any *grant* of armorial insignia (*i.e.* to exercise the Prerogative) might have consequences well recognised (even in other circumstances) in Shakespeare's day :

. . . an eye-sore in my golden coat,
Some loathsome dash the herald will contrive, to cipher me.
(*Lucrece*, ll. 205-7)

points in evidence cleared up, the formal " Letters Patent " on parchment, signed by the Lord Lyon and sealed with his Seal of Office, containing a fully illuminated drawing of the arms, is obtained,[1] but—being a Government Department— *only after payment* to the Lyon Clerk of the Treasury fees, which amount to about £59. A copy of the Letters Patent, including the painting of the arms, is made in the Lyon Register, from which further " Extracts " can at any future time be obtained. Where an applicant has instructed searches in any of the national Records or otherwise, and these have been made through the Lyon Court, the cost of these searches must be paid in addition ; whilst if the petitioner has employed professional assistance in drawing his Petition and proving his case, that may involve additional costs, which necessarily vary according to circumstances.

UNTO THE RIGHT HONOURABLE
THE LORD LYON KING OF ARMS

> The Petition of JOHN SMITH OF GLENSMITH in the County of Blankshire, D.S.O., Merchant in Glasgow, and Captain (retired) Blankshire Highlanders ;

HUMBLY SHEWETH

1. That he is the eldest son of the late Alexander Smith of Glensmith, Chartered Accountant in Edinburgh, and his wife Janet, third daughter of the late Sir Charles MacSporran of that Ilk in the said County of Blankshire, Baronet.

2. (*The petitioner may here briefly insert as much additional information regarding his ancestry as he desires included in the Letters Patent, provided he confines his statement to facts which he can actually prove—and he will be required to prove them all by*

---

[1] The Letters Patent, size 19 × 24 in., bear that Lyon has *devised* and does by these presents assign, ratify, and confirm to the petitioner the arms specified, and the parchment is of similar appearance to the Extract Matriculation in Plate XVI. (Smaller—19 × 12 in.—parchments are again popular.)

documentary evidence when they are outwith the period of his own personal knowledge or verification.)

3. That the Petitioner is desirous of bearing and using such Ensigns Armorial as may be found suitable.

MAY IT THEREFORE please your Lordship to Authorise [1] the Lyon Clerk to prepare Letters Patent granting unto the Petitioner and his descendants (*the words " According to the Laws of Arms " are here understood, and if the Petitioner desires that the " destination " be extended to " heirs of entail ", or to " the other descendants of " some specified ancestor, or restricted to heirs male or to the heirs in some estate or dignity, the prayer of the Petition must be worded accordingly*) such Ensigns Armorial as your Lordship may find suitable and according to the Laws of Arms.

And your Petitioner will ever pray.

(*Signature of Petitioner or his Agent*)

(*Example shows a laird's signature in terms of statute 1672, cap. 47.*)

J. SMITH OF GLENSMITH.
Date, 23rd January 1960.

A schedule of proofs should be annexed to the Petition, setting out, in numbered paragraphs corresponding to the numbered Condescendances of the Petition, a list of the sources, documents, or records proving each statement in that particular paragraph. (See page 106 for sample.)

Sovereigns have always claimed the right to nobilitate foreign nationals whom they desired to honour, and similarly the Lord Lyon has in special circumstances, where expedient, exercised the power of granting nobility to aliens of Scots descent, a power which, however, is sparingly exercised, for unless special considerations arise, the natural course is to obtain the initial grant of " nobility " and its relative armorial

---

[1] This word is used where the Writ to be prepared is " Ministerial " and the phrase " Grant Warrant " in the case of matriculation or other judicial directions.

PLATE XIX

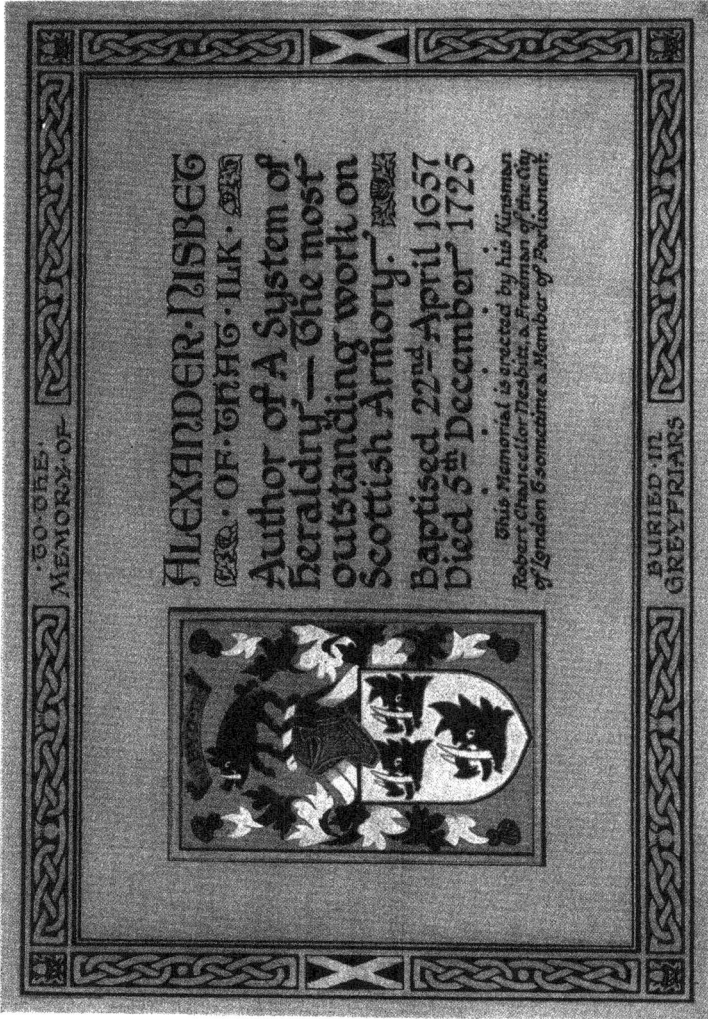

Bronze and enamel heraldic memorial plaque.

Erected in Old Greyfriars Kirk, Edinburgh, by Robert C. Nesbitt, M.P., in memory of Alexander Nisbet, writer, author of *A System of Heraldry*, who became Chief of the Name of Nisbet, which house bore, argent, three boars' heads erased sable, armed or and langued gules, anterior to the year 1672, and from which R. C. Nesbitt matriculated in cadency, 4th Oct. 1933, *Lyon Register*, xxx. 73.

ensigns from the Sovereign of the State in which one is domiciled—through that Sovereign's King of Arms.[1]

Where the petitioner is a foreigner, *e.g.* an American citizen, or domiciled in another jurisdiction, and might have difficulty in getting a Scottish grant of arms,[2] he may indeed, if he can prove his pedigree back to some Scottish ancestor,[3] word his petition to the Lord Lyon so as to obtain from his Lordship a grant of arms to that *ancestor and his descendants.* The petitioner himself can then apply for rematriculation in his own name of the undifferenced arms, if he be the heir under the grant, or, if he be a junior descendant, the properly differenced version applicable to his own position in the family.[4] Such proceedings are of considerable family interest, and the applicant gets two illuminated parchments : (*a*) the armorial grant, and (*b*) the extract matriculation. This double procedure, costing about £77 altogether, in addition to giving the statutory advantages of Scottish heraldry, in the case of Americans and other foreigners of Scottish ancestry is often the only way to obtain substantive armorial bearings.

Another quite usual course is for a foreigner to get one of his kinsmen in Scotland to obtain a grant with a suitably wide destination, and rematriculate a differenced version for himself.[5]

English and Irish arms can be matriculated in Lyon

---

[1] *Heraldry in Scotland*, p. 66 ; see below, as to British Dominions.

[2] Any descendant of a Scottish armigerous family can matriculate in Lyon Register, even though the petitioner be an alien, and the possibility of qualifying for such a matriculation should always be investigated.

[3] *Harkness*, 2 December 1930, Lyon Register, xxix, 56. Posthumous grants are almost as old as heraldry itself, and often needed for memorials, windows, and tombstones. In Ireland likewise " Ulster retains the power of ennobling ancestors ", Sir N. Wilkinson, *To All and Singular*, p. 183.

[4] *G. Stewart*, 31 August 1939, Lyon Register, xxxiii, 74 ; *A. Adams*, 7 November 1940, *ibid.*, xxxiv, 22.

[5] *Adams*, 7 November 1940, *ibid.*, xxxiv, 22 ; *Stewart*, 30 August 1939, *ibid.*, xxxiii, 74.

Register. This is legally necessary if their owners settle in Scotland [1] and, *e.g.*, take a Scottish designation, or suchlike. Matriculation, though competent, is not considered essential to entitle armigerous spouses to display a matrimonial escutcheon impaling the arms of a non-Scottish wife, for impaling is a temporary marshalling (see p. 145). Her own or paternal arms must be legally constituted in her jurisdiction of origin, or she may get a Scots patent.

Certain "honorary arms" recently given to foreigners, and some foreign recordings of purported (*faux*) arms, are not accepted in Scotland [2], but *armes de petite noblesse* are.

In the British Empire [3] there are no Dominion Kings of

---

[1] Green's *Encyclopaedia*, *s.v.* Heraldry, par. 1386; *Waring*, Lyon Register, xxvii, 76; *Northern Assurance Co. Ltd.*, 27 May 1930, *ibid.*, xxix, 20; *Ambrose*, *ibid.*, xxvi, 73; *Herraghty*, 3 July 1939, *ibid.*, xxxiii, 70.

[2] Cf. an inquiry, for *von Redlich*, 16 February 1932 (Honorary arms granted in England, 12 November 1931). He was already a Hungarian noble and also had a grant of arms and the dignity of Baron from the King of Montenegro, 27 December 1919. The dignity of Baron could not (save in certain special Scottish circumstances) be officially recognised as a title without, in England, a licence from the Crown, though it could be considered in Scotland in relation to " equivalent rank " in a birthbrief, and the foreign arms (substantive and connoting basic degree of " nobility ", *anglice* " gentility ") would in Scots Law be cognisable as ensigns armorial *qua* " tokens of nobility " (Balfour, *Heraldic Tracts*, p. 12, sec. 48) and admissible for matriculation if the petitioner established that he ought to obtemper the Statute 1672, cap. 47. Seven years later, following a petition by *Adams* for matriculation of honorary arms in Lyon Register in 1939, inquiry whether the grant had made the grantee a member of the *noblesse* of England, as described in old English armorial patents (*Webbe*, 1550, Misc. Gen. et Her., 3rd ser., ii, 156; *Bolney*, 5 November 1541, *ibid.*, 1868, i, 304; *Bell*, 26 June 1542, J. Dallaway, *Her. Inquiries*, p. 172), elicited a reply in the negative; it was held by Lyon that " honorary arms " do not fulfil the requirements of " arms " as defined in 1592, cap. 125, as " substantive " English (or foreign) arms do, and that " honorary arms " are inadmissible for matriculation in Lyon Register, per said decision of Lord Lyon Grant.

[3] Dominion and Empire are *not*, as some modern folk imagine, oppressive or dominatory words. They import " sovereign under God " ; and " imperial " applied to a Crown just indicates a " king of kings". " King ", and " imperial ", in that sense are kindred terms, the former derived from " house ", the family-home. They have a happy and liberal concept as compared with most " republic " terms, which smell of slavery-state origins.

Arms, and from time to time various views have been expressed as to which office overseas applicants for initial grants (*novi homines*) should apply,[1] it having latterly been indicated that in case of dispute the wishes of the applicant should prevail. The term "jurisdiction" in the foreoing connection[2] is incorrect, since the legal position regarding arms remains analogous to that regarding English and Scottish peerage creations between 1603 and 1707. Moreover, the Court of Session has reaffirmed that arms in Scotland are *feudal heritage*[3] (rather like a feudal barony[4]), which heritage any British subject is capable of acquiring by the feudal grant where Lyon, in exercise of the Royal Prerogative, sees fit to make the grant,[5] which in the case of overseas subjects he normally does where the Petitioner establishes Scottish ancestry. Lyon's jurisdiction, however,

---

[1] *Heraldry Explained*, p. 19. Arms are an incorporeal hereditament; that hereditament is either Scottish, English, or Irish; each hereditament is equally "British"; from whichever source a Briton has acquired his hereditament, it is his property, subject as regards use to any laws of the jurisdiction wherein he uses the arms. The position of arms and the hereditary "dignity of Gentleman" remain just as the dignity of peerage (of Scotland, England, and Ireland) stood between 1603 and 1707. There is no "U.K." or "G.B." coat of arms. The view of successive Lord Lyons has been: Scotland is an equal partner in the Union, and as regards Imperial jurisdiction there is nothing in the status or titles of the Great Officers of England not equally applicable to those of Scotland, though each has a certain privative jurisdiction in his original territory, not of course to the extent of precluding an Englishman getting ennobled in Scotland or *vice versa* where expedient, but recognition and usage of such *noblesse* in the "other" part of Great Britain depends on the grantee obtempering the local Law of Arms. A good deal of the misunderstanding arose from an English rule that a grant made by one English King of Arms in the "Province" of another is apparently null or reducible (*Heralds and Heraldry*, 77). Scotland is, however, in no sense a "Province" but a land with laws of its own, and a *noblesse* of its own.

[2] An opinion of the Law Officers—here on largely irrelevant information—is merely an "opinion of counsel", indeed inconsistent with legal decisions *infra* which govern the matter. See also *Souter*, 1955 Scots Law Times, Lyon Court.

[3] *Maclean of Ardgour* v. *Maclean*, 1941 S.C., 683, line 35, reaffirming *Macdonell* v. *Macdonald*, 1826, 4 Shaw 374.

[4] Mackenzie, *Works*, ii, 583, 615.

[5] *Macdonell* v. *Macdonald*, *supra*.

H

depends *inter alia* on the construction of statutes, and the Scottish Court of Appeal has laid down that he has a judicial function of determining in each case, whether he has jurisdiction or not.[1] So in every application he must as a judge give the petitioner the benefit of his decision.[2] Where a Dominion applicant is of Scottish ancestry or connection, the wishes of the petitioner are usually made quite plain. If the arms are ever to be used in Scotland, registration in Lyon Register is essential under 1672, cap. 47, and Lyon Court Act, 1867, which ensure statutory protection.

Any British subject lawfully in possession of English (or other) arms,[3] or even a foreigner[4] if he be obliged to use arms in Scotland or its heraldic dependencies, can apply for matriculation of them in Lyon Register in terms of 1672, cap. 47 ; and in granting warrant for matriculation, the Lord Lyon will difference them so far as Scots Law requires.[5] Such matriculation is essential to comply with the Scots Statutes if an Englishman or foreigner becomes domiciled in Scotland,[6] or in any permanent manner sets up or uses armorial bearings, for otherwise the purpose of the Public Register would be defeated. The Statute strikes at *whosoever* shall use unregistered arms in *any* manner of way. The tendency has been to treat an Englishman who merely owns an ancillary sporting estate, etc., as a " non-Scottish noble ", unless he begins behaving as a Scots noble and assuming a Scots feudal style. Conversely, a born Scot who resides in or about London by reason of duty or appointment in or about the Imperial capital, is regarded under the Lyon Court Acts

[1] *Royal College of Surgeons* v. *Royal College of Physicians*, 1911 S.C., 1055.
[2] Maclaren, *Court of Session Practice*, p. 75.
[3] *Northern Assurance Co. Ltd.*, 27 May 1930, Lyon Register, xxix, 20 ; *Houldsworth*, 8 November 1868, *ibid.*, xiii, 10.
[4] *Grosset*, 1737, *ibid.*, i, 320 ; *Hallen*, 30 June 1894, *ibid.*, xviii, 38.
[5] *Waring*, 2 March 1926, *ibid.*, xxvii, 5.
[6] *Northern Assurance Co. Ltd.*, above ; *Belenie*, 18 April 1951, *ibid.*, xxxviii, 70.

as a "well-deserving person" in the heraldic sense, and not as an Englishman, and Lyon grants him arms accordingly.

LEGAL EFFECTS OF A GRANT OF ARMS

The effect of a grant of arms in Scotland is to confer, in addition to a formal recognition by the Crown that the grantee and all his descendants—members of his "family"—are "noble", the following rights:

1. The grantee is entitled to use (that is, "the same to bear, use, show, set forth, and advance in shield, or ensign or otherwise, observing and using their due and proper differences according to the Laws of Arms and without let, hindrance, molestation, interruption, controlment or challenge by any manner of person or persons whatsoever")[1] the coat of arms either complete, or the shield alone, or the crest and motto alone, during his life. After his death each successive "heir" in terms of, and within the limits of, the grant is entitled to the same privilege for all time coming,[2] subject, of course, to "making up progress of title"[3] by rematriculation. One cannot just select an old coat in Lyon Register and assert one is "the heir". Beyond two or three

·DONALD·WALTER·CAMERON·
OF·LOCHIEL·

FIG. 47.—DONALD WALTER CAMERON OF LOCHIEL (arms conjoined with those of his wife, LADY HERMIONE GRAHAM). Two coats impaled—Dexter, gules, three bars or (*Cameron of Lochiel*). Sinister, quarterly, 1st and 4th, or, on a chief sable, three escallops of the field (*Graham*); 2nd and 3rd, argent, three roses gules, barbed and seeded proper (*Montrose*). *Crest*—A wreath of five arrows, tied with a band, gules. *Supporters*—Two savages, wreathed about the head and middle with oak, each holding in his exterior hand a Lochaber axe, all proper.

---

[1] Lyon Register, xxxvi, 24; cf. Sir James Balfour's patents; Mackenzie, *Works*, ii, 580.

[2] Mackenzie, *Works*, ii, 583.

[3] See *Law of Succession in Ensigns Armorial*, p. 45.

generations' " possession on apparency " the right must be
made up, just as with land, but unless there is any change
in the arms a rematriculation by progress needs no painting-
costs, but the coat of arms can only belong to one person at
a time, that person being the grantee or his subsequent
" Representative " in terms of the grant.[1] The coat of arms
is thus a hereditary decorative " monomark ", which can only
represent one individual at a time, viz. the chief or head of the
house or line whose founder the shield in question denoted.

2. If the grantee (or his heir for the time being) is married
to an armigerous female, he may divide his shield,[2] placing his
own arms on the *dexter* side and his wife's arms on the *sinister*
side (Plate xxx, Carr of Carrs-Carr, and Fig. 59), so
long as the marriage subsists (afterwards, if he or she does
not remarry), and in any event upon their tombstone, or on
architectural works erected by him or her during their
marriage.   Rules exist for impaling the arms of several
wives, but this is merely for purposes of record upon a family
tombstone or pedigree, and it is quite wrong to decorate a
motor-car or bookplate with arms suggesting bigamy or
polygamy.   A wife may also use her husband's arms alone,
of which Stevenson cites several instances.[3]

3. The eldest son (or failing him the heir-presumptive, a
term including the eldest daughter, if the arms are not
tailzied)[4]—who will eventually succeed his father in the

---

[1] *Maclean of Ardgour* v. *Maclean*, 1941 S.C., pp. 687, 713.

[2] As an alternative he may use two shields—the dexter showing his own arms
and the sinister his wife's arms—either inclined towards each other (the Continental
practice) or set together side by side—when they are termed *accollée* (see Fig. 72).
Impalement is usually preferred nowadays, but in some cases, *e.g.* a fireplace or
door lintel (Plate XXXV, and Figs. 72 and 73), separate shields may be more easily
depicted on the area available.

[3] J. H. Stevenson, *Heraldry in Scotland*, p. 160 ; Nisbet, *Heraldry*, ii, 35, 37.

[4] *Fenton of Baikie*, W. R. Macdonald, *Scottish Armorial Seals*, pp. 915-17.
A daughter is heiress-*presumptive*, because her parents might yet have a son.
Hay of Kellour, 1672, Lyon Register, i, 161 (heir-presumptive of *Erroll*) ; Robert

undifferenced arms—bears them, including supporters, if such there be,[1] during his father's lifetime differenced with a "label", as seen in the arms of H.R.H. the Duke of Rothesay [2] (Prince of Wales), and in the achievement of John, Lord Leslie, eldest son of the Earl of Rothes, upon his Archery Medal (Fig. 48). The grandson (second heir) bears the arms with a label of five points, but if by death of his father he becomes first heir, then such grandson takes up the three-point label.[3]

4. Daughters are each entitled to bear the undifferenced arms upon a *lozenge* during their lifetime, and to impale them with their husband's arms, but so long as a brother or a brother's descendants exist, no woman (except a few "heiresses of entail" under special grants) can transmit to her issue a right in her father's arms. If "heiress or next of blood" to her predecessor's arms, she or her issue inherits the whole armorial property, including crest, motto, and supporters. No woman, however, is entitled to crest or motto

FIG. 48.—Archery Medal of John, Lord Leslie, Master of Rothes (1715), eldest son of John, 8th Earl of Rothes. Quarterly: 1st and 4th, argent, on a bend azure, three buckles or (*Leslie*); 2nd and 3rd, or, a lion rampant gules, surmounted of a riband sable (*Abernethy*). Over all for difference, a label. *Crest* —A demi-griffin proper, beaked, armed, and winged or. *Motto*—"Grip Fast." *Supporters*—Two griffins proper, beaked, winged, and armed or.

unless she has become head of her house or branch, but there are numerous instances in which females have, on such succession, made up titles to the arms, crest, motto, and

Montgomery of Giffen, Master of Eglinton, *Scots Peerage*, iii, 442; Nisbet, *System of Heraldry*, i, 385.

[1] *Fergusson-Cunningham, younger of Caprington*, 2 November 1920, Lyon Register, xxiv, 68; *Earl of Dumfries* (Master of Bute and Dumfries), 9 November 1948, *ibid.*, xxxvii, 31.

[2] Also H.R.H. the Duke of Albany and York, 1672, *ibid.*, i, 26.

[3] *Chisholm of Chisholm, ibid.*, xxxiii, 12; A. C. Fox-Davies, *Complete Guide to Heraldry*, p. 487.

H 2

supporters.[1] Scottish women freely display their father's or husband's crest-badge in brooches, since the laws of arms do not debar a woman from being a " follower " and wearing a badge.

FIG. 49.—Swinton arms differenced with a bordure engrailed ermine and a mullet gules.

5. When arms descend to an heiress (ordinarily a woman with no brothers, or descendants of brothers) the English practice is for the husband to put her arms upon a " shield of pretence " in the middle of his own shield. This has sometimes been done in Scotland, but it is not Scottish custom.[2] Sir W. St John Hope criticises this English system of inescutcheon of pretence as " ugly and most inconvenient ", and advises that the arms of an heiress should either be impaled or quartered, which he says was the old law even in England.[3] Inescutcheons do spoil unquartered shields. The Scots law of arms in relation to *cumulatio armorum* (for we are here treating only of occasions where the arms of both families are to be perpetuated, marshalled together) is exactly as we would have wished. Our national practice is simply to

[1] *Duchess of Buccleuch*, 1672, Lyon Register, i, 34; *Graden of Earnslaw*, 1672, *ibid.*, i, 314; *Farquharson of Invercauld*, 11 April 1815, *ibid.*, ii, 130; 3 December 1936, *ibid.*, xxxii, 34; *Macleod of Macleod*, 28 November 1935, *ibid.*, xxxi, 74; *Douglas of Brigton*, 21 May 1941, *ibid.*, xxxiv, 33; *Maclean of Ardgour*, 10 October 1941, *ibid.*, xxxiv, 42; *Maclachlan of Maclachlan*, 3 July 1946, *ibid.*, xxxv, 72. [2] Mackenzie, *Works*, ii, 622.
[3] *Heraldry for Craftsmen and Designers*, p. 253.

impale the arms, unless or until the heiress has a child, when either that child or the husband *may* apply to the Lord Lyon to rematriculate the arms with the heiress's arms as a quartering.[1] Such a matriculation, which is also the normal practice where arms are taken up as an " heir of entail ", costs about £20. No one can vary their existing registered achievement by quartering the arms of an heiress mother, or taking arms as heir of entail, without applying to Lyon for a rematriculation or letters patent, as the case may be.[2]

6. Every younger son[3] of the grantee is entitled to petition the Lord Lyon King of Arms for a " matriculation " of the paternal arms with a suitable difference indicating his position in the family, as explained in the next chapter. Until this has been done, no younger son may use the arms, except whilst living as a " child " in his father's dwelling, when he bears the arms by courtesy with the appropriate " difference of seniority "[4] in a manner analogous to the " Hon." prefix of a peer's younger son. Sometimes his parents apply for the matriculation[5] whilst he is still a child, or his god-parents may concur in doing so.[6] The " difference " mark is usually a bordure of some sort,[7] the presence of which shows that the arms are not newly granted.

[1] *Encyclopaedia of the Laws of Scotland*, s.v. Heraldry, par. 1387 ; Nisbet, *Heraldry*, ii, 38 ; *Lord President Dalrymple of Stair, c*. 1672, Lyon Register, i, 136.

[2] Moir of Leckie, *Morrison's Dictionary of Decisions of the Court of Session*, No. 15537.

[3] In the case of a co-heiress, a junior heir-portioner desirous of obtaining a substantive version of the family arms, she must petition for a matriculation with due difference, which her son will inherit if he takes her name. *Jabez Mackenzie*, 1806, Lyon Register, ii, 9 ; *Law of Succession in Ensigns Armorial*, p. 48. Similarly, where a younger sister requires a difference, she is entitled to obtain one. *Heraldry in Scotland*, p. 281 ; *Mackenzie*, 1806, Lyon Register, ii, 9.

[4] Nisbet, *Heraldry*, ii, iii, 17.

[5] *Dunsmure*, 29 April 1867, Lyon Register, vii, 63 ; *Jas. P. Fraser, second son of Reelig*, 17 December 1932, *ibid.*, xxx, 45.

[6] *T. G. Innes, third son of Raemoir*, 24 July 1923, *ibid.*, xxvi, 19.

[7] Fig. 49 shows a differenced version of the Swinton arms.

7. Adopted children. Since family arms can only in the most exceptional circumstances, and by re-grant, be transferred to " strangers in blood ", and in armorial inheritance, 1672, cap. 47, explicitly required the claimant to lodge evidence of " verity of descent ", adopted children with no blood-connection cannot inherit, or receive matriculation of arms, nor can they be entered in an official (or indeed *any*) pedigree.[1]

The adoption as heir, by a chief, of some member of his own blood or family, is quite a different matter, see p. 125.

In England a person can only have one coat of arms,[2] but in Scotland, as on the Continent, the same individual may, by legal succession to registered arms, become in right of more than one,[3] when he may use either. The Duke of Buccleuch, for example, has a distinct coat of arms as proprietor of Granton Harbour.[4] When a cadet succeeds to the undifferenced arms of his chief he necessarily drops the " cadenced version ", as he must rematriculate in order to establish his right of succession, and make it indefeasible against any competing claimant.

[1] In rare cases arms have been *granted* with a destination specifically including an adopted child, but even in that case it gets the arms only with a *canton voided* to denote absence of blood-descent. *Stewart*, 28 July 1948, Lyon Register, xxxvi, 150; *Mirlees, ibid.*, xxxvii, p. 99; Erskine of Shielfield, 25 March 1953, *ibid.*, xxxix, 74; 1954 Scots Law Times.

[2] J. Dallaway, *Heraldic Inquiries*, p. 369.

[3] *Proc. Fiscal of the Lyon Court* v. *Earl of Rosebery*, 9 July 1773, regarding the arms of the Viscounty of Primrose.

[4] Lyon Register (1886), vii, 41.

PLATE XX

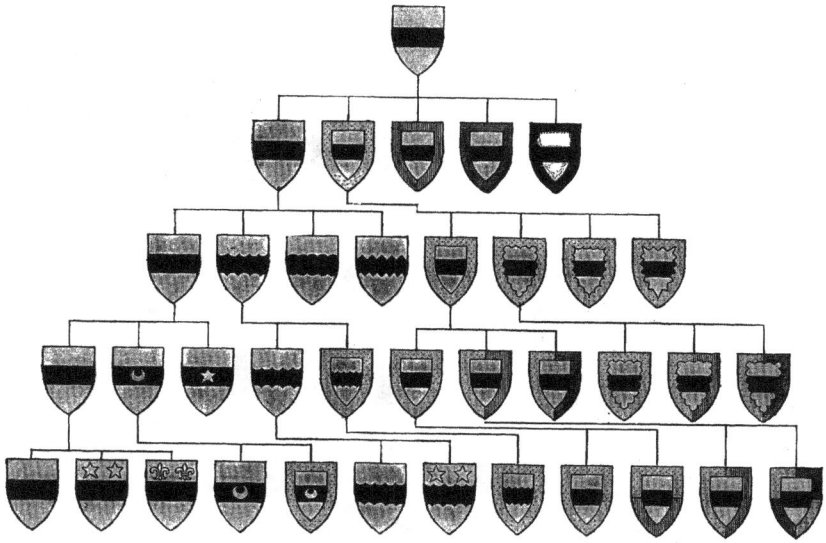

SCOTTISH ARMORIAL DIFFERENCING SCHEME.

When a younger son establishes an independent position or marries, he must matriculate the parental arms with a difference, usually based on this scheme, and then abandon any "courtesy" minute difference borne as an unforisfamiliated child in his parents' household (Nisbet's *Heraldry*, vol. ii; pat. iii; p. 14). These minute differences of seniority borne by courtesy by sons living in their father's household, or until marriage, are the armorial equivalent of the courtesy title "Honourable" in peerage families. They are in each generation coloured, as far as possible, in the tincture precedence on p. 53, and placed on the field on an ordinary or suitable charge, as best suits the tinctures. These minute temporary differences are:

Heir or first son, the Label

Second son, the Crescent

Third son, the Mullet

Fourth son, the Martlet

Fifth son, the Annulet

Sixth son, the Fleur-de-lys

Seventh son, the Rose

Eighth son, the Cross moline

Ninth son, the Double-quatrefoil

PLATE XXI

Achievement of the Hon. Sir LAUNCELOT DOUGLAS CARNEGIE, G.C.V.O., K.C.M.G.

Photograph of the painting in Lyon Register.

Argent, an eagle displayed azure, beaked and membered gules, charged on its breast with three mullets of the field in allusion to his maternal descent from the noble house of Stewart-Murray of Dunmore. Above the shield is placed a helmet befitting his degree, with a mantling azure doubled argent, and on a wreath of his liveries is set for crest a thunderbolt or, winged argent, and in an escrol over the same this motto, " Dred God ", and in a compartment below the shield are set for supporters, on the dexter a talbot, and on the sinister a lion argent armed and langued gules, and both gorged with a collar paly or and sable. The shield is surrounded by the collar of the Royal Victorian Order, and the circlet of a K.C.M.G. (*Lyon Register*, xxiii. 65, 20th September 1918, matriculation as second son of the 9th Earl of Southesk, with grant of supporters as G.C.V.O.)

PLATE XXII

(a) The Right Honourable
LORD HORNE OF STIRKOKE, G.C.B.
(*Lyon Register*, xxiv. 29).

(b) SIR JOHN R. CHANCELLOR, G.C.M.G.
(*Lyon Register*, xxv. 75).

INSIGNIA OF KNIGHTS GRAND CROSS OF ORDERS OF CHIVALRY.
Examples of cadets, with differenced arms, who have attained high chivalric insignia.

PLATE XXIII

Extract of Matriculation of the Arms of Carnegy of Lour, Baron of Lour (cadet of Carnegy, Earl of Northesk), including *chapeau* for the feudal barony of Lour. Matriculated by Warrant of Lord Lyon, Sir Francis Grant, 28th February 1945 (*Lyon Register*, xxxv, 24), and emblazoning the impaled escutcheons of the Barons of Lour ensigned of their baronial *chapeaux*. Inclusion of these Shields related to the devolution, under entail, of Lour and Kinfauns.

CHAPTER VIII

CADENCY, AND REMATRICULATION OF ARMS

AVING stated the rules for the grantee, his wife, eldest son, and daughters, now we must speak of his younger sons. These inherit, not a " right to use the arms ", but a right to obtain a rematriculation of their father's coat with such congruent difference as the Lord Lyon considers suitable. Herein is the vital feature of Scottish heraldry, and one of those in which it preserves the armorial purity and the practical aspect of mediaeval heraldry. Every younger son (except when using by courtesy a shield as a child in his parent's house with the " minute " and temporary cadency marks)[1] must obtain his correct " difference " before he may use the ancestral arms. The " scheme of differencing " used in Scottish heraldry is shown in Plate xx

DOUGLAS OF EGILSAY. Ermine, a heart gules on a chief azure, three mullets argent (differenced by tincture).

[1] Nisbet, *System of Heraldry*, ii, iii, 17, emphasises that marriage of a younger son is one of the contingencies on which " courtesy differencing " terminates—the son establishes a household of his own.

(p. 100), where, however, it is only possible to show the simplest forms of cadency. There are numerous other varieties of bordure. Normally, each son of the main line gets a simple *bordure* of some different colour, but sometimes a

FIG. 50.—STEWART OF BALNAKEILLY. Quarterly: 1st and 4th, or, a fess chequy azure and argent, surmounted by a lion rampant gules, armed and langued of the second (*Stewart of Albany*); 2nd and 3rd, azure, three garbs or (*Buchan*); all within a bordure parted per saltire argent and sable. *Crest*—A dexter hand holding a dagger erect in pale, proper.

" maternal difference ", a charge taken from his mother's arms, or his wife's, proves more convenient. Younger sons of younger sons, again, get various additional differences, *e.g.* the bordure engrailed, embattled, etc., or the bordure itself may be parted per pale, per fess, quarterly, per bend, per saltire, per pairle, or gyronny,[1] or it may be charged with appropriate objects. Sometimes the addition of a quartering is sufficient to difference the arms,[2] but is rightly criticised as ambiguous.[3]

An analysis of differencing in the first volume of Lyon Register shows the relative frequency : bordure, 1080 ; varying of boundary lines of ordinaries, 563 ; additional figures, 428 ; change of tincture (a bad system), 155 ; canton, 70.[4] Cantons have frequently been used to display augmentations, and sometimes bear complete maternal arms,[5] but are more properly employed to include arms or charges included

---

[1] A bordure gyronny of eight is simply a bordure divided into eight sections, just as a " bordure quarterly ", or " bordure per saltire " (*Stewart of Balnakeilly,* 23 October 1903, Lyon Register, xvii, 55) is divided into four.

[2] Cf. Fig. 19 (Duke of Argyll), with Fig. 16 (*b*) (Marquis of Breadalbane). Fraser of Reelig (Plate XVI) is likewise differenced from Lord Lovat by quartering. MacEwen of Moniack ; *Stewart-Mackenzie,* 1922 S.C. (H.L.), 39.

[3] Nisbet, *Heraldry,* ii, iii, 21, 23 ; cf. p. 138 *infra.*

[4] Balfour Paul, *Heraldry in relation to Scottish History and Art,* p. 74.

[5] *Boswell of Auchinleck,* 28 July 1809, Lyon Register, ii, 33.

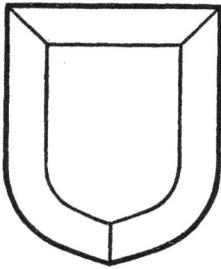

Bordure tierced in pairle.

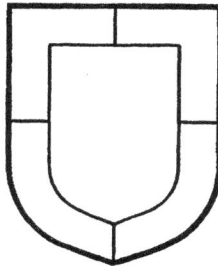

Bordure quartered.

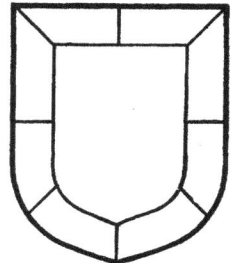

FIG. 51.—PARTED BORDURES.

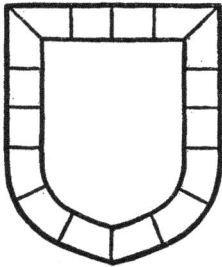

Bordure gyronny.

FIG. 52.—Bordure compony.[1]

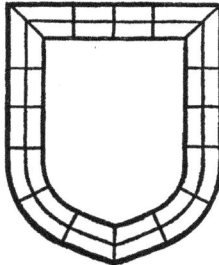

FIG. 53.—Counter compony.[2]

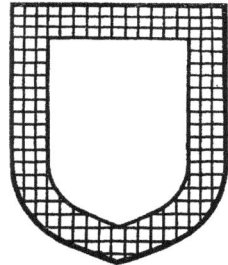

FIG. 54.—Bordure chequy.[3]

[1] In mediaeval times the baton and riband sinister seem to have indicated complete illegitimacy and the bordure compony to have (from the fifteenth century) denoted descent from one or other of the illegitimate but socially recognised connections less than canonical marriage, such as the issue of handfast marriages. Since 1672 it has invariably been used to denote illegitimacy, *vide Lundin of Lundin*, 10 November 1679, Lyon Register, i, 180; *Notes & Queries*, 22 November 1940, *s.v.* Heraldic Legitimation; also *Douglas*, 25 February 1952, Lyon Register xxxviii, 143, and 1953 Scots Law Times.

[2] The bordure counter-compony is not a mark of illegitimacy (Nisbet, *Heraldry*, iii, ii, 13, 1.33) and seems to have been used for cadets branching off in the fifteenth century.

[3] The bordure chequy always denoted a legitimate and ascertained cadet, and in seventeenth-century practice was normally used for cadets who came off a second or third son of the main line, or off a dominant chieftain's or cadet's line in the sixteenth century. Sometimes it connotes a maternal Stewart connection. It is now normally used (in cadency from more modern patents) in those cases where the " proper " bordure under the modern cadency-scheme would be a bordure of the field-tincture.

for some special reason where quartering is not admissible.[1]

In applying tinctures and variation of bordure lines as congruent differences under 1672, cap. 47, the Lord Lyon has laid down the following order of precedency : [2]

Colour of Bordure		Variation of Bordure Lines	
1. Or	8. Tenné	1. Engrailed	8. Raguly
2. Argent	9. Ermine	2. Invected	9. Nowy
3. Gules	10. Contre-ermine	3. Indented	10. Contre-nowy
4. Azure	11. Erminois	4. Embattled	11. Dovetailed
5. Sable	12. Pean	5. Wavy	12. Potenty
6. Vert	13. Vair	6. Nebuly	13. Urdy
7. Purpure.	14. Potent	7. Rayonee	14. Round embattled

The foregoing order is that of the cadets as they come off the stem or branch, and not in any particular generation, and at various junctures suitable maternal differences may be used when the opportunity arises.

The colour-on-colour rule is not strictly applicable in the case of bordures, but nowadays in any cases where a shield argent would fall to be embordured argent or suchlike, the practice is to employ a bordure chequy or counter-compony for that cadet.

In each case the " differenced " coat descends to the " heir " of the man in whose favour it was matriculated, and if any special limitation is desired, this should be stated in the petition, when a destination will be inserted in the matriculation.[3]

The procedure of matriculation is to present a Petition somewhat as follows :

[1] *Campbell of Barcaldine*, 25 April 1817, Lyon Register, ii, 164.
[2] Hospital Management Boards, 1949, *ibid.*, xxxvii, 152.
[3] *Fullarton of Craighall*, 9 March 1720, *ibid.*, i, 305, see *Laing Charters*, No. 3091 ; *Graham of Balgowan*, Lyon Register, i, 157 ; *Seton of Pitmedden*, *ibid.*, i, 214 ; *Macpherson of Pitmain*, 27 February 1940, *ibid.*, xxxiv, 7.

UNTO THE RIGHT HONOURABLE
THE LORD LYON KING OF ARMS

The Petition of FERGUS SMITH,
Banker in the City of New York,
U.S.A.

HUMBLY SHEWETH

1. THAT he is the second son of the late George Smith, Rancher at Redskin Gulch, Alberta, in the Dominion of Canada, by his wife Margaret, daughter of Joseph Taylor, Manufacturer, Chicago, U.S.A.

2. THAT the said George Smith was the sixth son of the late John Smith of Glensmith in the County of Blankshire, D.S.O., Captain in the Blankshire Highlanders, and his wife Anne, daughter of John Campbell, Chartered Accountant in Edinburgh.

3. THAT arms were matriculated in the Public Register of All Arms and Bearings in Scotland upon the seventh day of March 1950 in name of the said Captain John Smith of Glensmith (*If a claimant is craving matriculation, not as a cadet but in virtue of a Testamentary Name and Arms Clause, as heir of tailzie under a settlement, or in virtue of a resignation,*[1] *the ground of claims and terms of the deeds founded on should be set forth here*) and that the Petitioner is desirous that the foresaid Ensigns Armorial should be matriculated of new in his own name with a suitable difference. (*If an alteration of destination*[2] *or a specified line of descent is to be inserted, or any alteration upon existing arms is desired, such matters should be clearly set forth here. The prayer will then run:*

      " May it therefore please your Lordship to maintain, ratify, and confirm unto the Petitioner and his (*here insert the exact destination craved*) the foresaid ensigns armorial (*here specify any alteration or addition desired*) and to Grant Warrant . . .")

(*If the Petitioner is of knightly or baronial rank and desires a badge, add after the words* " own name " *or* " difference ", *the phrase* " and

---

[1] *Hamilton of Binning,* 20 July 1687, Lyon Register, i, 329; *Scott of Harden,* 9 November 1700, *ibid.,* ii, 189; *Myreton of Cambo* (text of resignation), 10 November 1700, *Scottish Notes & Queries,* 1939, p. 187.

[2] *Heraldry in Scotland,* pp. 67, 127.

to allow the Petitioner for Badge a . . . and ordain the same to be displayed on a standard befitting his degree along with the motto/slogan . . ." [1])

In an ordinary petition for matriculation, the prayer will read :

MAY IT THEREFORE please your Lordship to Grant Warrant to the Lyon Clerk to matriculate of new in the Public Register of All Arms and Bearings in Scotland in name of the Petitioner the foresaid Ensigns Armorial with a suitable difference. (*If a specific destination is desired* (*in an initial cadet-matriculation*), *add here :* "and limited unto his . . .", *specifying the precise destination craved.*)

And your Petitioner will ever pray.

(*Signature of Petitioner or his Agent*)

F. SMITH.
Date, 9th September 19——.

To the Petition, which should be typed on *foolscap size paper* with a broad margin, should be annexed on a separate sheet a "Condescendance of Proof" with paragraphs numbered to correspond with those in the Petition, each headed, *e.g.* :

To prove proposition 2nd (*i.e. second paragraph in the Petition*).

1. Birth certificate of the said George Smith, No. 102 of Guggleton Reg. District, Blankshire, year 18——.
2. Commission, John Smith in Blankshire Highlanders, 2 March 18——.
3. London Gazette, D.S.O. Captain John Smith, 14 June 18——.
4. Extract Will of Captain John Smith, 8 February 19——, Reg. Books of Council and Session, 3 March 19——, referring to five elder sons.

The Petition is lodged with the Lyon Clerk, along with the tabulated pedigree and Statement of Proof, and with documents, certificates, or other satisfactory proof of the pedigree, and thereafter the Lord Lyon gives judgment

---

[1] An inventory of all the "productions" should also be lodged.

granting warrant to the Lyon Clerk to matriculate the arms in the Lyon Register with such additional bordure or other difference as his Lordship considers appropriate. The fees

in this case are about £19, and depend to some extent on whether quarterings are included or other matters arise rendering the arms more complicated. On payment of these Treasury fees, the petitioner receives, not, as in the case of a "grant", Letters Patent from the Lord Lyon, but an illustrated parchment[1] from the Lyon Clerk which, like a " Birth Certificate ", is an *Official Extract* of the facts which have been entered in the Public Register of All Arms and Bearings.

FIG. 55.—Archery Medal of Robert Hay of Strowie (1705). Argent, three escutcheons gules, a bordure of the second, charged with eight crescents of the field (for difference, indicating a younger son of a younger son). *Crest*—An ox's yoke impaled gules, ensigned on the top with a crescent argent. *Motto*—" Cresco sub jugo ".

This, of course, bears an officially illuminated drawing of the coat of arms, as differenced, whilst the document is sealed, and in all respects as imposing as an original grant, and nowadays usually finds a place in an oak frame upon the walls of dining-room or library. The point, however, is that a matriculation is not a " newly devised " coat of arms. It is, as Nisbet observes,[2] a distinct heraldic

[1] See Plate XVI, p. 79, Extract of Matriculation of the Arms of *Fraser of Reelig*, Lyon Register, xxx, 22. [2] *System of Heraldry*, i, 176.

fief to which the cadet gets " a feudal title ". It is a " differenced " version of *the old arms* (technically an " incorporeal appanage-fief " allocated out of what we might call the " waste " of the chiefly " armorial estate ", just as a cadet was often given a farm out of the chief's " territorial property "), indicating the precise position of the cadet in the family from which he has proved his descent, and it is a valuable legal proof of the ancestry to which it testifies, being the decision of a National Court of Justice, and is *res judicata* for subsequent matriculations.

Much of the business in the Lyon Court consists of these numerous applications by cadets of ancient Scottish families for rematriculation of the family arms, with requisite differences and with the addition of quarterings for heiresses whom their ancestors have married. These rematriculations form a convenient opportunity for obtaining judgment establishing and putting on record in the Public Register the intervening pedigree back to the main line, or to the ancestor who last matriculated, and for bringing down the " progress of title " of the arms as a " noble fief ".[1]

Even the bastard—perhaps on account of the old Scottish custom of " handfast marriages "—is favourably treated in Scots Heraldic Law.[2] On proof of his paternity, he matriculates exactly like any lawful cadet, and simply obtains some

---

[1] *Douglas of Brigton*, 21 May 1941, Lyon Reg., XXXV; *Law of Succession in Ensigns Armorial*, p. 28; 1941 S.C., pp. 671-2. The procedure (judicial constitution of appanage-arms indicating position *in familia*) is as nearly equivalent as scientific differencing-enforcement admits, to the Scottish sub-infeudation system in land, on which the whole Scottish social system is built, and which differs fundamentally from everything English subsequent to Edward I's statute *Quia emptores*, which along with Henry VII's anti-livery Acts, struck heavily at " the family " as a social organism in England. In Scotland heraldic and land laws both retain the full feudo-celtic familial concept of expanding " erected " sub-households growing into great " branches ", each sub-organised. Every matriculation actually or potentially " founds " an additional (sub-)house.

[2] *E.g.* A. and A. Donald, *The Clan Donald*, iii, 159.

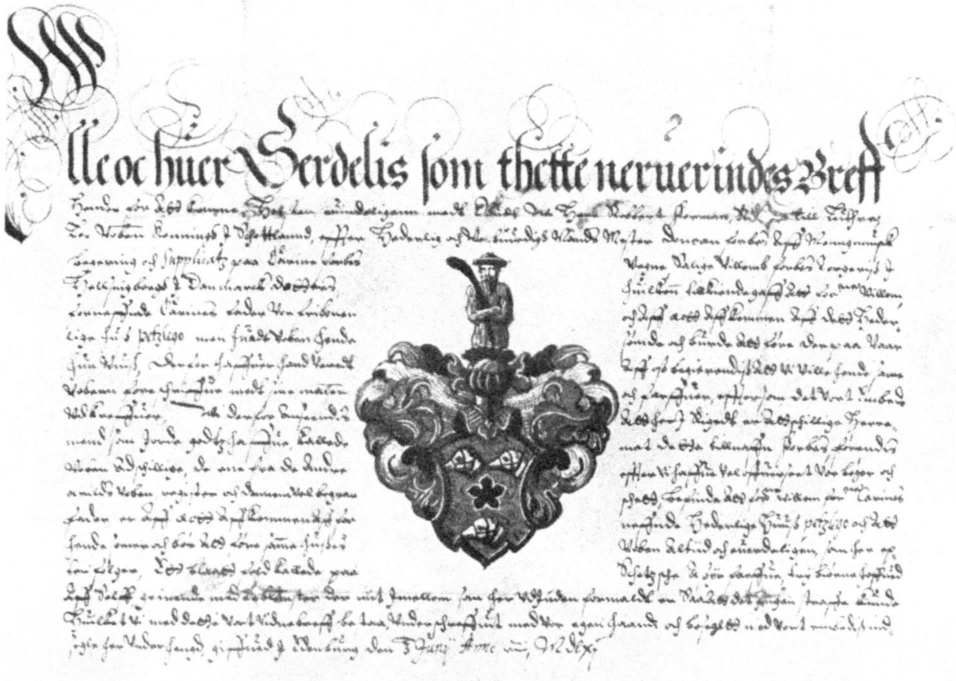

PLATE XXIV

Extract of Matriculation and Confirmation, of the arms of Katharine Forbes, as a cadet of the Family of Forbes of Pitsligo, by decree of Sir Robert Forman of Luthrie, 3 June 1561, *Liber Curiarum et Processus* of Lyon Court, 1561, fol. 27. *Cf.* Spalding Club. *Antiquities of Aberdeen and Banff*, vol. III, p. 502. This is the Danish copy of the Original Extract of Matriculation sent overseas to avouch her nobility in Denmark. This shows that the jurisdiction and procedure were established (and the same as subsequently found in operation) long before any statutory enactments regarding Lyon Court.

PLATE XXV

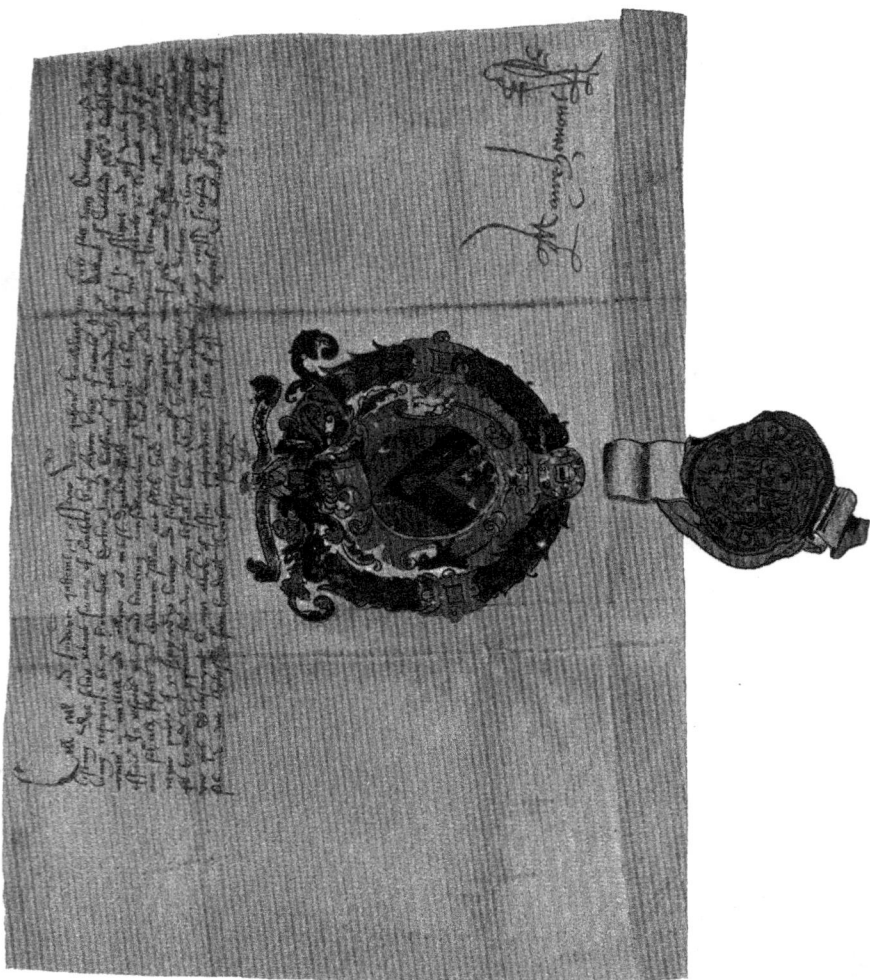

Extract of the Matriculation and Confirmation, of the arms of Sir James Balfour of Pittendriech, as a cadet of Balfour of Balfour, as confirmed by Sir Robert Forman of Luthrie, Lord Lyon King of Arms, 2 April 1567. (*Edinburgh Heraldic Exhibition*)

form of the specific "bordure compony",[1] or baton or riband sinister, the purpose of which is merely to show that he is not actually in the legal line of succession;[2] but far from being reckoned a *filius nullius*, he is treated as a member of his father's clan, and as having a hereditary right to the ensigns armorial which indicate his actual paternity, and quarterings, if any (or "legitimated" by marrying an armigerous heiress).[3] A girl-bastard in whose name arms have been matriculated becomes an "heiress" in that bastardised coat, which can be quartered by her descendants.[4] This is sometimes a good way of acquiring a quartering of the arms of some great house.

Nowadays, even the successive heirs to the principal or undifferenced coat of arms usually rematriculate after a few generations, or bring up to date a pedigree in the Public Register of Genealogies, both for the purpose of putting on record the intervening pedigree since last registration. It is much easier, and less costly, to prove a pedigree of three to four generations than to let matters slide and oblige some descendant to prove links over a period of two centuries or so, in order to establish that he is actually the heir in right of the coat of arms recorded by the ancestor he represents.

There are actually about five principal varieties of matriculation:[5]

1. Initial Matriculations, placing on record arms of ancient user, after proof. These may often contain a destination.

2. Matriculations by Cadets—obtaining cadet-arms which may or may not contain a specific destination—as circumstances require.

---

[1] Fig. 52, p. 103. [2] A. C. Fox-Davies, *Art of Heraldry*, pp. 355, 357.
[3] *Notes & Queries*, 22 November 1940, vol. 179, p. 362.
[4] A. C. Fox-Davies, *Complete Guide*, p. 554; Hamilton quarter in Lyon Register, xxx, 59.
[5] *Scottish Law Review*, 1941, vol. lvii, p. 129, Lyon Court Procedure.

I

3. Matriculation by Progress, the equivalent of special service in other feudal heritage, and whereby title is made up either to chief-arms or to existing cadet arms.

4. Matriculation to alter arms ; sometimes to vary or correct the existing coat on further research, and sometimes to include fresh quarterings and form a *cumulatio armorum*.

5. Matriculation for Redestination (see p. 126, *infra*). This is the equivalent in Armory of a Royal Confirmation of a tailzie or settlement of heritage, as set forth by Sir George Mackenzie,[1] and that an alteration of destination is made by matriculation is indicated by Stevenson.[2]

---

[1] *Works*, ii, 616 ; and *Notes & Queries*, clxxviii, 273, and see *infra*, pp. 123, 133, n. 5.

[2] *Heraldry in Scotland*, p. 129. See also analysis of this passage in " Scottish Armorial Tailzies ", article in *Notes & Queries*, clxxviii, 273 ; *Maclachlan of Maclachlan*, 3 July 1946, Lyon Register, xxxv, 72 ; *Campbell of Dunstaffnage*, 11 November 1943, *ibid.*, xxxiv, 71.

CHAPTER IX

SUCCESSION TO ARMS

HAY, EARL OF ERROLL. Argent, three inescutcheons gules.

HEN the direct line of descent of a family is interrupted, questions may arise as to who is entitled to the undifferenced arms. The fundamental principle in Scottish Armorial Succession [1] was laid down in 1824 by Lord Lyon the Earl of Kinnoull :

" There does not seem any rule necessary for deciding questions for competition for particular sets of arms, for such questions must be settled according to the ordinary rules of law, and in all cases decided in favour of the party establishing the best right to the character of Representative or heir of line [2] to the family whose arms they claim to bear, and the same rule must always hold in deciding the claims of individuals for arms or supporters as a matter of right, which fall only to be awarded to the

[1] For detailed exposition of this subject see Innes of Learney, *Law of Succession in Ensigns Armorial*, 1941, and *Notes & Queries*, 1939, vol. 177, p. 164; vol. 178, pp. 74, 131, 254, 362; vol. 179, p. 308; vol. 180, p. 128; vol. 181, p. 2; vol. 183.

[2] Kinnoull correctly treats " Representative " as a broader character than " heir of line ", and which could include nominees or heirs of tailzie, including heirs-male in a case where male tailzie operates.

party establishing the character in virtue of which the claim is advanced." [1]

This principle was reaffirmed by Lord Lyon Grant on 8 Dec. 1838 in determining as between heir-male and heir of line:

I find that the petitioner, as eldest daughter, is now in right . . . to the said arms of their father, as there is no entail or destination of the same on record,[2]

and this (subject to the excision of a phrase referring to the younger sisters as heirs-portioners, which the Lord Justice Clerk held inconsistent with law of superiorities to which he held the substantive right to undifferenced arms analogous) [3] the Court held to be a correct statement of Heraldic Law.[4] The Court of Session, however, also held Lord Jeffrey's view [5] that the inheritance of the old family estate, where such existed, was a material element ; and this was followed by the Lord Lyon in the case of The Mackintosh. [6] The Lord Justice Clerk's principle that for an heir-female to succeed, her husband and her children must " become members of the heiress' family either by adoption or by taking of the name " [7] is also accepted as the Law of Arms and was already the recognised principle in the seventeenth [8] and eighteenth centuries.[9] There are, however, a few dis-

---

[1] Excerpt from Lord Kinnoull's criticism of the evidence of Interim Lyon-Depute Tait (printed in the *10th Report on Scots Courts of Justice*, 1822). Kinnoull had been pressed into appointing Tait, who immediately began undermining the Scottish heraldic jurisdiction and subverting the old Scots Law of family and armorial succession, and for this Kinnoull dismissed Tait in 1823.

[3] *Ibid.*, p. 687.　　　[4] *Ibid.*, pp. 687-708, *i.e.* regarding non-"lorded" arms.

[2] *Maclean of Ardgour* v. *Maclean*, 1941 S.C., p. 662.

[5] *Cuninghame* v. *Cunningham* (11 Dunlop 1139).

[6] *Mackintosh of Mackintosh* v. *Mackintosh of Clan Chattan*, 9 April 1947, Lyon Register, xxxvi, 36 and 40.

[7] *Maclean of Ardgour* v. *Maclean*, p. 684.

[8] *Lundin of Lundin, Notes & Queries*, 22 November 1940.

[9] *Douglas of Douglas*, 1771, Lyon Register, i, 189, and see *Douglas of Douglas-Support, ibid.*, iii, 93, where the heir-male is symbolically represented as a reptile to be trodden under foot (30 February 1832).

tinctions in the Law of Arms, such as that a quartered *cumulatio armorum* on failure of direct descendants would split up again, *paternis paterna, maternis materna,* so that where a coat has descended through an heiress it genealogically follows back the line from whence it came, as was the rule in old Scottish feudal succession,[1] even for a Crown (*e.g.* the Crown of Scotland, which in 1292 passed *maternis materna* to John Baliol, the heir of line of the Maid of Norway, and not to her father, the King of Norway). To this Sir George Mackenzie of Rosehaugh equates the Law of Succession to arms.[2] The Law of Armorial Succession thus preserves many aspects of our really ancient Scottish feudal law, *i.e.* the *Law of the Family* or clan, in which the undifferenced arms demonstrate the *Chiefship of the Family,* and in the words of Sir George Mackenzie, its Gaelic equivalent, the *Headship of the Clan.*[3] Likewise in the unanimous opinion of the Law Lords in *Seaforth* v. *Allangrange,* the undifferenced arms denote the Chief of the *Clan.*[4]

Concerning the terms of destinations of arms, Stevenson lays down that :

a grant to a person and his descendants, or, in earlier phrase, posterity, is a grant to heirs of his body in contradistinction to heirs-male of his body. A grant, or, failing the grant, the entry of it in the Register of Arms, declaring the existence and nature of the arms of A. B., without restricting the right in them to A. B. alone, is equivalent to a grant to A. B. and his heirs, a term which includes collateral heirs.[5]

Arms the destination of which is unknown, and those destined to the patentee and his *heirs,* go to the collateral *heir* on the extinction of the patentee's descendants in the same way that those destined to

---

[1] *Countess of Atholl,* Scots Peerage, i, 423 ; F. Adam and Innes of Learney, *Clans, Septs, and Regiments of the Scottish Highlands,* 1955 ed., pp. 31, 33.

[2] *Works,* ii, 615.   [3] *Ibid.,* ii, 616.

[4] 1922 S.C. (H.L.), 39 ; see *Tartans of the Clans and Families of Scotland,* 1948 ed., p. 28, n. 2, and p. 50 ; *Clans, Septs, and Regiments of the Scottish Highlands,* 1952 ed., p. 190.

[5] *Heraldry in Scotland,* p. 335.

his *heirs-male* go on the extinction of his male descendants to his *heir-male* collateral.[1]

The word " heir " is here used as heir-general in pointed distinction to "heir-male", and this was equally well recognised in 1816, when Lyon-Depute Home expounded that :

A patent to a person and his descendants is much more extensive than a patent to a person and his heirs-male (*of the body*).[2]

The principle and practice of armorial succession in Scotland may thus be set down as follows : When the direct line of an armigerous family goes to an heiress and a collateral heir-male exists, then (1) where the grant itself defines the succession, no difficulty arises, provided the destination is free from ambiguity,[3] (2) otherwise, since (per Sir George Mackenzie)

Arms descend to the (patentee's) heirs " as they would succeed to a crown " and (per Lord President Stair) " what cannot be claimed by a special title either as being conquest *or special provided by the tenor of the infeftment,* befalleth to the heirs of line, and therefore in dubious cases what doth not appear to belong to other heirs appertaineth to these ".[4]

And in the Law and Practice of Arms under the Scottish Acts the matriculation in Lyon Register is the " infeftment " or record of sasine of the Arms.[5]

Arms accordingly devolve on the heir of line, provided such is—or " within due time " *becomes* (by taking or *retaking* the family name)—a member of the family, unless there is a special destination to heirs-male or of tailzie and investiture thereof on record in Lyon Register. Stair continues :

[1] *Heraldry in Scotland,* p. 344.
[2] *Fyffe,* 18 August 1816, *Notes & Queries,* vol. 179, p. 308, n. 3, *Erskine of Linlathen*—where Lord Lyon Burnett's opinion is printed.
[3] Lord Aitchison in *Maclean of Ardgour,* 1938, S.L.T., p. 57.
[4] Lord President Stair's *Institutes of the Law of Scotland,* iii, v, 8.
[5] *Law of Succession in Ensigns Armorial,* pp. 28, 44 ; 1941 S.C., p. 672.

Heirs-portioners are amongst heirs-of-line, for when more women or their issue succeed, failing males of that degree, it is by the course of law that they succeed . . . and though they succeed equally, yet rights indivisible fall to the eldest alone without anything in lieu thereof to the rest; as (1) The dignity of Lord, Earl, etc.; (2) The principal mansion being tower, fortalice, etc.; (3) Superiorities, etc.[1]

Here emerges the " Jeffrey " principle approved in *Maclean of Ardgour* v. *Maclean*, 1941 (since in both military and civil life undifferenced arms are synonymous with and demonstrative of Chiefship/Representation). This principle is that the "Inheritor" of the old family estate is the Represener (*i.e.* the Chief) of the Family, where there is (*a*) no special destination of arms, (*b*) no explicit or implied[2] settlement of arms. The arms necessarily carry the relative chiefship[3] and *then* the "arms of that description" (*i.e.* recorded in Lyon Register under the "title" of such feudal or chiefly family) will (agreeably to what in Peerage Law is termed " attraction "[4]) follow the principal fief or the part thereof settled as the *caput* of such fief. This is normally the chief *chymmes* or castle-stead,[5] so long as such *chymmes* or *caput*[6] descends within

---

[1] Stair, *Institutes*, ii, 5. 11, quoted in *Law and Practice of Heraldry*, p. 338.

[2] As in *Mackintosh of Mackintosh*, 1947 ; see 1950 Scots Law Times, 2.

[3] *Multa cum universitate transeunt quae singulariter prohibentur.* This *universitas* is the " universal succession " or Representation Chiefship which passes from each patriarch to his successor (*Notes & Queries*, vol. 178, p. 274; *Albany's Observations*, p. 43).

[4] Since 1941 such " attraction " is definitely accepted as part of the Law of Arms. *Maclean of Ardgour*, S.C., pp. 687, 700, 705.

[5] *Earldom of Mar in Sunshine and Shade*, i, 120. Sometimes, however, another special locus is specified or reserved as such *caput*. W. C. Dickinson, *Baron Court Book of Carnwath*, p. xxii.

[6] The *caput* may even be the principal hearth, within the mansion, as has sometimes occurred in France (F. Brentano, *Old Régime in France*, p. 44). Indeed, as at Cromartie Castle, the fireplace lintel (Plate XI), a concept of family-representation which carries us back to the *hearths* of the Iron Age tribal hut-settlements (see *Proc. of Soc. of Antiquaries of Scot.*, lxxix, p. 116, n. 2, and cf. *Dalyell of the Binns* charter to National Trust).

the family (*i.e.* in the blood and name). It was along with the mansion that the old " heirship movables " descended. These included " the family seal of arms ",[1] the shield, of course, originally the Chief's shield of arms,[2] and the " ornament ", *i.e.* escutcheon of the family seat in church, under which the Chiefs were anciently buried.[3]

The seal of arms, chiefship, and sepulchre descend together, according to the same principles as govern the Scottish Crown, Earldoms, and Baronies, each of which were simply tribal chiefships.[4] Arms are feudal heritage [5] and an incorporeal fief, and descend as such unless "attracted ".

The principle and practice in Scottish Armorial succession is accordingly quite simple, and results in the original arms descending at common law, essentially like the castle or mansion of a Scottish estate, so long as the heir bears the name incident to the " armorial fief ", *i.e.* its " description ", really *nomen dignitatis nobilitatis minoris.* In the case of an ascent to collaterals the ancient principle of *paternis paterna, maternis materna,* which was, and remains, the rule in Scottish honours,[6] the ancient Law of Scotland, and still rules in the Law of Arms.

Armorial bearings being heritage whereof the title is " matter of record ", its devolution becomes the subject of a legal progress-of-titles,[7] " revesting ",[8] whether by confirma-

---

[1] *Maclean of Ardgour,* 1941 S.C., p. 713, Finding 27; *Proc. of Soc. of Antiquaries of Scot.,* lxxvii, 171, n. 3; Agnew, *Hereditary Sheriffs of Galloway,* p. 111.

[2] This originally *hung,* and was later *carved* over the hall fireplace.

[3] *Law of Succession in Ensigns Armorial,* pp. 33-48.

[4] *Tartans of the Clans and Families of Scotland,* p. 26, cf. *Notes & Queries,* vol. 181, p. 2, *re* Sir George Mackenzie of Rosehaugh on armorial succession.

[5] Lord Justice Clerk in *Maclean of Ardgour,* 1941 S.C., p. 683, line 35.

[6] *Vide* Atholl, *Scots Peerage,* i, 423; *Clans, Septs, and Regiments of the Scottish Highlands,* 1952 ed., pp. 31, 33.

[7] Mackenzie of Tarbat, " heir be progress of Macleod of Lewis ", Lyon Register, i, 184.

[8] *Miscellanea Genealogica et Heraldica,* 1880, iii, 298, Garter to See, 1536.

PLATE XXVI

LIVINGSTONE OF THAT ILK.

Example of the achievement of a Scottish Chief and minor Baron before elevation to the peerage. Arms: quarterly, 1st and 4th, *Livingstone*; 2nd and 3rd, *Callendar*.

PLATE XXVII

LIVINGSTONE OF WESTQUARTER.

Achievement of a cadet of Livingstone of that Ilk, showing arms differenced with a bordure quarterly or and gules. (*Lyon Register*, v. 58.)

tion, or redestination (or resignation *in favorem*),[1] and may be by a simple letter of renunciation [2] or by a "matriculation by progress "[3] for the purpose of making up the title to the arms.

Even in the case of higher dignities, our ancient practice was for the heirs to be retoured,[4] or otherwise satisfactorily connected to their predecessors in the honours,[5] and in heraldry the statutory means of making up title to arms on succession is to get the arms rematriculated in one's own name in Lyon Register, the equivalent of recording a progress of title to land in the Register of Sasines.[6] The Lord Lyon's judgment and subsequent matriculation in Lyon Register is analogous to the modern recorded decree of Service as a title to land. In this, armorial conveyancing from 1672 was two centuries ahead of land conveyancing. A rematriculation by progress is the equivalent of a general retour as regards representation, and a special retour as regards title and pedigree, and of great value in succession to honours, including Baronetcies [7] and higher honours.[8] The Act 1672, cap. 47, intends that this should be done within a year and day at every succession; [9] however, just as many proprietors of land were content to possess on apparency for a generation

---

[1] Myreton of Cambo, 10 January 1701, *Scottish Notes & Queries*, 1933, p. 187; Grant of Auchernack, 31 December 1777, Lyon Register, i, 515; *Encyclopaedia of Legal Styles*, v, 286.

[2] Hamilton of Binning, 20 July 1687, Lyon Register, i, 329, printed in *Notes & Queries*, vol. 178, p. 293.

[3] *Notes & Queries*, 27 April 1940, p. 294.

[4] J. Riddell, *Inquiry into the Law and Practice in Scottish Peerages*, pp. 141, 640.

[5] *Earl of Mar*, 7 July 1933; Lyon Register, xxx, 67; *Earl of Selkirk, ibid.*, xxxv, 28; *Kinloss*, 18 July 1947, *ibid.*, xxxvi, 61; see p. 125 *infra*.

[6] 1941 S.C., p. 672.

[7] Home Office letter in *Grant-Suttie*, 5 June 1947 (Case 921, 215); *Strathspey*, 27 January 1950 (1950 Scots Law Times, p. 17).

[8] *Selkirk*, Lyon Register, xxxv, 28, and note; *Kinloss, ibid.*, xxxvi, 61.

[9] *Notes & Queries*, 22 February 1941, p. 131, col. 2.

or two, most people are content to hold the arms their immediate predecessor had registered on that same footing, since the heirship is still common knowledge, though if " used ", the Fiscal could charge the heir to rematriculate, and additional expenses beyond the matriculation fee would then be incurred.[1]

Beyond two or three generations, if no steps are taken, the time may come when that heirship will be difficult or impossible to establish.[2] Such a descendant might be unable to make out his claim, or answer a complaint by the Fiscal, so in cautious families it is the rule for even the direct to rematriculate about every third generation. When succession passes through a female, the husband's change of name should be " officially recognised " in the rematriculation.

The foregoing rule explains the descent of the arms *per se* and, *e.g.*, through a non-armigerous husband and irrespective of the cumulation by marshalling with other arms, paternal or by inbrought heiresses (which is treated of under " marshalling "). Quartering is important and often genealogically interesting, but when a family is one of standing, with well recognised arms, it is preferable that the well-known achievement of the House, emblazoned on its flags and plate, should descend unaltered ;[3] and this is also the case where inbrought

---

[1] This "possession on apparency," to use the old feudal term, has even been allowed in the case of heirs-female and in relation to Thistle stall-plates. *Buccleuch*, 1911—arms of Scott alone ; *Erroll*, 1911—arms of Hay alone ; the Erroll arms were rematriculated *inter alia* under an appointment of arms dated 1672 in the present line of Earls in the person of Diana, Countess of Erroll (Lyon Register, xxxiv, 44) ; *Colquhoun of Luss*—arms of that house alone without any paternal grant arms. In each case the arms set up were " on record " in Lyon Register, but succession through a female had subsequently occurred.

[2] Possession on Apparency is not recognised beyond eighty-one years, as beyond that it is a mere *ipse dixit* (Lord Lyon's report to the Lord Chamberlain on Territorial Designations, 1948).

[3] For Nisbet's distinction between heiresses and such as are " Representatives ", *i.e.* senior, or by settlement some specific heir-portioner, *Notes & Queries*, 25, May 1940, p. 364.

paternal or other quarterings would render the coat over-complicated.[1] Sir George Mackenzie considers that the name and arms of the heiress should be borne by her heirs alone and unquartered,[2] and for enforcing this she may—apart from any tailzie or settlement—"make the paction herself",[3] and, if an eldest daughter's child bears her name, devolution is through her as "heiress herself" by operation of Heraldic Succession.[4]

The label is the charge appropriate to be borne by the heir-male who is not the heir-of-line of his house when the principal (*i.e.* undifferenced) arms have gone to the heir-of-line.[5]

This is logical, since the heir-male is heir-presumptive until his niece has a child bearing her name, so he bore a label as first heir and it became convenient for his brisur to continue hereditarily for his line.[6] Since plain labels of three and five points are borne automatically by the son and grandson as 1st and 2nd heirs-apparent, and the plain three-point label may be automatically and temporarily taken by the 1st heir-presumptive, it is expedient that all hereditary labels be charged,[7] and this is now the expressly approved practice when the label is assigned to an heir-male who has

[1] Lord Lyon Burnett, *Erskine of Linlathen*, 20 May 1870, *Notes & Queries*, 25 May 1940, p. 364.

[2] *Works*, ii, 490 (a passage jurists have overlooked), 622, l. 1.

[3] *Ibid.*, ii, 616, l. 4, analysed *Notes & Queries*, 2 September 1939, p. 166, n. 6.

[4] Mackenzie expressly distinguishes this succession *by right* from the cases of tailzies involving "the Prince's consent"; see *Notes & Queries*, 5 July 1941, p. 2; *i.e.* in a settlement with name and arms clause, on an *eldest* daughter, she and her child are also *alioqui successuri* in the arms.

[5] J. H. Stevenson, *Heraldry in Scotland*, p. 300; Nisbet, *System of Heraldry*, 1722, i, 449, ii, iii, 8; *Cuninghame* v. *Cunyngham*, Session Papers, 1848, p. 27.

[6] *E.g.* Master of Maxwell, Lord Herries, officially allowed to retain the label in his Maxwell coat, *Heraldry in Scotland*, p. 121, pl. 6, p. 88; Nisbet, i, 449; ii, iii, 8, 15. Also the Abercorn line of Hamiltons *did* use such a mark (Mackenzie, *Works*, ii, 616, l. 42, 617; *Scottish Armorial Seals*, No. 1216; Stoddart, *Scottish Arms*, ii, 109) prior to their differencing by the inescutcheon of Chatelherault, cf. Crecq, p. 97; Sir W. Fraser, *The Douglas Book*, ii, 624.

[7] Cf. *R. V. Macpherson*, 16 December 1941, Lyon Reg. xxxiv, 45. Plate XVIII.

not become the Chief.[1] A similar label charged with the Crown is the difference borne, in conformity with the foregoing, by H.R.H. the Duke of Windsor, since upon his abdication he ceased to be King and Chief of the Royal House. Another well-known instance is Lindsay of Spynie, heir-male of Crawford, 1652–72.[2] Many heirs-male have merely got an additional charge [3] or variation of an ordinary,[4] conforming to Sir George Mackenzie's ruling [5] that where the line of the heretrix succeeds to the Chiefship, the heir-male is simply a cadet.

Where the succession has fallen to a female who desires to renounce, the heir-male petitions *with consent* of the renouncing heiress, who signs the petition as Consenter.[6]

The wife of the fiar of the arms is entitled to use them (during wifehood or widowhood), and the heir-apparent, as such, to use them with a three-point label. When the arms devolve on an heiress, her husband is, as with any other feudalised inheritance, entitled to use of them by the courtesy of Scotland.[7] If the heiress has herself matriculated, her

[1] *Mackintosh of Clan Chattan*, 9 April 1947, Lyon Register, xxxvi, 36, charged label in the Mackintosh quarter in respect of his not having succeeded to the Chiefship of Mackintosh (see Plate XLVI, p. 220).

[2] The label-differenced arms, confirmed in *Lindsay-Carnegie-Torrie*, Lyon Register, xxxiii, 17. The Earldom, Chiefship, and undifferenced arms had in the seventeenth century been diverted by a tailzie, and Spynie, the disinherited heir-male, was duly bearing the label difference.

[3] *Nicholson, Bt.*, heir-male of Carnock, 3 April 1901, Lyon Register, xvi, 40 ; *Hamilton*, " heir-male of Westburn ", 1774, *ibid.*, i, 504.

[4] *Hunter*, heir-male of Hunterston, 15 July 1881, Lyon Register, x, 86.

[5] *Notes & Queries*, 20 April 1940, vol. 178, p. 274, for analysis of the passage in Mackenzie's *Works*, ii, 616, l. 36.

[6] *Pringle of Lynedoch*, Lyon Register, xxxiii, 43 ; *Notes & Queries*, 27 April 1940, p. 294. Renunciation may be by a separate " Letter " (*Hamilton of Binning*, 1686, Lyon Register, i, 329).

[7] Lord Advocate in *Balfour of Burleigh* Peerage, 1867, proceedings, 166 ; *Notes & Queries*, 9 September 1939, p. 185 ; 3 February 1940, p. 76, n. 8 ; Erskine, *Institutions*, ii, ix. sec. 54 ; *Smith-Cuninghame*, 1829, Lyon Register, iii, 71 ; *Seton of Touch*, 1771, *ibid.*, i, 489 ; *Carnegy-Arbuthnott of Balnamoon*, 1898, *ibid.*, xv, 18 ; *Mackenzie of Cromartie*, 6 January 1905, *ibid.*, xviii, 21.

incoming-husband (whose assumption of name will be recognised under Schedule B) may exercise the courtesy without himself matriculating—provided he enters her armorial family by assuming her name, cf. Lord Aitchison in *Maclean of Ardgour*, 1941 S.C., p. 684, this being laid down by our authorities, Seton, Stevenson, and Macpherson, as "indispensable" and a *sine qua non*.[1]

In the case of heirs-portioners the "armorial fief analogous to the feudal law of property is (failing words of limitation) divisible between the sisters; but as all daughters enjoy "daughter privilege" (*i.e.* a courtesy life-use of their parents' arms) no "difference" is essential during their lives.[2] Beyond their generation the Law of Arms (1672, cap. 47) requires all arms to be "distinguisht", and, failing settlement in tail, *the right of the fee of the undifferenced arms (being an indivisible dignity like a mansion or superiority)* pertains to, and is transmissible only through, the eldest heir-portioner, whose husband alone can enjoy courtesy of the undifferenced arms.

A junior heir-portioner may at any time have her share of the armorial fief "distinguisht" by a suitable difference,[3] and this is necessary if her husband is to bear it.[4] She, or the heir of her body, would get the arms differenced (by matriculation), and such arms, so differenced for her, devolve (if

---

[1] *Maclachlan of Machlachlan*, notice of Lord Lyon's warrant for the husband by the courtesy of Scotland, *Scotsman*, 3 December 1948. The husband is normally required to take the heretrix's name alone, cf. Mackenzie, *Works*, ii, 490.

[2] *Notes & Queries*, 3 February 1940, p. 77, n. 19; 22 May 1940, p. 365. This is a non-transmissible use analogous to "Honourable" derived by peers' children from their noble parents. It is now called a "derivation" right.

[3] *Heraldry in Scotland*, p. 281; *Law and Practice*, p. 339.

[4] *His* arms, of course, could form such a "difference", but quartering is not necessarily a difference, and in the issue of the elder heir-portioner is often mere *cumulatio* of dignities in cases where there is no practical reason against taking in an extra quartering.

desired, irrespective of paternal arms) on the heir of her body bearing her (the mother's) name.[1]

The more important judgments of Lyon Court in regard to Succession and other matters are now—since 1950—reported in the Scots Law Times Law Reports.

The *clan*, a word meaning " children ", is, like other noble groups, *hereditary*, so that we find its chiefship in the reign of David II subject of grant by charter, and in 1672 Lyon recognised this in declaring it a subject which descended to, and through, a " heretrix ". In 1937 an effort was made (on ideas inspired by Clan societies seeking powers to allocate Celtic titles and heraldic supporters) to have it laid down that clan-chiefship had no relation to arms. At the subsequent proof this ridiculous idea was negatived by the expert witnesses, it being established that " *Clan and Family mean exactly the same thing* ", and Sir George Mackenzie, whose *Science of Herauldrie* was declared authoritative,[2] laid down that heraldic differencing was expressly for distinguishing cadets from " *the chief, for so we call the Representative of the Family . . . and in the Irish* (Gaelic) *with us, the Chief of the Family is called the Head of the Clan* ". This expressly relates clan-headship to family-chiefship, and *both* to ownership of the " undifferenced arms ", which was also the unanimous opinion of the House of Lords.[3]

[1] *Jabez Mackenzie*, 1806, Lyon Register, ii, 9 ; *Notes & Queries*, 3 February 1940, p. 77, and 24 February 1940, p. 132, *re* n. 19. A *junior* heir-portioner *ordinarily* merely carries her share of the armorial estate into her husband's family to be marshalled as a quartering with his armorial property by the issue, as her share of the land is added to their landed property.

[2] *Works*, ii, 618. *Chief* of the Family is the term used in Scotland and France, " Head of the Family " being an English phrase.

[3] See Innes of Learney, *Clans, Septs, and Regiments of the Scottish Highlands*, 1952, pp. 190 and 609 ; *Tartans of the Clans and Families of Scotland*, 1948, pp. 28, 50 ; an attempt by Lord Sumner to suggest the arms and chiefship would be in the heir-male was at variance with the other Lords' opinions, which equated arms with feudal heritage, 1922, S.C. (H.L.), 39 *et pag. cit.* In a subsequent litigation, Lyon was expressly held entitled to adjudge between contestants the chiefship of an

Lyon Court thus in Scotland determines, and usefully by relation to the arms (and banner) whereby chiefly authority was exercised in peace and war, the legal succession to the headship of these " Honourable Communities ", as the *Priom Aralt na Eireann* does in Eire, and so provides for continuity and certainty of succession in our ancient tribal civilisation on which so much of the vigour and romance of Scotland depends.

ENTAILS OF ARMORIAL BEARINGS

A settlement of " Name and Arms " is in its nature a decision by the Head of an armigerous family on who shall be his successor as Representative (*i.e.* chief) of the Founder and of the Family. It is thus a perpetuation, under the efficient legal machinery of Feudalism, of most ancient tribal principles.[1]

Entails, or, to use the more appropriate Scottish word, " tailzies ", have been very usual in Scotland,[2] but if these

armigerous family, and Chiefship of Name and Arms (1941, S.C., p. 687, analysed in *Farquharson of Invercauld*, Lyon Court, 20 July 1949), see also *Maclachlan of Maclachlan*, 3 July 1946, Lyon Register, xxxv, 72 ; *Mackintosh of Mackintosh* v. *Mackintosh of Clan Chattan*, 9 April 1947, *ibid.*, xxxvi, 36.

[1] Sir H. Maine, *Ancient Law*, 1930, pp. 211, 266. Sir Fred. Pollock alludes to the analogy of the Scottish Trust Settlement to the Roman procedure (p. 238), but under chivalric forms, though settlement is often, indeed usually, for " grave and weighty considerations ", we disdain the idea of a *familiae emptor*. For analogous French feudal practice, see F. Brentano, *Old Régime in France*, pp. 21, 42, and as regards Tanistry, Innes of Learney, *Tartans of the Clans and Families of Scotland*, pp. 40, 44 ; and *Clans, Septs, and Regiments of the Scottish Highlands*, 1952 ed., p. 172.

[2] Mackenzie, *Works*, ii, 616 ; Sir George wrote of these settlements prior to the " Strict Entail Act " of 1685, so the Law of Arms relates in principle to the old feudal tailzies adjudicated on in *Stevenson* v. *Stevenson*, 1677, Mor. 15, 475 ; Nisbet, *System of Heraldry*, iii, 56, 63 ; see " Scottish Armorial Tailzies " in *Scottish Notes & Queries*, 1940, pp. 254, 272, 292 ; " Transfer of Armorial Bearings ", *ibid.*, 1933, p. 188, also " Armorial Conveyancing ", *ibid.*, 22 February 1941, p. 128, where it should be observed the footnote from 11 onwards should read 13 onwards to 47. In these articles the principle and practice are analysed in detail, see also p. 232 *infra*, *s.v. Cockburn* and *Rintoul*, 22 November 1948, Lyon Register, xxxvii, 47 ; 1950 S.L.T. (Lyon Court), p. 12.

are to be effective, the correct procedure in Lyon Court must be followed.[1] Nowadays when fresh entails of Scots landed estates have ceased to be legal, it is important that testators should recollect that the old " Dispositions " of armorial bearings are still quite lawful,[2] if properly carried out.[3] By such means arms, and in some cases supporters as well, if the owner is careful, can be passed to series of heirs who otherwise could not have taken them up, and where a dormancy would otherwise probably occur. A name and arms clause may be inserted in any will or trust settlement.[4] In principle this seems essentially a constructive resignation in Lyon's hands,[5] and it depends on Lyon's grace whether it be completed. Its terms should be carefully considered, for where the heir " takes " under it, the Lyon Court will look closely to the terms of the Deed, and to the Testator's own title to the Bearings, when the Petition is lodged for the essential re-matriculation. No one can entail, or resign in favour of anyone else, a coat of arms to which he or she has not a legal

---

[1] Green's *Encyclopaedia of the Laws of Scotland*, s.v. Heraldry, pars. 1379-1781.

[2] *Maclean of Ardgour* v. *Maclean*, 1941 S.C., 684, per Lord Aitchison, " the lawfulness of conditions of this kind . . . is recognised by all the heraldic writers ".

[3] *Maclachlan of Maclachlan*, 3 July 1946, Lyon Register, 72, and Lord Lyon's *Note*; *Mackintosh of Mackintosh*, 9 April 1947, Lyon Register, xxxvi, 40; *Scotsman* report, 28 March 1947; Nisbet's *Heraldry*, ii, iii, 56, 58, 59; Mackenzie, *Works*, ii, 616, and see vol. 181, *Notes & Queries*, " Scottish Armorial Tailzies ", 5 July 1941, p. 2, expounding implications of Lords Aitchison and Jamieson's opinions in *Maclean of Ardgour* v. *Maclean*, 27 March 1941.

[4] *Dunbar of Seapark*, 13 June 1906, Lyon Register, xviii, 78; *Bruce of Sumburgh*, 14 November 1939, *Notes & Queries*, vol. 179, p. 310, Lyon Register, xxxiv, 77.

[5] This will be seen in the terms of the settlement of the Arms and Representation of *Scott of Synton*, 29 November 1700 (Lyon Register, ii, 189, analysed in detail in *Notes & Queries*, 27 April 1940, p. 293). For a " designation " or disposition of a peerage, without actual resignation (and so analogous to the usual " name and arms clause "), completed by the Crown's assent, cf. the Lordship of Sinclair in 1677 (Riddell's *Peerage Law*, 55), also Sempill, 1685 (*ibid.*, p. 52).

PLATE XXVIII

Rear-Admiral LACHLAN MACINTOSH OF MACINTOSH, THE MACKINTOSH.

Achievement confirmed to him as Chief of the Clan Mackintosh, 25th March 1947, *Lyon Register*, xxxvi. 40; 1950 *Scots Law Times* (Lyon Court) 5.

Quarterly : 1st, or, a lion rampant gules; 2nd, argent, a dexter hand couped fessways grasping a heart paleways gules; 3rd, azure, a boar's head couped or, armed proper, langued gules; 4th, or, a lymphad, sails furled, azure flagged and surmounted of her oars in saltire gules. Above the shield is placed an helmet befitting his degree with a mantling gules doubled or, and on a wreath of the liveries is set for crest a catamountain salient gardant proper, and in an escrol over the same this motto, " Loch Moigh ", and on a compartment below the shield embellished with red whortleberry fructed proper as being the badge of Clan Mackintosh, along with this motto, "Touch not the cat bot a glove", and set for supporters two catamountains gardant proper.

right in their own person.[1] In several cases, arms have been transferred *inter vivos* (between living persons) by Deeds of Resignation in the Lyon Court Books, followed by rematriculation.[2] Indeed, the "renunciation" can be by "Letter",[3] but is only competent if an estate, or the *universitas*, *i.e.* the "universal representation" of the testator, is settled along with the arms; that is, one way or another the headship or "representation" of the settler's family.[4] It has been held that the chief of a clan is entitled to nominate his successor from amongst the members of the chiefly family, and consequently to settle upon him the supporters incident to the chiefship.[5] There is nothing unusual in this, for many Scottish peers formerly had the power of nominating the successors to their peerages, a practice which was a survival of the old law of Tanistry,[6] but if made by a nomination within the "posterity" of the grantee's family, *i.e.* within the limitation of the arms, it seems the view was that such a settlement was made "by right" as chief, whereas a settlement on a stranger[7] can only

[1] Richards-Strachan, Lyon Court, 4 April 1900. Similarly a cadet can only resign his own version of the arms, and could not bar even his own descendants from obtaining other differenced versions of them; *Lamont of Lamont*, 1953.

[2] *Myreton of Cambo*, 10 November 1701, Lyon Register, i, 504, and Register of Genealogies, i, 227; *Grant of Auchernack*, 31 December 1777, Lyon Register, i, 515, and Register of Genealogies, i, 229; *Steuart of Allanton*, 15 April 1813, Lyon Register, ii, 101; *Lamont of Lamont*, 10 July 1953, *ibid.*, xxxix, 172.

[3] *Hamilton of Binning*, 20 July 1687, Lyon Register, i, 329.

[4] Mackenzie, *Works*, ii, 618; *Scottish Notes & Queries*, vol. 178, p. 293; Nisbet, *Heraldry*, iii, iii, 57, l. 23—but Nisbet has missed the real import of "*universitas*"; *Scott of Harden*, 1700, Lyon Register, ii, 189.

[5] *Macneil of Barra*, 27 May 1915, Lyon Register, xxii, 60; see p. 92, l. 2, *re* arms, and Innes of Learney, *Tartans of the Clans and Families of Scotland*, pp. 40, 44.

[6] *Sources and Literature of the Law of Scotland* (Stair Soc.), p. 433.

[7] Settlements on a "stranger in blood", such as an "adopted child" with no blood connection, are viewed with stern disapprobation, being utterly subversive of the natural (biological) family. *Ross of Balnagowan*, Lyon Register, i, p. 208, is one of the relatively few instances.

K

be carried through with Lyon's approval.[1]

The law, as now laid down, in accordance with the principles of early feudal heritage, is that all such diversions are subject to the reinvestiture (by confirmation-matriculation, or re-grant, according to circumstances) at Lyon's pleasure.[2]

It is, of course, Lyon's practice, in so exercising H.M. Prerogative, to give effect to all reasonable resettlements, just as the Kings of Scots, and the Kings of France, were in use to do in regard to family settlements including even high peerage honours.[3]

The disponer who intends to perpetuate his name and arms must look carefully to the terms of his Deed, and should bind " the heirs male and female, and the husbands of heirs female, to assume and thereafter to bear, use, and constantly retain, the name [4] [and designation (or title [5])] of *Glenfern of Blairbracken* as their only name [and designation (or title)] and the arms of *Glenfern of Blairbracken* allenarly ", but if the inclusion of additional quarterings is not to be barred, the arms clause may run " and the arms of *Glenfern of Blairbracken* as their principal arms ". If a disponer merely

---

[1] See Mackenzie, *Works*, ii, 618, and *Tartans of the Clans and Families of Scotland*, p. 44, and compare J. Ferne, *Glove of Generositie*, 1586, p. 67.

[2] *Mackintosh of Mackintosh*, 18 March 1947, 1950 S.L.T. (Lyon Court), p. 3.

[3] Settlers who contemplate some unusual order of succession to either estates or armorial honours, or both, should approach Lyon antecedently, since in certain cases, Lyon, like the Crown of old, may express advice, or warning, of the prerogatival attitude to certain proposals. (Cf. Brentano, *Old Régime in France*, p. 162.)

[4] The term " name " alone—as " name Maclean of Ardgour " (Ardgour settlement, 1930, see p. 148)—following the precedent of "Crauford of Auchinames ", effectively ties the heirs to use the designation in modern daily life, which is otherwise sometimes neglected.

[5] The highly effective Leckie entail read " to use the name and title, to carry the arms of Moir of Leckie without any addition, diminution, or alteration of any kind " (Morrison, *Dictionary of Decisions of Court of Session*, No. 15538).

binds the heirs to " bear the name and arms " without further restrictions, a family such as *Hunter of Hunterstone* may survive only as " *Hunter-Weston* ",[1] though that is not the correct interpretation of the provision.[2] " Double-barrelled surnames " are in heads of county families [3] only justifiable when two historic inheritances are conjoined,[4] but are now recognised as irreconcilable with the inheritance of Chiefship.[5] One must, in Scotland, belong to one family or another, and not attempt, like a chameleon, to pass off as belonging to both, and end by legally representing neither. Reluctance in abandoning a patronymic on marrying an heiress or succeeding to the representation of an ancient family is a modern and lower-class English feature, and the husband who in such circumstances sticks to his own name or pushes it into that of an ancient house is usually a second-rate type. The supersession of historic styles such as *Cameron of Inverailort*, *Cunninghame of Caprington*, and *Rose of Holme* by such names as " Cameron-Head ", " Smith-Cunninghame ", and " Lang-Rose ", is un-Scottish and deplorable. Such families thereby " advertise ", if not a break in the line, at any rate a break in their style and title, by varying it, create the idea that an " interruption " has occurred, and materially lessen their local importance.

A new formula, by less-informed solicitors, of substituting for a precise Name and Arms clause a " desire " that the heirs will take the name and arms, is bad law and bad practice. First, it is inconsistent with a settlement of armorial

---

[1] Cf. Mackenzie, *Works*, ii, 490.

[2] *Hunter* v. *Weston*, 1882, 9 Rettie, 492 ; Mackenzie, *Works*, ii, 622 ; *Smollett of Bonhill*, 1952, Lyon Reg., xxxix, 72 ; *Hunter of Hunterstone*, 1954, *ibid.*, xl, 49.

[3] They form a useful distinction for landless cadets and younger children (see p. 206), but are inappropriate to the representative of the " house ".

[4] *Carnegy-Arbuthnott of Balnamoon and Findowrie* (Lyon Register, xxv, 76) combines Carnegy of Balnamoon and Arbuthnott of Findowrie.

[5] Campbell-Gray, Lord Gray, 1950, *ibid.*, xxxviii, 56.

heritage, and second, it is vague and only leads to litigation.[1] Sensible testators and wise solicitors—looking to the real interests of a family—will insert a clear and imperative Name and Arms clause with a forfeiture-over. The younger line can then take up the succession.[2] Solicitors should make clear to their clients that the taking up of their historic coat of arms is just like succeeding to a Peerage or Baronetcy, and that failure to do so is endangering the social position of the heir and his successors—and a coat of arms or supporters once lost and dormant are often not easily recovered.

[1] *Murray of Taymount*, 2nd Div., Court of Session, 13 February 1948. These " desires " spring from England, where the law has become different and markedly anti-familial.

[2] *Stevenson* v. *Stevenson*, 1677, No. 15475.

PLATE XXIX

Extract of Matriculation, by progress, of the arms of Chisholm of Chisholm, with Official recognition of Captain Roderick Chisholm of Chisholm (formerly Gooden-Chisholm) in the surname of *Chisholm of Chisholm*, and finding that his grandson and heir-apparent, Alastair Chisholm of Chisholm ygr. is entitled, by decease *vitæ patris* of his father, to bear the arms of Chisholm of Chisholm with a three-point label for difference as now heir-apparent. (29 March 1937, *Lyon Register*, xxxiii. 12.)

CHAPTER X

HERALDIC SUPPORTERS

HE creatures which support the shield, or, as in older examples, scramble on it and support the helmet (see Fig. 10), are generally supposed to be derived from display of a badge or animal on either side of the shield in seals. In old Scots Patents they are usually termed " bearers ". In early times sometimes only one is found, and a few such instances survive in Scots Heraldry. The arms of the City of Perth are set on the breast of a double-headed eagle,[1] and those of the Burgh of Falkirk are held by a lion

FORBES, LORD FORBES. Azure three bears' heads couped, argent muzzled gules.

rampant *affronté* gules crowned with a mural crown argent.[2] The Campbells of Craignish and Askomel,[3] and Campbell of Inverneill,[4] have their arms supported on the mast of a galley, which is one of the most picturesque as well as unusual achievements in all the heraldry of Europe (see Fig. 56).

Apart from such instances, the " single supporter " is now seldom seen except when used to support an armorial banner or standard [5] pertaining to a person entitled to supporters,

---

[1] Lyon Register, i, 455.   [2] *Ibid.*, xviii, 66.   [3] *Ibid.*, xxviii, 32.
[4] *Ibid.*, ix, 88.   [5] See Plates XVI, p. 79, and XLVI, p. 220.

and supporters are now regarded as one of the highest heraldic honours.

In Scotland the Law of Supporters is very different from that of England, the social system being Celto-feudal and different from that south of the Border. In England they are almost exclusively confined to peers, and Garter has no power to assign them to others without a special warrant. Lyon grants supporters to the arms of (*a*) all peers of Scotland, (*b*) United Kingdom peers whose arms are Scottish, or who receive Scottish titles,[1] and no peer may use supporters in Scotland until these have been so constituted in Lyon Register. In Scotland, not only peers, but the heirs[2] of the many minor barons, or "Lairds", who were liable to be called to Parliament prior to 1592, and Chiefs of Clans and "old families" and certain knights, are entitled as of right[3] to obtain grants of supporters from the

FIG. 56.—CAMPBELL OF INVER-NEILL AND ROSS. Gyronny of eight or and sable, a bordure azure. The shield placed in front of a lymphad, sails furled and oars in action, sable, flags and pennons flying gules. On a helmet having a mantling, gules doubled argent, and a wreath of the liveries, is set for crest a boar's head erased or.

[1] At the beginning of this century, a claim was made that Garter alone should grant supporters to British peers, however Scottish. This came to a head in the case of the great jurist, *Lord Dunedin* (cr. 9 March 1905), who declined to have supporters until the matter was settled, matriculating without them 25 January 1907 (Lyon Register, xix, 24) and then *with* supporters *from Lyon*, 30 December 1907 (*ibid.*, xix, 65). This great Lord Justice-General thus got Scottish heraldic right in relation to British peers vindicated, and an attempt to "anglicise" the whole British peerage, as an institution, was justly prevented (Fig. 57).

[2] It appears that each erection of such a barony creates a separate supporter-claim, and whether a resettlement of the barony covers the supporters depends on whether the charter of resignation refers to the arms, and a reinvestiture has followed thereon. Since 1672 this can only be established from a rematriculation.

[3] *Seaforth* v. *Allangrange*, 1920 S.C., 764, per Lord Sands at p. 803.

Lord Lyon.[1] Since the Statute 1587, cap. 120, was a relieving and not a disenabling Act,[2] the right could only be lost by negative prescription, so that all barons *ante* 1633 seem entitled to claim. In other cases people may be able to prove the use of supporters anterior to 1672, when there is a presumption that a regular grant must have existed. The Lord Lyon, however, having by Statute the exercise of the Sovereign's *whole* armorial jurisdiction [3] (excepting, of course, power to grant *any part* of the Queen's own arms without an order from Her Majesty,[4] has always had the power to grant supporters in such cases as he considers suitable, and has exercised this power from the Middle Ages [5] onwards. Acting as he does in this matter as the Queen's representative, and also under statutory powers, such grants fall " entirely within the ambit

FIG. 57.—GRAHAM-MURRAY, LORD DUNEDIN. Quarterly: 1st and 4th, or, three piles sab. within a double tressure flory counterfl. gu. ; on a chief of the second a crescent between two escallops of the first (*Graham*) ; 2nd and 3rd, az., a cross patee between three mullets arg. within a double tressure flory counterflory, or (*Murray*). Above the shield is placed his coronet (as matric. 1907—he was cr. a Viscount 1926), thereon a helmet with mantling gu. doubled erm. and on a wreath of the liveries, is set for crest a buck's head couped proper ; in an escrol over, this motto : *Macte virtute*, and on a compartment beneath the shield are set for supporters two doves proper (Lyon Reg., xix, 65). Two swords in saltire behind shield as Lord Justice General.

---

[1] See Plate XVI, Matriculation of Arms of *Fraser of Reelig*, 10 February 1932, Lyon Register, xxx, 22, containing a patent of supporters as " Baron of Moniack " *ante* 1587.   [2] Acts, iii, 509.

[3] *Sundry Barons* v. *Lord Lyon*, 1673, *Fountainhall's Decisions*, 393.

[4] *Macdonell* v. *Macdonald*, 1826, 4 Shaw & Dunlop 371, per Lord Robertson.

[5] Sir R. Forman's (Lyon Office) Register, at large ; *Law of Succession in Ensigns Armorial*, pp. 21, 23.

of his ministerial power " and cannot be called in question by anyone.[1] This is, however, a power exercised in the most sparing manner, and nowadays never without some unexceptionable reason.[2]

Supporters are an indivisible right [3] and descend, like a peerage, to only one person at a time (though, contrary to the English rule, an heir-apparent may with us bear his

FIG. 58.—Archery medal of David, Lord Rosehill, Master of Northesk, 1719, eldest son of the 4th Earl of Northesk. Quarterly: 1st and 4th, or, an eagle displayed azure, armed and membered sable (*Carnegie*); 2nd and 3rd, argent, a pale gules, as a coat of augmentation, over all a label—as heir. *Crest*— a leopard's head full-faced, proper. *Motto*—"Tache sans tache." *Supporters* — Two leopards full-faced, proper.

[1] *Seaforth* v. *Allangrange*, 1920 S.C., 764, particularly per Lord Justice-Clerk at p. 792, and 1922 S.C. (H.L.), 39, particularly per Lord Shaw at pp. 46 and 48 and Finding 4 (*ib.* 1920 S.C. 805) that such grantees "have right to use the said supporters ".

[2] Heraldic writers usually characterise the grant to Sir Edmund Antrobus of Antrobus and Rutherford, Bart., of the supporters of the dormant Lord Rutherford, 13 February 1815 (Lyon Register, ii, 123) as *ultra vires* and " egregious ". (A. C. Fox-Davies, *Art of Heraldry*, p. 309; Seton, *Law and Practice of Heraldry*, p. 310.) The critics have overlooked that as Laird of Rutherford, Sir Edmund Antrobus—if he was to use arms in Scotland at all—was bound to matriculate them under 1672, cap. 47. In these circumstances, whilst a grant of supporters was uncalled for, it was within the Lord Lyon's prerogative, and the decision of the House of Lords a century later in *Seaforth* v. *Allangrange* has shown that the grant of Lord Rutherford's *alleged* supporters (two horses—to which that peer had never legally established his own right) was not only unchallengeable in itself, but that a precedent had occurred in Lord Lyon Sir Charles Erskine's grant to Mackenzie of Seaforth of the savages with blazing heads formerly borne by the Macleods of Lewis from whom he had bought that island (*Seaforth* v. *Allangrange*, 1920 S.C., 773). In view of the theory that supporters evolved from the badge (A. C. Fox-Davies, *Heraldry Explained*, p. 48) a more detailed scrutiny of those incidents might have helped Fox-Davies to elucidate the mystery of " How the Badge descends " (*Art of Heraldry*, p. 331). We may assume that it passed with " the following ", and that these otherwise surprising concessions were simply a survival of the "badge" conception in matters of supporters.

[3] Nevertheless, one person may be *de jure* in right of several sets of supporters and these may be governed by different destinations.

parent's supporters [1]), so whilst younger sons can rematriculate the family arms with suitable difference, they are not entitled to their Chief's supporters. The descent of supporters and the " principal armorial honours " of a family are sometimes not necessarily either in the " heir-male " or in the " heir-of-line ", but may be governed by destination of Chiefship,[2] by the clauses of different entails,[3] or by the succession to the " principal representation " of the family.[4] In some cases the Lord Lyon has held that what was formerly a male line of descent has altered to heirs-female,[5] or has exercised his feudal prerogative to effect or confirm such an alteration in their line of descent, and it can only be said that whenever a question of right to supporters arises, the claimant will be well advised to take Counsel's opinion, especially as more than a single " right " may be involved.[6]

[1] *Fergusson-Cunninghame, younger of Caprington*, Lyon Register, xxiv, 68. (Cf. Archery Medals of John, Lord Leslie, eldest son of the Earl of Rothes, Fig. 48 ; and David Lord Rosehill, eldest son of the Earl of Northesk, Fig. 58.)

[2] *Scott of Harden*, 9 November 1700, Lyon Register, ii, 189 ; *Stirling of Keir*, 30 December 1903, *ibid.*, xvii, 63 ; *Wemyss of Wemyss*, 2 November 1910, *ibid.*, xxi, 1 ; *Mackintosh of Mackintosh*, 9 April 1947, *ibid.*, xxxvi, 40 ; *Lord Macdonald*, 1 May 1947, *ibid.*, xxxvi, 44.

[3] *Campbell of Dunstaffnage*, 11 November 1943, Lyon Register, xxxiv, 71 ; *Murray-Usher of Broughton*, 5 May 1936, *ibid.*, xxxii, 17.

[4] *Cunninghame*, 1849, 11 Dunlop, S.C. 1139 ; *Innes-Lillingston of Lochalsh*, 20 June 1939, Lyon Register, xxxiii, 67 (a perpetuation of Innes supporters in such a subsidiary double-name would not, however, now be sanctioned) ; *Macdonald-Lockhert*, L.C. 16 Dec. 1947, *cf. Carnegy of Lour*, 9 December 1944, L.R., xxxv, 24.

[5] Cf. Mackenzie, *Works*, ii, 570 ; *Mackenzie of Seaforth*, 1815, 1891, 1935, when Lady Hood-Mackenzie of Seaforth, having inherited the achievement as nearest *heir of line* " conventionally alive ", took a *narrower* destination, which subsisted until her grandson got it re-extended by means of his Trust Settlement and matriculation following (Lyon Register, xxxi, 56) ; cf. also *Hon. Isolde Borthwick*, 23 October 1923, *ibid.*, xxvi, 4, where the supporters which had passed collaterally to heirs-male of some of the later Lords Borthwick were, on the dormancy of the peerage, transmitted inexplicably per the Lord Lyon's interlocutor to the daughter and heiress of the 21st Lord, whilst *Borthwick of Borthwick and Crookston* (the Laird of Borthwick) acquired a right to other supporters, 26 July 1944, *ibid.*, xxxv, 14.

[6] See note 3, p. 132, *supra*.

A grant of supporters may be either hereditary or for life. Occasionally they are conferred as special marks of Royal favour under Warrants directed to Lyon.[1] Royal Warrants authorising supporters to be granted to Knights Grand Cross of the several Orders of Knighthood, for life only, have been directed to the College of Arms. Garter King of Arms had no general power to grant supporters to anyone under the rank of a peer, and formerly every such grant to an English commoner required a special Royal Warrant.[2] In the case of English Knights Grand Cross, this practice has now been superseded by the General Warrant referred to.

The Lord Lyon, on the contrary, has a discretionary power to grant supporters to *any person* upon whom he elects to confer the honour, and limited either for life or with such destination as his Lordship considers expedient.[3] The Royal Warrants connected with Knights Grand Cross conferred on Garter the power to do what he could not hitherto perform for English Knights Grand Cross, but naturally did not confer on the Lord Lyon a power which was already inherent in his armorial prerogative.[4]

A Scottish Knight Grand Cross,[5] therefore, applies to

---

[1] *Dundas of Fingask*, Lyon Register, i, 448 ; *Wingate, ibid.*, xxiv, 23.

[2] *Heraldry in Scotland*, p. 313.

[3] *Law of Succession in Ensigns Armorial*, p. 21. In *Seaforth* v. *Allangrange* the especial object of the pursuer was to reduce an *ex gratia* patent of 7 February 1908. The Court of Session and House of Lords held he could not do so, and that the Defender was entitled to what she had been granted (1920 S.C., p. 805, Findings 3 and 4). The "Note of Evidence" produced by Lyon-Depute Tait within six weeks of taking office (and printed both by Stevenson and Fox-Davies) is of no evidential value, and is amongst the things for which Tait was dismissed in 1923.

[4] For Achievements of a Scottish Knight Grand Cross, see *Hon. Sir Lancelot Douglas Carnegie*, G.C.V.O., K.C.M.G., 20 September 1918, Lyon Register, xxiii, 65, pl. xxii ; also pl. xxi, *Chancellor*, K.C.M.G.

[5] Lyon restricts such grants to life only, but made an *ex gratia* hereditary grant to life-peer *Lord Normand* from his Lord Presidentship (24 July 1947, Lyon Register, xxxvi, 72) on precedent in Lord President *Dalrymple* (Erskine's Lyon Office Journal, p. 6).

Lyon for his Patent, and should incidentally bear in mind that the use in Scotland of supporters granted elsewhere is a statutory offence until they have been rematriculated in Lyon Register.[1]   During the period 1804–20 some undesirable grants were made by the Lyon-Depute, so in 1822 the Lord Lyon ordained that no patents of supporters should be issued except on Warrants under Lyon's own hand, terminology which puzzled Seton.[2]   During the later 19th century a practice arose of granting supporters (and knights' helmets!) to virtually any corporation that asked, and indignation culminated in such grants to distilleries.   Accordingly this sort of thing has ceased and normally only corporations created by Royal Charter or special Act of Parliament are so honoured.

As regards grants of supporters, there being heraldically no legal distinction between natural and corporate *personae*, both are now subjected to approximately similar tests of eligibility.[3]

[1] *Northern Assurance Co. Ltd.*, 17 May 1930, Lyon Register, xxix, 20.

[2] *Law and Practice*, p. 316, quoting Lyon Register, iii, 47, 23 November 1826.

[3] Except where very special circumstances arise, supporters are not granted to corporations other than those established by special Act of Parliament or Royal Charter.

CHAPTER XI

MARSHALLING OF ARMS AND QUARTERING

ERALDRY does not merely indicate the individual, but is capable of demonstrating a succession of marriages, and the combination of inheritances either by heirship or family settlements. This accordingly relates not to the rights in or devolution of a single coat of arms, but the manner in which several arms can be conjoined.[1] It has already been explained [2] how a man, by impalement, demonstrates his marriage to an armigerous wife. Should his wife be non-armigerous, he can, if she comes of " virtuous and well-deserving " parents,

LORD HALIBURTON OF DIRLETON. Quarterly: 1st and 4th, or, on a bend azure, three mascles of the first (*Haliburton*); 2nd, or, three bars gules (*Cameron*); 3rd, argent, a bend gules (*Vaux*).

obtain a grant of arms either for herself or some selected ancestor of whom she is the representative. If she is an heiress, his son (or even himself after she has issue) may obtain a rematriculation, including her arms as a quartering, and if her arms are quartered already, all or some of her quarterings may be included. The son of a man with a simple shield by an heiress with a simple lozenge may matriculate a

---

[1] Cf. Mackenzie, *Works*, ii, 622.　　　[2] See pp. 55, 96, 146, and 157.

PLATE XXX

Armorial panel with genealogical display of sixteen noble branches (great-great-grandparents) of John Carre of Cavers-Carre (1700) and showing his achievement impaled with that of his lady, Margaret Wauchop.

Two coats per pale; dexter, gules, on a chevron argent, three mullets of the first within a bordure chequy of the second and first; sinister, quarterly, 1st and 4th, azure, a crescent between two mullets in chief argent and a garb in base or; 2nd and 3rd, or, a cross engrailed sable. (Kerr of Cavers, *Lyon Register*, i. 172.)

quartered shield having his paternal arms in the 1st and 4th quarters[1] and his mother's arms in the 2nd and 3rd quarters. Should this man also marry an armigerous heiress, then their son may rematriculate with the arms of this second heiress in the 3rd quarter—and so on. In England this is done by the individual at his own hand, and extraordinary shields

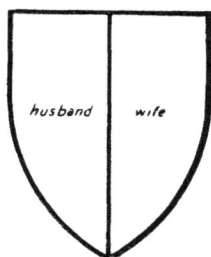

FIG. 59.—Husband and Wife.

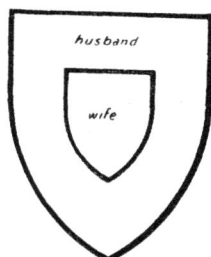

FIG. 60.—Inescutcheon of Pretence (English system).

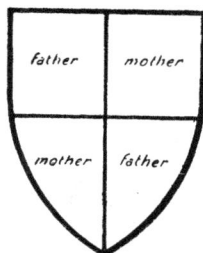

FIG. 61.—Quartering for Heiress.— Mother.

are seen, some with over 300 quarterings.[2] Such a shield is useless for any practical purpose, and Scottish heraldry being essentially scientific and practical, quartering is not only discouraged, but is *not permitted* without rematriculation, when the arrangement of the quarterings is laid down in the Lord Lyon's decree, and must be adhered to until altered by another " rematriculation ". Moreover, the Scottish shield has only four quarters, and if more than that number are to be shown, " grand quartering ", *i.e.* subdivision of one or more of the quarters, has to be adopted. In practice, " quartering " is confined to the arms of those heiresses who for some reason are of real importance, *e.g.* through whom some substantial asset has come to their descendants, or through whom one has become connected with some particular property. In this way the simplicity of Scottish heraldry is maintained, and

[1] For the numbering of quarters, see p. 55.
[2] Fox-Davies, *Armorial Families*, s.v. Lloyd of Stockton.

whenever a quartering is added, it is done scientifically, through the Lyon Court, and with a sound reason. Chiefs have, moreover, often been very slow to quarter other arms with the simple arms of their name—and wisely so, since quartering *can* be a difference, and might so create ambiguity.

Quartering may also depend on the terms of an entail,[1] and these are very usual in Scotland. A tailzie requiring use of " Name and Arms of Keith " occurs as early as 1324.[2] In these cases, the Lord Lyon considers the terms of the entail and the nature of the arms registered, and the arrangement of the quarterings depends to some extent upon her-

FIG. 62.—HOPE-DUNBAR OF BALDOON, Baronet. Quarterly : 1st, gules, a lion rampant argent, armed and langued azure, a bordure of the second, charged with ten roses of the field, barbed and seeded vert (*Dunbar of Baldoon*); 2nd, azure, on a chevron or, between three bezants, a bay leaf slipped vert, a mullet of the second in chief for difference (*Hope*); 3rd, argent, a man's heart imperially crowned, proper, on a chief azure three mullets of the field (*Douglas*); 4th, counter-quartered : 1st and 4th, gules, three cinquefoils ermine (*Hamilton*); 2nd and 3rd, argent, a lymphad, sails furled sable, flagged gules (*Arran*). *Crest*—A horse's head couped argent, bridle gules. *Motto*—".Firmior quo pariatior ". *Supporters*—Two lions rampant guardant argent, armed and langued gules, each holding in one of the forepaws a rose slipped vert, proper (Lyon Register, xxiii, 26).

aldic expediency. The wishes of the petitioner are given effect to as much as possible. Scots armory gains romance in possessing feudal arms and hereditary official arms appertaining to various heritable offices, and in this respect it is more akin to Continental heraldry than to English practice.[3] Con-

---

[1] Technically a "simple tailzie ", not necessarily a " strict entail " ; Mackenzie, *Works*, ii, 616.   [2] Acts, i, 482.
[3] J. Woodward, *Heraldry, British and Foreign*, p. 138.

sequently, we find many quarterings which represent not personal heiresses, but feudal lordships, estates,[1] heritable offices, or special augmentations,[2] and in addition to inclusion as quarterings, these arms sometimes appear on inescutcheons, which in England are used almost exclusively to represent an heiress wife. In Scotland the inescutcheon is often reserved for a Royal augmentation (*e.g.* Earl of Marchmont, Earl of Winton),[3] or some highly important feudal fief [4] or heritable office,[5] or in other cases for the paternal arms where the shield

FIG. 63.—EARL OF EGLINTON AND WINTON. Quarterly: 1st and 4th grand quarters counterquartered; 1st and 4th, azure, three fleur-de-lis or (*Montgomerie*); 2nd and 3rd, gules, three annulets or, stoned azure (*Eglinton*); all within a bordure or, charged with a double tressure of flory counterflory gules. 2nd and 3rd grand quarters counterquartered: 1st and 4th, or, three crescents within a tressure flory counterflory gules (*Seton*); 2nd and 3rd, azure, three garbs or (*Buchan*). Over all, in an inescutcheon parted per pale, gules and azure, the dexter charged with a sword in pale proper, pommelled and hilted or, supporting an imperial crown, the sinister charged with a star of twelve points argent, all within a double tressure flory counterflory, gold. *Crests*—Dexter, a lady dressed in ancient apparel, azure, holding in her dexter hand an anchor, and in her sinister the head of a savage couped, suspended by the hair, all proper. *Motto*—"Garde Bien". Sinister, a ducal coronet or, and issuing therefrom a wyvern vomiting fire, his wings elevated proper. *Motto*—"Hazard, yet Forward". *Supporters* —Two wyverns vert, vomiting fire, proper.

[1] Nisbet, *System of Heraldry*, iii, 63, 77; *Maitland of Dundrennan*, 21 November 1806, Lyon Register, ii, 11.

[2] *Loomis*, 23 April 1920, Lyon Register, 58, impaling the municipal arms of Cambrai and Mons by grant from these cities in recognition of service in war.

[3] *Earl of Linlithgow*, Lyon Register, i, 55, and Plate XXXI; *Strathmore, ibid.,* xxxiii, 46.

[4] *Livingstone*, Earl of Linlithgow, Plate XXXI; James, 9th Earl of Douglas—for Galloway—W. R. Macdonald, *Scottish Armorial Seals*, No. 677; David Lindsay, 5th Earl of Crawford and Duke of Montrose—for Montrose—*ibid.,* No. 1645; *Leslie, Lord Lindores*, 1672—for Lordship of Lindores—Lyon Register, i, 96.

[5] *Hereditary Constable of Aberdeen*, 1672, Lyon Register, i, 149.

itself is occupied with quarterings of fiefs and heiresses.[1] In some cases the arrangement seems to have been temporary, and the escutcheon *en surtout* has subsequently become a

FIG. 64.—ROYAL BURGH OF ANSTRUTHER AND KILRENNY. Tierced in pairle reversed: 1st, sable, an anchor argent (*Anstruther-Easter*); 2nd, gules, three fish fretted in triangle proper (*Anstruther-Wester*); 3rd, on the sea in base azure and of the field, an open boat rowed by four mariners, steersman at helm, a hook suspended by a chain, and in chief the rays of the sun issuant from a cloud, all proper (*Kilrenny*).

FIG. 65. — SUTHERLAND OF DUFFUS. Per fess, and in chief per pale; 1st, three stars (for *Sutherland*); 2nd, three cross crosslets fitchée (for *Cheyne*); 3rd, a boar's head erased (for *Chisholm*). (From a carved stone at Duffus.)

quartering,[2] whilst in others a quartering has subsequently been rematriculated *en surtout*.[3]

The Scottish practice is therefore very much that of the Continent, where in the case of family arms its use often indicates the chief of the family.[4] When, however, the

---

[1] Earls of Douglas and Angus.

[2] Marquess of Tweeddale, *Scottish Armorial Seals*, Nos. 1280-83; cf. Lyon Register, xx, 61, *surtout* disallowed as reflecting on Erroll.

[3] *Earl of Mar and Kellie*, 28 September 1923, Lyon Register, xxvi, i; *Earl of Kintore*, 22 July 1895, *ibid.*, xiv, i.

[4] *Douglas of Douglas*, 20 May 1771, Lyon Register, i, 143; *Duke of Sutherland*, 22 November 1839, *ibid.*, iv, 42; *Mackintosh of Clan Chattan*, 9 April 1947, *ibid.*, xxxvi, 36; *Macdonald of Macdonald*, 1 May 1947, *ibid.*, xxxvi, 40; 1950 S.L.T. (Lyon Court), p. 8.

LIVINGSTONE, EARL OF LINLITHGOW.

Quarterly : 1st and 4th, *Livingstone*; 2nd and 3rd, *Callendar*; over all on an inescutcheon the arms of the Earldom of Linlithgow. (*Lyon Register*, i. 55.)

inescutcheon bears the arms of a fief, the use of this marshalling indicates cadency,[1] (unless such inescutcheon is coroneted[2]), *e.g.* the Duke d'Arshot bears the arms of Croy and Renty quarterly, without brisur, thus indicating chiefship. The junior branches, Counts of Rœux and Solré, and the Lords of Crecq, respectively, add inescutcheons of their fiefs —indeed the Lords of Crecq, being cadets of Rœux, actually bear the arms of d'Arshot charged with the inescutcheon of Rœux, and that inescutcheon itself charged with another of the arms of the Lordship of Crecq.[3] When the inescutcheon bears arms of augmentation conferred by Royal Warrant, it does not import cadency.[4]

FIG. 66.—Matrimonial achievement parted per fess at Burgie Castle. Mr ALEXANDER DUNBAR, Dean of Moray (*d.* 1593) (three cushions in chief), and his wife, KATHERINE REID (a stag's head in base). Stone carved by their son, Robert Dunbar of Burgie, in 1602. (Initials, R. D., below.)

It is important that students of Scottish heraldry should realise its affinity, in this and many other respects, to Continental practice.

[1] The Duke of Abercorn, heir-male but cadet in the Hamilton family, bears an inescutcheon of " his " Dukedom of Châtelherault. In Scotland his predecessors bore a label (Nisbet, *Heraldry*, ii, 8).

[2] *Mar and Kellie*, Fig. 68 ; *Strathmore*, Lyon Register, xxxiii, 46.

[3] Jehan Schohier, *L'Estat et Comportement des Armes*, p. 67.

[4] *Mar and Kellie*, 28 September 1923, Lyon Register, xxvi, 1 ; *Strathmore*, 26 December 1938, *ibid.*, xxxiii, 46.

Another Continental form of marshalling, *tierced in pairle reversed*, is found in Scotland (see Fig. 64) usually where a petitioner desires to include arms which for technical reasons would be inadmissible as a quartering.[1] Sometimes the sides of the pairle are curved, and such a partition is then termed *entee en point*.[2] Yet another somewhat similar partition is *per fess and in chief per pale*. This is found in the arms of Sutherland of Duffus.

FIG. 67.—Seal of Alexander Innes, fourteenth of that ilk, 1542, showing Innes and Aberchirder marshalled as a " composed " coat of arms.

Where one coat consists of a cross, this " ordinary " is sometimes placed *en surtout*, dividing the quarterings.[3] This is essentially a Scandinavian form of marshalling—noticeable in the Royal Arms of Denmark and Sweden—and evidently came into Scottish heraldry through the Norwegian associations of the Earls of Orkney, who originally held that fief as Norwegian *jarls*.[4]

In a number of sixteenth- and seventeenth-century carvings, shields are found on which two coats are conjoined *per fess*, instead of *per pale*.[5] In every case investigation has shown that these were matrimonial achievements. This form of marshalling the arms of husband and wife has never

[1] *Burgh of Anstruther and Kilrenny*, 12 July 1930, Lyon Register, xxix, 31.

[2] *Art of Heraldry*, p. 379.

[3] *Sinclair, Earl of Caithness*, 6 January 1673, Lyon Register, i, 59, see Plate XLIII, and cadets of his house ; *Douglas of Brigton*, 26 December 1900, *ibid.*, xxiv, 33, see Plate XXXIII.

[4] J. Woodward, *Heraldry, British and Foreign*, p. 136.

[5] *E.g.* Dunbar and Reid at Burgie Castle, Forres ; Innes with Reid and Gordon at Coxton Tower, Elgin ; Leslie and Gordon, at Warthill House, Aberdeenshire.

received official sanction in Lyon Court, except as an integral part of a new and independent coat of arms.[1]

Composed Arms.[2]—When representation of two houses devolved on one man, the earliest plan for combining the two inherited coats, and that used before the invention of marshalling by quarterings, was to combine the charges from both arms in the same field. The system was unsatisfactory, because it spoilt the identity of each coat. It was soon superseded by quartering, but examples of " composed arms " are found as late as the sixteenth century in Northern Scotland.

OFFICIAL ARMS AND INSIGNIA

There are a number of offices to which specific heraldic insignia belong, and which the holders are entitled to bear *virtute officii*, or to include in their personal heraldic achievements. Frequently such official insignia consist of " exterior ornaments ", such as badges,[3] batons or swords of office (Figs. 57, 68). Amongst such are the batons of the Earl Marshal, the Master of the Household, and the Lord Lyon,[4] or the crossed swords of the Lord Justice General of Scotland.[5] Sometimes, however, an office has a coat of arms of its own, *e.g.* the official coats of the Lord Lyon King of Arms and of the Usher of the Green Rod. In England every bishopric has an official coat, and it seems a pity that official arms are not assigned to the Moderator of the Church of Scotland.

[1] *Helensburgh*, Lyon Register, xxviii, 70.   [2] *Heraldry in Scotland*, p. 149.
[3] Dean of the Order of the Thistle, 30 November 1951, Lyon Register xxxviii, 129.
[4] See Arms of Lord Lyon G. E. C. Swinton in Plate XLI (at side) and of the Lord Lyon on the title-page.
[5] *Viscount Dunedin*, 26 January 1907, Lyon Register, xix, 24, and 30 December 1907, *ibid.*, xiv, 65 (Fig. 57); *Hereditary Keeper of the Quigerich of St Fillan-Dewar*, *ibid.*, xxviii, 78 ; *Hereditary Captain of Dunstaffnage*, 11 November 1943, *ibid.*, xxxiv, 71 ; *White Rod*, 31 October 1877, *ibid.*, x, 34 ; *Keeper of the Abbey of Dundrennan*, 21 November 1806, *ibid.*, ii, 11.

These official arms may be borne alone, but if the official be himself armigerous, then the official arms may be impaled with the personal arms of the holder of the office: Dexter, the official arms; sinister, the personal arms (see Lyon, title-page). In these circumstances, if the holder of an office desires at the same time to display the arms of his wife, he resorts to an achievement consisting of two shields ; the dexter bearing his official arms impaled with his personal arms, and the sinister shield his personal arms impaled with his wife's arms. Where the official arms include a collar,[1] this must in the latter case surround the dexter shield only, because the wife has no share in, and derives no rank from, her husband's office,[2] and in the case of Orders of Chivalry has no right to wear her husband's collar. To make the achievement balance, the sinister escutcheon impaling the wife's arms is in these circumstances surrounded

FIG. 68. — EARL OF MAR AND KELLIE. Quarterly : 1st and 4th, argent, a pale sable (*Erskine*); 2nd and 3rd, azure, a bend between six cross crosslets fitchée or (*Mar*). Over all, on an escutcheon gules, the Royal Crown of Scotland, proper, within a double tressure flory counterflory or, ensigned with an earl's coronet (*Kellie*); behind the shield are placed in saltire a key, wards outwards, or, and a baton gules, garnished or, and ensigned with a castle of the last (Insignia of the office of Hereditary Keeper of the Castle of Stirling). *Crests*—Dexter, on a cap of maintenance gules, turned up ermine, a dexter hand holding a skene in pale argent, hilted and pommelled or. *Motto*— "Je pense plus". Sinister, on a cap of maintenance gules, turned up ermine, a demi-lion rampant guardant gules, armed argent. *Motto* — "Decori decus addit avito". *Supporters* — Two griffins gules, armed, beaked, and winged or.

---

[1] For similar rule and other specialities relating to collars and circlets of Knighthood, see pp. 47, 66, 148.   [2] Mackenzie, *Works*, ii, 551.

with a chaplet of leaves, as shown in Fig. 73.

The arms of Green Rod [1]—a subsequent Green Rod, who did not claim the official coat, did get the rod (two set in saltire behind the shield) [2]—and the Hereditary Office of Constable of Aberdeen, which is annexed to the lands of Carnmucks, now Ellon Castle in Aberdeenshire, are exceptions to this rule. The latter is borne on inescutcheon [3] instead of being impaled. Green Rod quarters his official arms.

When a Trades Incorporation or similar body has registered arms, and the Deacon thereof is also himself armigerous, the Lord Lyon has sanctioned the use of an impaled coat during such Deacon's term of office ; dexter, the arms of the Incorporation ; sinister, those of the Deacon.[4]

Since this rule has been laid down in the case of one corporation, it follows that in Scotland the *preses* of any corporate body who is himself legally in right of a personal coat of arms may impale these arms (sinister) with those of the corporation (dexter), provided that the arms of the corporation are also duly recorded in Lyon Register. This ruling would apply to Lord Provosts and Provosts of burghs during their term of office, Presidents and Chairmen of Companies. Series of these impaled shields will no doubt in due course form one of the most popular features of decoration in corporate buildings.

ARMS OF ALLIANCE

Since the English practice of placing the arms of an heiress upon an Inescutcheon of Pretence is foreign to Scottish

---

[1] *Brand*, 4 February 1721, Lyon Register, i, 123.

[2] *Mansfield*, 30 October 1907, Lyon Register, xix, 1.

[3] *Forbes of Waterton*, 1672, Lyon Register, i, 149, and xxxvii, 42 ; *Forbes-Robertson*, 28 June 1927, *ibid.*—a bad award as not *in* the office titules.

[4] *Wrights' Incorporation of Glasgow*, letter from the Lord Lyon, 1932.

L 2

heraldry,[1] our matrimonial achievements are normally reduced to the simple rule that the shield or lozenge is impaled with

FIG. 69.—Impaled achievement, married gentleman.

FIG. 70.—Impaled achievement, married knight.

the husband's arms on the dexter, and wife's paternal arms on the sinister. If the wife's arms, as last matriculated, include quarterings, these should appear in the impaled arms.[2]

If the arms of either husband or wife are surrounded by a bordure, the portion of the bordure next the palar line is omitted, a provision which does not apply to an orle, or necessarily to a tressure. This is the relic of an old form of marshalling, termed dimidiation.[3] Sometimes, instead of one impaled shield, the arms

FIG. 71.—Impaled achievement, married peer.

[1] Mackenzie, *Works*, ii, 622; Nisbet, *Heraldry*, ii, iii, 37.

[2] The English practice is to impale the paternal arms of the wife's family alone, and impalement of her family quarterings is actually forbidden.

[3] *Heraldry in Scotland*, pp. 151, 162.

of the two spouses are displayed on adjoining shields, close together, which are then termed *accolée*.

FIG. 72.—WILLIAM KING OF NEWMILN (*d.* 1715), Provost of Elgin, and his wife, MARGARET CUMMING OF LOCHTERVANDICH. Two shields accolée : dexter, azure, on a fess between a lion's head erased in chief, and a mullet in base argent, three round buckles gules (*King of Newmiln*) ; sinister, azure, three garbs or (*Cumming*). [The congruent difference for *Lochtervandich and Auchry* is a buckle, and has been improperly omitted.] *Crest*—A hand holding a dagger proper. *Motto*—" Audaces fortuna juvat ".

Where the husband's arms are surrounded by a collar or the circlet of any Order of Knighthood, *i.e.* if he is a Companion, Knight Commander, or Knight Grand Cross of any

Order, then two escutcheons must be used, because the circlet and collar are personal to the husband alone. The dexter escutcheon shows the husband's arms alone, or impaled with his official coat of arms, if any, and is surrounded with the circlet and collar. The sinister escutcheon, surrounded with a chaplet of leaves, displays the impaled arms of husband and wife. The principal star or decoration usually hangs from a ribbon between the bases of the two escutcheons, which are inclined towards one another, and above them appear the husband's helmet, crest, and motto, and his coronet if any.[1] Should the wife have any decoration of her own, such as rank in the Order of the British Empire, or of St. John of Jerusalem, the relative insignia is suspended from the chaplet surrounding the impaled escutcheon.

Fig. 73.—Achievement of married K.C.M.G. Dexter, husband's personal escutcheon within the collar of the Order; sinister, matrimonial escutcheon within a wreath, bearing impaled arms of husband and wife.

Fig. 74. — Gentleman married to a peeress in her own right.

When the wife is a peeress in her own right, the husband, whether he be peer or not himself, may display her arms upon an inescutcheon of pretence, ensigned with her coronet. This form of

---

[1] Fig. 73. Where the wife is a Dame (the escutcheons are hers anyway), they are shown oval or lozenge-wise, badge centrally pendant, no helmet (*Lady Muriel Barclay-Harvey*).

marshalling is evidently based on treatment of the peeress's arms as those of a fief, and in that sense is consistent with the principles of Scottish heraldry, though use of the inescutcheon for a mere heiress-in-blood is not.[1]

QUARTERINGS

The theory of inheritance and marshalling of quarterings has been dealt with at p. 136, and it is unnecessary to trouble the student with the principle on which these are arranged, because a Scottish quartered shield has to be taken as it is found recorded in the last matriculation in Lyon Register. No quarterings can be added, nor their order changed, without rematriculation, when the Lord Lyon will see that any addition or rearrangement is technically correct. In Scotland, the shield has only four quarters (see p. 55). If more quarterings are to be displayed, one or more of the quarters has to be grand-quartered, and such of the grand quarters as are subdivided are termed "grand quarters counterquartered". A good example is the shield of the Duke of Atholl (see Fig. 16 (a) and Plate XLI). In blazoning such a shield, each "counter-quartered grand quarter" is described in detail, exactly as if it were itself a quartered shield.

FIG. 75. — MACKINNON OF MACKINNON. Quarterly: 1st, vert, a boar's head erased argent, holding in its mouth the shankbone of a deer proper; 2nd, azure a castle triple towered and embattled argent, masoned gable, windows and post gules; 3rd, or, a lymphad sails furled and oars salterwise sab., flags gu.; 4th, arg., a dexter hand couped fesswise holding a cross-crosslet fitchée sab. (Lyon Reg., xxxvi, 153).

[1] Cf. p. 120 and Lord Advocate's opinion, that the husband of a peeress in her own right has a courtesy right to her whole achievement, which had already been claimed and admitted by Lyon Court in *Seton of Touch*, 29 April 1771, Lyon Register i, 489, and *Smith-Cuninghame of Caprington*, 18 June 1829, *ibid.*, iii, 71.

If a coat of arms is complicated by numerous quarterings or grand-quarterings, it is considered admissible in small work, including seals, signet rings, etc., or in carvings of a small size or at great altitude, to display the first quarter only, along with any relative bordure or other difference. Indeed, this practice of temporary simplification is followed for the design of the stained-glass windows and stall-plates in the Thistle Chapel. Simplification of this nature has been regarded as permissible both in Scotland and on the Continent from the Middle Ages onward.[1]

Non-armigerous Husband.—The theory of quartering presumes that an armigerous husband has married an armigerous heiress. It is necessary also to consider the heraldic consequences when a heraldic heiress marries a non-armigerous husband. It is often stated that the descendants can inherit no arms whatever.[2] This, however, is not the law in Scotland, since it is open to descendants of the marriage to take the name, and petition for their mother's arms by matriculation,[3] the non-armigerous husband being simply ignored. To be the child of an heiress itself nobilitates,[4] that is, if the child remains in, and bears the name of, its mother's family. The arms (*indiciae* of its nobility) then pass irrespective of the husband. On the same principle an armigerous female bastard transmits her arms to her issue, who are her only " heirs ".[5] If an heiress has herself made her right to the undifferenced arms indefeasible by re-

---

[1] J. Schier, *L'Estat et Comportement des Armes*, p. 67.

[2] C. A. H. Franklyn, *The Bearing of Coat Armour by Ladies*, p. 88 ; Dallaway, *Heraldic Inquiries*, p. 372.

[3] Mackenzie, *Works*, ii, 490, 616. If a *grant* were made, the " new arms " would not be " the mother's arms " at all—which arms, Mackenzie says, may pass to her issue " if the Prince consent ", *i.e.* if Lyon interpone the Royal authority (see pp. 116, 123).

[4] *Heraldry in Scotland*, p. 344.

[5] *Art of Heraldry*, p. 359 ; *Douglas of Timpendean*, 25 February 1952, Lyon Register, xxxviii, 143.

matriculation, not only is her eldest son in practice allowed to succeed without further rematriculation (which is none the less desirable), but the Lord Advocate has expressed the opinion (and Lyon Court practice shows) that even a non-armigerous husband is entitled to bear her arms by the " courtesy of Scotland ",[1] and, even as regards supporters, this is recognised in Lyon Register.[2] Obviously he cannot transmit them to anyone except his issue by the heiress.

Two recent matriculations illustrate the practice : (*a*) On 28 March 1898, " Arthur Risdon CAPEL-CARNEGY-ARBUTH-NOTT (formerly Arthur Risdon CAPEL) OF BALNAMOON ", having married " Mary Anne Jemima Carnegy-Arbuthnott of Balnamoon and Findowrie ", daughter of " James Carnegy-Arbuthnott (formerly Knox) of Balnamoon and Findowrie ", the son of Andrew Knox of Keithick by Helen, daughter of " James Carnegy of Balnamoon " by his wife " Margaret Arbuthnott of Findowrie ", obtained, by matriculation, the arms of Carnegy and Arbuthnott quarterly,[3] no claim being made that either Capel or Knox was armigerous. (*b*) His son left three co-heiresses, of whom the second, " Mistress Enid CARNEGY-ARBUTHNOTT OF BALNAMOON AND FINDOWRIE, and Lieutenant-Colonel Wilmot Boys CARNEGY-ARBUTHNOTT (formerly Wilmot Boys ADAMS), her husband ", obtained the undifferenced arms of 1898 by a matriculation, 21 June 1923, with official recognition of *their* having assumed the " name and designation of CARNEGY-ARBUTHNOTT OF BALNA-

---

[1] *Balfour of Burleigh Peerage Case Proceedings*, 1867, p. 166. It would follow that he must assume her name—as most Scots entails would oblige him to do.

[2] *Carnegy-Arbuthnott of Balnamoon and Findowrie*; *Fraser-Mackenzie of Allangrange* (see below). Cf. *Seton of Touch*, Lyon Register, i, 489, a principle explained by *Lorimer* v. *Gilmour*, 1709, M. 3114 ; and *Hog* v. *More*, 1740, M. 3119. Mrs. Fraser-Mackenzie had got her supporters by *patent*, so there was no ground for " courtesy ". See also *Lundin of Lundin*, Lyon Register, i, 180 ; *Dalyell of the Binns*, 1 March 1938, *ibid.*, xxxiii, 8.

[3] Lyon Register, xv, 18.

MOON AND FINDOWRIE ",[1] notwithstanding Adams held by courtesy only, and was otherwise non-armigerous. The Register shows two achievements: (1) Mistress Enid's lozenge, (2) the full-crested achievement for her husband.

The same practice is found in the case of Mrs. Fraser-Mackenzie of Allangrange and Robert Scarlett Fraser-Mackenzie, her husband,[2] but it is noticeable the "courtesy" is not extended to the supporters granted to her *ex gratia*.

Obviously a husband using his wife's arms "by courtesy" cannot also impale them—that presumes that he has arms of his own, and that he is continuing to use them.

Divorce.—In Scotland, the heraldic practice would simply follow the principle of Scots Law, that the guilty spouse becomes *civiliter*

THOMAS DUFF
GORDON-DUFF

Fig. 76.—GORDON-DUFF OF DRUMMUIR (Lyon Register, xix, 31). Quarterly: 1st vert, a fess dancettée ermine between a buck's head cabossed in chief and in base two escallops accompanied by a mullet, or (*Duff*); 2nd and 3rd, azure, a dexter hand vambraced, grasping a sword erect in pale proper, hilted and pommelled or, between three boars' heads couped of the third, langued gules (*Gordon of Park*); 4th, vert, a buck's head cabossed between three escallops or (*Duff of Drummuir*). *Crests*—1st, a man's heart gules winged or; 2nd, a sinister gauntlet. *Supporters*, dexter, a savage wreathed about the middle with laurel, in his exterior hand and resting on his shoulder a club all proper; sinister, a stag proper attired unguled, collared and chained or.

[1] Lyon Register, xxv, 76. Adams took the existing family name *per se*, though it was already a "double" one. Following on *Munro of Foulis*, 1939, and *Campbell-Gray, Lord Gray*, 1950, *ibid.*, xxxviii, 1, it is unlikely Lyon would allow courtesy or matriculation of either undifferenced arms or the supporters to "hyphenates", even as a purely temporary expediency of conjunction (but a husband's arms may be quartered when there is no good reason against it, cf. *Dalyell of the Binns*, 1 March 1938, Lyon Register, xxxiii, 8); *Maclachlan of Maclachlan, ibid.*, xxxv, 72, and *Scotsman* advert., 3 December 1948.

[2] Lyon Register, xix, 66.

mortuus and the innocent spouse derives all the advantages which would have accrued had the guilty spouse been actually dead, *e.g.* an innocent wife who divorces a guilty husband bears arms just as if she were his widow. A *guilty* wife is no longer entitled to the impaled coat, and could only bear her maiden lozenge.[1]

The husband who marries, and subsequently divorces, a guilty heiress, and has " made up titles " to her arms, is clearly entitled to continue bearing these ;[2] indeed, if rematriculation had taken place prior to the divorce of a guilty husband, he could hardly be divested ; but if he were possessing on " courtesy ", the decree against him would terminate that right.[3]

Special Marshalling of Quarterings.—In exceptional cases (for example Gordon-Duff of Drummuir, see Fig. 76, page 152) the 1st and 4th quarters differ, whilst the 2nd is repeated in the 3rd.[4] This usually occurs where the 1st and 4th quarters are of similar type (*e.g.* Orkney and Caithness), or where they are the arms of different branches of the same family repre-

---

[1] Wheeler Holohan takes the same view in *Boutell's Heraldry* (1913), p. 93.

[2] *E.g.* Graham-Wigan of Duntrune (*Armorial Families*, 7th ed., p. 794).

[3] In the case of a patent, the quartering was allowed but the *whole* was abated by a *gusset*. The first wife's arms, so included on a petition at the instance of the son, were subsequently removed on the father's petition, as unpalatable to him. (See *infra.*)

The law of arms provides for abating the arms of an adulterer by two gussets sanguine, and where the bearing of arms is necessary this, and one gusset (they will be close-gussets) for non-adulterous divorcees, are, at least in Patents, applied in the case of divorcees. On the other hand, nobiliary and tribal marriages contemplate an *intention to have issue,* and a recent appealed decision that wilful declination does not involve nullity might not preclude a suitable " demonstration " in the Law of Arms. Jurists might consider that a deliberate non-breeding wife should be treated as a quasi-prostitute, and that her husband might be entitled to insist on impalement per bend sinister. Since her conduct may extinguish the family, she is worse than an adulteress, who can be divorced, and she should be clearly and specially stigmatised in feudal society.

[4] *Earl of Caithness,* Plate XLIII; *Gordon-Duff of Drummuir,* Fig. 76 : *Arbuthnot-Leslie of Warthill,* 6 May 1947, Lyon Register, xxxvi, 52.

sented by two lines of succession (see Fig. 76), or where a cadet in right of some early and highly differenced coat is also allowed to quarter the paternal arms of the family, *e.g.* Douglas, Earl of Morton, and Douglas of Tilquhillie.

CHAPTER XII

THE ARMS OF A LADY

EDIAEVAL Scottish seals show that ladies simply bore their father's arms upon any of the ordinary varieties of shield.[1] Nevertheless it has long been laid down that the arms of a woman should always be displayed upon that particular variety of escutcheon called a Lozenge,[2] and that is now invariably the practice in Lyon Register. An heiress, representative of her family or chief of her clan, is allowed to record and use a crest and motto.[3] The external ornaments allowed to other ladies consist, when unmarried, of a True Lovers' Knot, which in Scotland is nowadays usually depicted in the livery colours of the arms, and has much the same effect as a

EARL OF MAR. Azure, a bend between six cross-crosslets fitchée or.

---

[1] *Heraldry in Scotland*, p. 147 *et seq.*; Seton, *Law and Practice*, p. 208.

[2] C. A. H. Franklyn, *The Bearing of Coat Armour by Ladies*, p. 59.

[3] *Buccleuch*, 1672, Lyon Register, i, 34; also Seal of Anne, *Duchess of Hamilton*, 1696, *Scottish Armorial Seals*, No. 1215; *Maclean of Ardgour*, 10 October 1941, 11 July 1944, Lyon Register, xxxiv, 42, xxxv, 15; *Countess of Erroll*, 26 November 1944, *ibid.*, xxxiv, 41; *Maclachlan of Maclachlan*, 3 July 1946, *ibid.*, xxxv, 72; *Rose of Kilravock*, 10 November 1946, *ibid.*, xxxvi, 8.

mantling. Several of these appear in recent volumes of the Lyon Register. A peeress in her own right, or any other lady entitled to supporters, is entitled to display these in her achievement, and as many Scottish supporters descend in the female line, there are numerous examples in Lyon Register. The arms of a peeress, whether in her own right [1] or by marriage, are ensigned with the appropriate coronet. Ladies substantively in right of arms have always been held entitled to display their arms (in the case of married women, the impaled arms) on banners,[2] and ladies with a " following " have frequently been awarded a badge and standard.[3]

FIG. 77.—NINA CAROLINE, COUNTESS OF SEAFIELD. On a lozenge, quarterly: 1st and 4th grand quarters counterquartered; quarterly, 1st and 4th, argent, a lion passant guardant gules, imperially crowned or (*Ogilvie*); 2nd and 3rd, argent, a cross engrailed sable (*Sinclair*). 2nd and 3rd grand-quarters, gules, three antique crowns or (*Grant*). The Countess's lozenge is ensigned with her Ladyship's coronet, and on a compartment are set for *supporters*—dexter, a lion guardant gules; sinister, a naked man wreathed about the loins and in his exterior hand a club, leaning upon the shoulder, all proper (Lyon Register, xxiii, 3).

Maiden Lady.—The arms of an unmarried woman are therefore, as above indicated, depicted upon a lozenge, with coronet and supporters if she be entitled to these, and where no crest or coronet exists, by a True Lovers' Knot, usually emblazoned in the heraldic

[1] *Countess of Seafield*, 20 July 1916, Lyon Register, xxiii, 3; *Duchess of Roxburghe*, 16 December 1904, *ibid.*, xviii, 14.

[2] *Duchess of Roxburghe*, 21 February 1905, *ibid.*, xviii, 19.

[3] *Maclean of Ardgour*, 11 July 1944, *ibid.*, xxxiv, 42; *Rose of Kilravock*, 10 November 1946, *ibid.*, xxxvi, 8.

PLATE XXXII

(a)

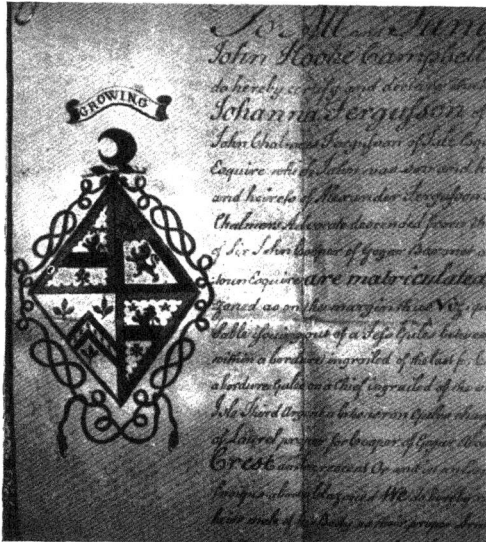

(b)

(a) Arms of Madam Myrtle Farquharson of Invercauld, as Chief of the Clan Farquharson (showing matriculation of arms of an Heretrix with wreath, crest, motto and supporters), 3 Dec. 1936, *Lyon Register*, xxxii. fol. 34. *Miscellanea Genealogica et Heraldica*, 5th ser. vol. x, p. 121. (b) Arms from Extract of Matriculation of Arms of Johanna Fergusson of Isle, 8th July, 1788, by Decree of Lord Lyon John Hooke Campbell of Bangeston, showing wreath, crest and motto, then allowed to the Heretrix of the Family. Also cordeliere as a widow. *Lyon Register*, vol. i, p. 548.

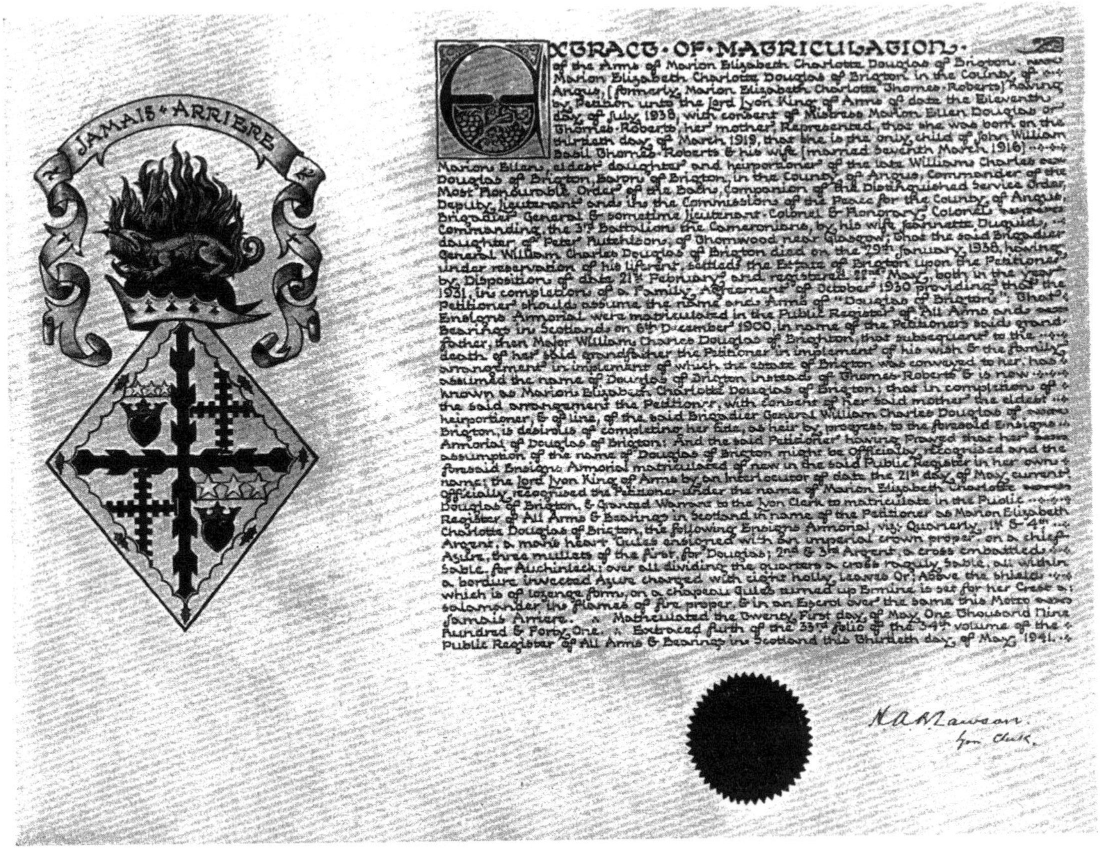

PLATE XXXIII

Extract of Matriculation of the Arms of Charlotte Douglas of Brigton, feudal Baroness of Brigton, in Angus. 21 May 1941. Showing achievement of a Heretrix and Feudal Baroness in the Baronage of Scotland, with crest on baronial chapeau. *Lyon Register* XXXIV. 33.

colours of the arms.[1] The use of this ribbon is, however, optional.[2]

Married Woman.—A good deal of speculation has surrounded the arms of married women,[3] principally because in England a married woman had no identity of her own, so English rules have merely dealt with what the husband did with the wife's arms. In Scotland, ladies were more independent, and mediaeval practice shows that in armorial matters both spouses were in much the same position as regards the shield. Either might continue to bear their own arms (in the lady's case her father's[4] arms) without

[1] *Heraldry for Craftsmen and Designers*, p. 222.

[2] *Brodie-Wood of Keithick*, Lyon Register, xxii, 72.

[3] A. C. Fox-Davies, *Art of Heraldry*, p. 387. In Scotland the wife may use her husband's shield of arms (Nisbet, ii, iii, 34), and use the household crested note-paper—though she or a daughter would not do that when living independently.

[4] The Scottish practice—shown both by mediaeval seals and subsequently by matriculations in Lyon Register—shows that on this point the Scots law differs

FIG. 78.—Armorial tombstone of Janet Kerr, Lady Restalrig, 2nd wife of Robert Logan, 7th of Restalrig (the Gowrie conspirator). Two coats impaled—Dexter, quarterly, 1st and 4th, or, three piles sable (*Logan*); 2nd, or, an eagle displayed sable (*Restalrig of that ilk*); 3rd, argent, three papingoes vert (*Hume of Fastcastle*). Sinister, gules, on a chevron argent, three mullets of the first (*Kerr*). The inscription does not infer that she was a peer's daughter. She is styled " Lady Restalrig " as wife of the Laird; she may have been a sister of the 1st Earl of Lothian.

fundamentally from the English rules enunciated by Dr. Franklyn (*The Bearing of Coat Armour by Ladies*, p. 93), who questions whether a woman, except a peeress *suo jure*, has any right to bear arms for herself when her husband is alive,

M

allusion to the other spouse,[1] and either party was at liberty to impale, the husband's arms in that case being shown on the dexter, and the wife's on the sinister, portion of the shield. The impaled shield of the man and wife are therefore identical, which is consistent with the theory of marriage. If supporters or coronet exist, the wife uses these also. The only difference is that, unless the lady be an heiress, representative of her family or clan, with crest and motto of her own, the husband's helmet and crest, as objects peculiar to the head of the house, are omitted from the wife's achievement. From modern practice it might follow that since a woman's arms are invariably displayed upon a lozenge, a

FIG. 79.—Seal of Princess Margaret of Scotland, Countess of Douglas (daughter of Robert III and wife of 4th Earl), showing arms of the Earl of Douglas, Duke of Touraine, impaling Royal Arms of Scotland.

and that " she may not use her father's arms alone but must impale. . . . When armory was in the making, no allowances were made for the bearing of arms by women." Dr. Franklyn, however, mentions on page 48 a number of cases, mostly Scottish, showing—as further research confirms—that married women could, did, and indeed were often legally obliged to, use armorial bearings on seals or otherwise, as they certainly did—with splendid effect—on their garments. The idea that heraldry did not cater for women is a fallacy which has grown out of the equally unfounded idea that heraldry was concerned with war, and not—as it really is— much more with civil and domestic life (*Heraldry in Scotland*, p. 31).

[1] J. H. Stevenson, *Heraldry in Scotland*, p. 151. It is noticeable that most of these impaled shields were those of the wife ; except where she was an heiress the husband continued to use his own arms alone.

married woman ought preferably to display the impaled coat upon that form of escutcheon. Nevertheless, the impaled shield is the more popular form, and quite consistent with mediaeval practice.

Where the lady is a peeress in her own right, or either spouse has certain insignia of knighthood, special considerations arise which are dealt with on pages 144, 178. In Scotland, however, even a Royal princess has her arms impaled with her husband's according to the old simple Laws of Armory.[1]

Widow.—Normally a widow displays a lozenge impaling her husband's arms on the dexter, and her own upon the sinister. Coronet and supporters, if any, will

FIG. 80.—Impaled achievement, widowed peeress.

appear, but the True Lovers' Knot is omitted. Sometimes a *cordelière* or tasselled rope, either sable or of the livery, is used, and denotes the arms are those of a widow.[2] In origin this is really the extinct French Order of the Cordelière, but has long been applied to widowhood. Where the widow is a peeress in her own right, she may display a lozenge of her husband's arms, bearing her own upon an Inescutcheon of Pretence, ensigned with her coronet—if she favours that form of marshalling (see p. 148).

---

[1] The arms impaled by a son-in-law of the King of Scots were the Scots Royal Arms undifferenced (Fig. 79), for just as the French Royal children were styled *Enfants de France*, Scottish princesses were, at their baptism, proclaimed *Cochtours of Scotland* (*Moysie's Memoirs*, p. 127). Impalement constituted a difference and no instance of an unmarried princess's seal survives.

[2] *Findlay*, Lyon Register, xxxvi, 116.

CHAPTER XIII

MODERN USE OF SCOTTISH HERALDRY

BRUCE, LORD BALFOUR OF BURLEIGH.
Quarterly: 1st and 4th, argent, on a chevron sable a setter's head erased of the 1st; 2nd and 3rd, or, a saltire and chief gules. The last charged with a mullet of the 1st.

RMORY was invented for the purpose of identification, and those who wish to use it should bear in mind that this is the acknowledged object for its display, and wherever it is honestly and correctly used for that purpose, its use is not only justifiable, but honest and pleasing. No more splendid form of decoration exists, for it is at once artistic and interesting, and affords a pleasure which meaningless tracery and "stock patterns" can never supply. In the Middle Ages armigerous people were surrounded by heraldry literally from the cradle to the tomb.

In the Middle Ages there was none of the modern snobbery which makes conceited "democratic" plutocrats ape humility and enjoy being "honoured" in tweeds and bowler hats, and makes lesser folk self-conscious and ashamed of their callings. Mediaeval dress and heraldry alike were designed to tell at once *who* you were and *what* you were, and people were straightforward and honest about both.

PLATE XXXIV

Staircase tower and armorial doorway, erected 1602, at Huntly Castle, Aberdeenshire.

The arrangement is as follows:

(*a*) Door lintel, four shields: (1) arms of Marquess of Huntly; (2) initials of Marquess and Marchioness; (3) arms of Marchioness; (4) date.

(*b*) Lower panel: impaled achievement of Marquess and Marchioness (Lady Henrietta Stewart).

(*c*) Central panel: Royal Arms of James VI impaled with Denmark.

(*d*) Third panel: symbols of the Passion.

(*e*) Circular panel: Order of St. Michael.

PLATE XXXV

Armorial fireplace at Huntly Castle.

Royal Arms above, as feudal superior, and on lintel beneath, achievements of: dexter, Marquess of Huntly; sinister, Duke of Lennox, father of Lady Henrietta Stewart, Marchioness of Huntly.

Dress no longer tells us that ; nevertheless heraldry still tells precisely who and what its user is—whether male or female, married or single, gentleman, chief, baronet, or peer. Those who wish to be honest and correct should always remember that when one uses heraldry at all, one really uses it for identification. The object should be to make that identification as instant and as complete as is possible by the medium of display. For successfully effecting this purpose, there are certain quite definite heraldic customs, and those who use their heraldry in accordance with these customs—hereinafter explained — need never fear that its use will be either " snobbish ", aggressive, or out of place. Indeed the *absence* of heraldry in certain places and on certain occasions is often much more noticeable than its presence, and if the man be a gentleman at all, one is led to wonder why his arms are *not* being used in certain places where that would normally be expected.

As regards practical identification : in these days of " standardised " motor - bodies, a well - illuminated coat of arms both adds to the appearance and simplifies identification of one's motor in parking-places, etc., but either on a motor-car or on a piece of notepaper the arms should be of a reasonable size, so that it can easily be recognised and so fulfil its proper purpose.[1] A microscopic piece of heraldry necessarily stands condemned, because it merely pretends to hint that the owner thinks himself a person of distinction, instead of performing the true function of enabling the casual observer to identify the owner. Monograms and " unostentatious " heraldry are therefore the badge of the *parvenu*, and such heraldry is usually bogus. Genuine arms are almost always displayed boldly and beautifully at

---

[1] The arms (shield included), not the crest, is the traditional and *correct* thing to emblazon on a carriage or motor. Unlike the crest, it identifies the owner with certainty.

M 2

every possible opportunity, indoors and out. They will bear examination, and their owners do not feel squeamish at the sight of their ensigns armorial. The use of heraldic devices in Scotland has been constant, and indeed wholesale, amongst all ranks of armigerous persons, and our heraldry is displayed in every conceivable manner. The cult of " unostentatious affluence " and " contempt of scutcheons ", is a product of the crabbed mentality of the industrial profiteer of the English middle class.[1] The vulgar self-consciousness of those who worry about " ostentation " is thus a product of modern class-consciousness, and never has had any place either in the Scottish character or the Scottish clan system.[2]

So popular is the brightness of heraldic display in Scotland, that even those who themselves have no claim to a personal coat of arms, or have obtained one but have no others to combine with it, will decorate a house or room with series of arms, such as (a) the owner's armigerous friends ; (b) the arms of neighbours in the portion of the County where the house is situated ; (c) arms of successive proprietors of an estate [3] (or of their wives) ; (d) the sixteen Scots representative peers at the date of the decoration,[4] and numbers of other such series—in themselves interesting, and which are heraldically unexceptionable, *provided the purpose and meaning of the series is made evident*, and the heraldry actually displayed is authentic and accurate.[5]

---

[1] Lady Strachey, *Memoirs of a Highland Lady*, xix, 361 (1928 ed.).

[2] " The Eclipse of Scottish History ", *Scots Magazine*, April 1931.

[3] *Heraldry in Relation to Scots History and Art*, p. 210.

[4] Balbegno Castle, *Heraldic Exhibition Catalogue*, pl. lxxiv.

[5] Lyon Office Circular regarding Ensigns Armorial, 19 June 1935. The foregoing is quite different from *wearing* or using otherwise, unwarrantably, other people's arms, as on brooches or sets of dinner mats (other than, *e.g.*, illustrating the alliances of the house). Such uses are bad form, at the least ; and usually—as the *wearing* of other people's arms is—illegal. (Cf. Coronation Souvenir regulations, 27 April 1952, which embodied sound heraldic principles.)

ENDURE FORT

Earl of Crawford and Balcarres

FIG. 81.

Before commencing to use heraldry, the first step is to find out whether you actually have a coat of arms, and whether the other coats of arms you intend displaying in any armorial series have a legal existence, *i.e.* whether they are matriculated in the Public Register of All Arms and Bearings in Scotland. All arms matriculated prior to 1903 will be found in Sir James Balfour Paul's *Ordinary of Scottish Arms*. If you believe the arms were registered subsequent to 1903, a search in the Lyon Office (Treasury search fee 5s.) will settle the matter, but no person has a right to any coat of arms (or crest) unless he is the "heir" to it for the time being, or the eldest son and "appearand heir", or a daughter, sister, or aunt (see p. 97). When you have ascertained that all the individuals to be represented do have lawful coats of arms, you can depict them about your house, or as illumination of pedigrees, books, etc., either in series of shields, each by itself, or rows of impaled shields with which one can make a handsome frieze, or indeed, any form of carved or painted illumination.

PRACTICAL APPLICATION OF HERALDRY

Even when armorial bearings have been correctly ascertained, people are often in doubt as to how the "achievement" should be used, and what liberties they may take with the official drawing. An eminent sculptor emphasised this difficulty in eleven questions to Sir W. St John Hope.[1] These questions and their answers [2] are typical, and may be set out as follows :

1. *Must a shield always be surmounted by a crested helmet ?* No ; the shield of arms alone may always be used. It is

[1] *Heraldry for Craftsmen and Designers*, p. 13.
[2] By the author : Sir W. St John Hope merely *stated* the questions but did not specifically *answer* them.

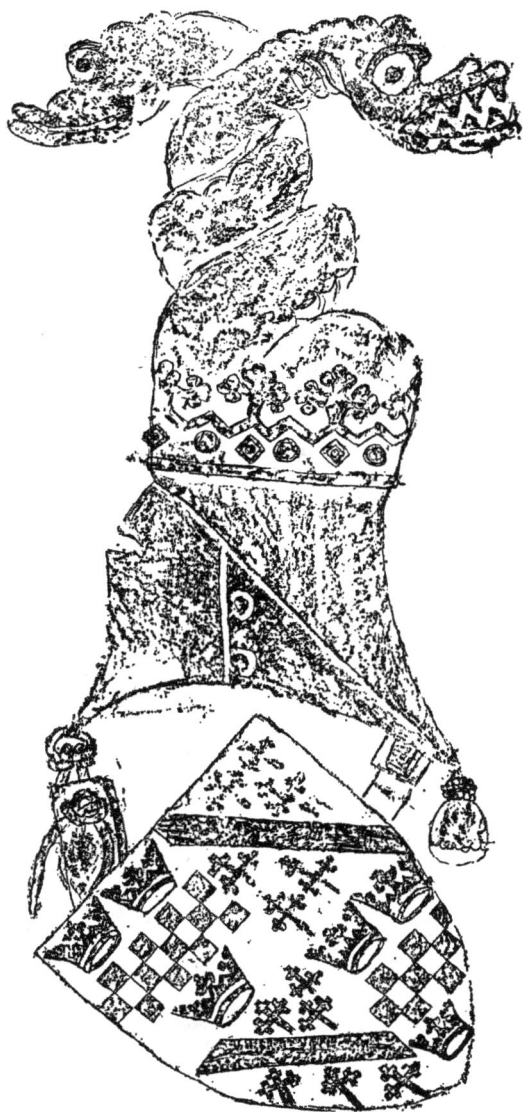

the foundation of the whole thing, and sometimes the only thing which exists. For example, Fig. 81 and the initial letter on p. 67 are both " the Earl of Crawford's Coat of Arms ".

2. *Must the shield always be the same shape as in the official drawing ?* No ; it may be of whatever shape is most suitable for the style of work or decoration in hand, and in period architecture, anachronisms should be avoided by choosing the right type of shield. The plain

FIG. 82.—STEWART, EARL OF MAR (1411–36). Arms at Bishop's Palace, Elgin. Quarterly : 1st and 4th, or, a fess chequy azure and argent, between three open crowns gules (*Stewart*) ; 2nd and 3rd, azure, a bend between six cross crosslets fitchée or (*Mar*). Above the shield is a tilting helmet with tasselled capeline, and thereon a coronet, from which issues this *Crest* — Two demi-serpents entwined (presumably proper). This carving shows the true proportions of helmet, crest, and shield, and has been called " the finest heraldic design in Scotland ".

The Marquis of Huntly

FIG. 83.

thirteenth-century "heater" type is best for twentieth-century architecture.

3. *What are the ordinary relative proportions which helmet and crest should bear to the shield?* The great mediaeval helmet was nearly as large as the shield itself. The crest towered high above it. If shield, helmet, and crest are each made one-third of the whole design, the result will not be wrong, whilst a proportion of one-half shield to one-half helmet and crest is the limit, if an absurdly small helmet is to be avoided (see Fig. 81, Earl of Crawford, which shows a splendid crest).

4. *May a shield be set aslant, as well as upright?* Yes; and when displayed with helmet and crest, old artists invariably do show the shield *couché*—the natural way a shield hangs from its belt or *guige*.

FIG. 84.—Crest with helmet and *owner's* name [1] in "belt and buckle" surround.

5. *Can a crest be shown without its shield?* No crest can exist without a corresponding coat of arms, but the crest when it exists can be depicted without the shield to which it belongs—indeed, is often depicted even without its helmet, though from an artistic and technical point of view it should, except on cap badges, always be depicted upon the helmet to which it belongs (see, however, Fig. 84, above).

6. *Should a wreath or torse be drawn with a curved or a straight line?* Whichever best suits the rest of the design.

7. *Should the helmet be shown full-face, or in profile?* Provided it is the correct pattern of helmet, appropriate to the owner's rank (see p. 29), it may face in whichever direction

---

[1] In this design, *with helmet*, the crest is evidently *not* a "badge" in the sense indicated on p. 180, and consequently a *brooch in which the helmet appears* should only be worn by the owner of the crest, and not by his retainers.

is artistically suitable. The crest should face the same
way as the helmet, and the nature of the crest will often
determine how the artist can best place the helmet. Normally,
a helmet in profile, like every other heraldic charge in profile,

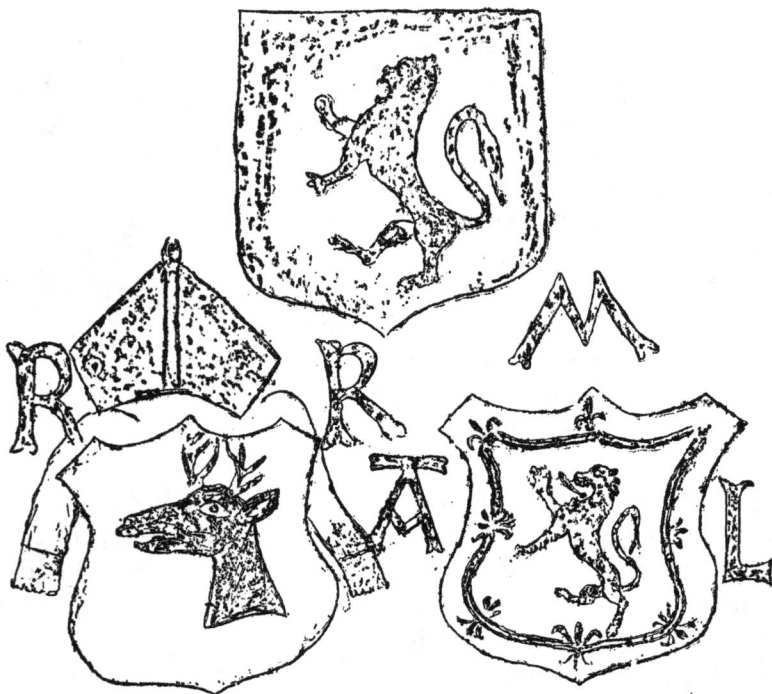

FIG. 85.—Arms on the Bishop's Palace, Elgin, showing three coats: (*a*) the Royal Arms
of Scotland, as feudal superior of the Bishopric; (*b*) Robert Reid, sub-Dean of Moray
and Abbot of Kinloss; (*c*) Mr Alexander Lyon, Chanter of Moray (*d*. 1541), younger
son of John, 4th Lord Glamis.

faces to the dexter, but if two helmets surmount the same
shield, they are usually made to " respect ", *i.e.* to face,
each other; so the dexter helmet (and, of course, its crest)
are *contourné* to face the centre line, but on any occasion
when the dexter crest is shown alone, it and its helmet will

PLATE XXXVI

Armorial ceiling at Earlshall, Fife.

Tempera painting on wooden-lined ceiling, early seventeenth century. (*Proc. Soc. of Antiquaries of Scotland*, xxviii. 161.)

PLATE XXXVII

(a) Armorial ceiling at Collairnie Castle, Fife, 1607. Tempera painting on boarding between the ceiling joists, which are also decorated. (*Proc. Soc. of Antiquaries of Scotland*, xxviii. 157.)

(b) Presentation salver, from the Duke of Alba and Berwick, Hereditary Great Constable of Spain, to the Hereditary Lord High Constable of Scotland (The Countess of Erroll), and engraven with the arms of the donor and the donee— a highly appropriate form of gift-decoration.

automatically revert to dexter, the reason for " respecting " having ceased.

8. *Must the mantling be as shown in an official drawing ?* No ; it may be quite plain, or as flourished and elaborate as you please. Much depends on the effect desired, the period style of the work, or the material.

9. *Is it necessary to represent the engraved dots and lines indicative of tinctures ?* No ; these are only for reference. They always look bad in artistic work and are never found on ancient seals and carvings. Engraving on plate is the only exception, because there the tincture lines help to make the design stand out. Coloured enamel, where possible, is, however, infinitely more attractive, and was the mediaeval practice for decorating silver and gold plate.

10. *May arms entitled to have supporters be represented without them ?* Yes ; but where a coronet exists, it is usual, though not essential, to depict this above the shield or lozenge, whether the supporters are shown or not.

11. *What are the simplest elements to which a shield of arms may be reduced, as for example in a panel some 60 or 70 feet above the eye, and when but a small space is available ?* Use a shield alone, of plain outline, and if possible omit all quarterings. Depict the charges in the simplest forms, cut in flattish sweeps, and let the whole design be carved in as deep relief as possible. The shields carved on the Thistle Chapel and Scottish National War Memorial are examples of how this may be done effectively.

It is almost impossible to enumerate the purposes to which heraldry has been put, and the manners in which it can be depicted, but the principal uses in Scotland are as follows :

Architecture.—Indoors and out, Scottish houses, from castle to cottage, have been decorated with armorial bearings.[1]

---

[1] Glamis, Huntly, Craigievar, Fyvie Castles, are typical examples of which illustrations are easily obtainable, *e.g.* Billings, *Baronial Antiquities.*

The doorway was lavishly ornamented, either the lintel-stone itself, or by the insertion of one or more panels above. These designs may include crest, motto, supporters, etc., but invariably the *shield* is the central object, and often the only part of the " achievement " displayed. In the Middle Ages the whole design would be painted and gilded. Frequently there is more than one achievement : (1) impaled arms of the builders ; (2) family arms alone ; (3) superior's—in the case

FIG. 86.—Door-lintel, 1674, displaying arms of David Fowler of Coulmauld, Bailie of Inverness, and his wife Margaret, daughter of Murdoch Mackenzie, Bishop of Moray. (From a carved lintel-stone showing the use of independent shields for each spouse.)

of a large castle, usually the Crown. Where a vassal holds his land of a subject-superior, he ought similarly to place his superior's arms above his own,[1] should he be making a really elaborate fireplace or doorway. On the sides of a tall tower he would place first his own, then his superior's. Plate x (*b*) shows the arms of Master Robert Irvine of Fornett, a cadet of Irvine of Drum, surmounted by the arms of the Earl Marischal, the feudal superior from whom he held the lands of Fornett. Having no supporters, the Gudeman of Fornett has placed the Irvine badge, a holly-bush eradicated, on either side of his shield. Smaller escutcheons of arms of former lairds, or heiresses, may be introduced to enhance the effect. The great doorway at Huntly Castle (see Plate xxxiv) is

[1] *Heraldry in Scotland*, p. 26, quoting *Bartolus a Saxaferrato*.

perhaps the most effective example, and even in its ruined state is a splendid piece of heraldic decoration. The tympanums of dormer windows are favourite places for heraldic display, whilst panels displayed on gables and around the walls often show impaled shields of the builder and his wife.

FIG. 87.—Kilcoy Castle, portion of armorial fireplace-lintel (dated 1679), size 99 ins. by 18 ins., containing three 15-in. circles of impaled arms of the first three Lairds of Kilcoy. Circle shown here represents Colin Mackenzie, 2nd of Kilcoy, and his wife, Lilias Sutherland of Duffus.

Interior Decoration.—In old houses, the fireplace is invariably surmounted by a full heraldic achievement, carved in plaster, wood, or stone, or maybe only painted. Usually it is emblazoned in full heraldic colours, but sometimes nowadays painted flat white. Where the proprietor is a Crown vassal, the Royal Arms of Scotland occupy this position, those of the owner taking their place on the lintel below. At Huntly Castle (Plate XXXIV) we see the large Royal Achievement above, whilst on the lintel below appear the complete achievements of the Marquis and his father-in-law the Duke of Lennox, for this produced a better effect than would the lozenge of Lady Henrietta Stewart, his Marchioness.   Sometimes a long carved lintel will display a series of impaled shields, the family escutcheon itself occupying the central position as at Kilcoy Castle (Fig. 87).

Windows.—Prior to the seventeenth century there was a good deal of domestic heraldic glass, but the use of sash-windows has deprived Scottish secular buildings of the leaded lights and coloured heraldic tracery found in other lands.

Ceilings.—These, whether open-beam or modelled plaster, have been freely used for heraldic display, and though modern people seem now to like shields modelled in relief upon a plain ceiling painted with flat white-wash, our ancestors preferred their heraldry in gilt and colour, whether it was on the modelled plaster,[1] or merely tempera painting on a boarded ceiling.[2]

FIG. 88.—RANDOLPH, EARL OF MORAY. Argent, three cushions within a double tressure flory counterflory gules.   Shield suspended from an oak tree.   (Carving on west façade, Elgin Cathedral.)

A series of small shields, carved or modelled, set in the cornice, adds to the appearance of any room, and will agree with most styles of decoration.

Panels.—Walls, windows, shutters and doors were carved, painted, or both, with all kinds of heraldic devices, from the plain shield of the family, to elaborate series of family alliances, *seize-quartiers*, and other combinations.   The Gothic style of fifteenth-century heraldry, with strong lines,

[1] *E.g.* Muchalls Castle, Kincardineshire ; Gorgie House ; Plates XIII, XXXIX (a).

[2] Crathes Castle, Delgaty Castle, Earlshall (see Plate XXXVI); also Paul, *Heraldry in Relation to Scots History and Art*, Fig. 69 ; F. J. Grant, *Heraldic Exhibition Catalogue*, Plates LXIX-LXXV.

PLATE XXXVIII

THE SCOTTISH ROYAL ARMS.

Fifteenth-century carving from a house in Exchequer Row, Aberdeen, attributed to William Rolland, Master of the Mint (*Aberdeen Booklover*).   In several fifteenth-century versions the unicorns are regardant.   Rolland's initials appear on the under-shield, and the panel evidently refers to his official status.

PLATE XXXIX

(*a*) Gorgie House. Plaster ceiling decorated with Royal Crest and Regalia. (*Proc. Soc. of Antiquaries of Scotland*, lxii. 279.)

Such insignia are usual decoration in the house of a Crown vassal. Regarding motto, *cf.* inscription formerly on Palace of Holyroodhouse. ˝(Grant, *Old and New Edinburgh*, ii. 73.)

(*b*) The Bute or Bannatyne Mazer (fourteenth century), showing heraldic boss in the bottom of the cup. (*Proc. Soc. of Antiquaries of Scotland*, lxv. 219.)

heavy helmets, and towering crests, is that most adapted to the age of oak. In England the crest never shared the popularity it has enjoyed in Scotland and on the Continent. In carvings where the shield alone is displayed, it may be suspended from a tree by the *guige*, and this looks well in a series of panels round a tomb, communion table, or sideboard.[1]

Furniture.—Chests and chair-backs, escritoires, and tables have all in Scotland been made the vehicle for displaying national love of heraldry,[2] not only in the age of carved oak. Lacquer, walnut, and mahogany have been used as means on which arms can be displayed, usually in colour. It is wonderful how lacquered heraldry brightens the monotonous surface of walnut and mahogany, but the design of shield in these cases must be carefully chosen to suit eighteenth-century panels. There is, indeed, hardly any article of

FIG. 89.—Archery Medal of James Durham of Largo (1752). Quarterly: 1st and 4th, argent, a crescent gules, on a chief azure, three mullets of the first, pierced (*Durham of Largo*); 2nd and 3rd, or, three piles within an orle gules, and in chief, as many martlets sable (*Rutherford*). Crest.—A dolphin proper. *Motto*—" Victoria non Praeda ".

furniture which cannot, by carving, lacquer, or embroidery, be enhanced by well-selected heraldic display. The brightness (not to mention the historic or family interest) obtainable will hardly be believed by those who have not enjoyed the pleasure of living with the fascinating glow of armorial bearings freely displayed around them.

[1] It is strictly in accord with tradition to decorate altar, communion vessels, and vestments with the chieftain's or donor's arms. *It relates the race to the church.* (Cf. *Clans, Septs, and Regiments of the Scottish Highlands*, 1952 ed., pp. 25, 74 ; cf. " Syon Cope " in St J. Hope, *Heraldry for Craftsmen and Designers.*)

[2] J. Gillespie, *Details of Scottish Domestic Architecture.*

N

Portraits.—A small shield or lozenge is frequently found on old portraits, and almost invariably prevents the subject degenerating into " gentleman unknown ". Name-plates may come loose, frames may be altered, and re-lining will destroy writing on the back of a canvas, but the arms on the painting itself will survive all these accidents. Such a shield ought to be of medium size, and unobtrusively set in one of the corners, painted in rather low colours so that it does not catch the eye. This is easily arranged. In a large painting, supporters and crest may be included, but in smaller portraits the shield, or shield and coronet, or lozenge of a lady, will supply the essential identification mark. In the seventeenth and eighteenth centuries it was the custom to surround engravings with the four or eight " branches " of the subject (see p. 191) whose full heraldic achievement appeared below. These engravings have a delightfully historical and artistic effect. In oil-paintings the shields might either be painted in an oval circlet on the canvas, or, where an oval gilt frame is used, the shields might be carved and emblazoned in heraldic colours.

Plate.—Although Sir David Lindsay of The Mount, the celebrated Lord Lyon King of Arms, had his " armis " engraven upon his spoons,[1] most people are content with a crest and motto, but on salvers, teapots, and larger articles, a shield—and preferably an impaled shield of the husband and wife in whose time the object was acquired—adds to the interest of the family plate-chest, as well as the appearance of the piece in question. In ecclesiastical or public plate, the arms of the donor normally appear—*e.g.* those of Sir Rory Mor Macleod of Macleod on the celebrated Duirinish communion cup (Fig. 44). Often, several shields can tell quite a story of successive owners of some object. A large piece, to which an impaled shield is added by each generation,

[1] J. Warrack, *Domestic Life in Scotland*, p. 74.

becomes indeed a family treasure.   Public or presentation
plate may include many series of arms, but in these cases
the officials should make sure that every coat is genuine
before its inclusion is per-
mitted.

*Book-plates and Note-
paper.* — The book-plate
should always display the
full achievement.   The
crest and motto alone
looks "cheap and nasty".
There are now many
processes cheaper than
copperplate and equally
effective, but even a "line
block", costing 15s. or so,
looks well if made from a
good drawing.[1] Coloured
book-plates reproduced by
the "three- or four-colour
process" are, however, in
the opinion of many
people, the finest of all,
for heraldry is meant for

FIG. 90.—Book-plate of the Earl of Moray.

display in colours.   The arms as emblazoned on the official
parchment[2] are photographed, using a process camera, and
three- or four-colour negatives are exposed and developed
as required.   A set of colour blocks made from these negatives costs about £16 for the minimum size of 30 square
inches.   Larger reproductions cost more, depending on size,

---

[1] See Fig. 92 (Duke of Montrose), Fig. 81 (Earl of Crawford and Balcarres),
as examples of high-class line drawing suitable for book-plates. Fig. 47 and
Plate XIV (*b*) and p. 187 show other examples in miniature.

[2] Plates XVII, XVIII, and XXVIII are examples of coloured book-plates.

but once the blocks are made, a few, or several thousand, colour plates can be printed from them.

On notepaper the owner's crest, and coronet if any, is the most usual and simplest device, but a Baronet of Nova Scotia will surround his crest with the orange-tawny ribbon and badge, and in these circumstances it is usual to inscribe the family motto upon the ribbon. Officers of Arms, Knights, and Commanders of Orders follow the same practice, and so do Peers who are knights or baronets, the ribbon, or collar, in their case being surmounted by the appropriate peer's coronet. In Scotland, however, it is quite usual, and much more informative and decorative, to display the whole armorial achievement upon one's notepaper, in cases where the detail is not too small to be effective. Indeed, the Royal notepaper at the palaces displays the full Royal Arms, which shows the correctness of this. Supporters, however, are seldom used on paper smaller than quarto, but often appear on the " correspondence-cards " of Chiefs, Peers, and Baronets.

A chief, chieftain, or laird's calling cards should bear his feudal title alone, without prefixed " Mr " or suchlike, and, as on the Continent, the custom was to display the crest or crests above. The full arms, or crest (with coronet if any), should always be used on formal invitation cards, wedding invitations, etc., on which the correct feudal or Celtic titles should also appear, and not anglicised stock-descriptions.

Furnishings.—China and porcelain, table-cloths and carpets,[1] curtains and screens, tapestry chair-backs, book-bindings, table dish-mats and napery are all adapted to heraldic display, and most of our old Scottish families possessed armorial napery. The steam-laundry has, it is to be feared, for all but the wealthiest, sounded the knell of heraldic linen ! Furnishings in general, either painted or embroidered, are, however, an excellent subject for heraldic decoration, and

[1] Carpet of *Charles le Téméraire*, B.M. Add. MSS. 36619.

coats of arms are of far more permanent interest than meaningless conventional designs.[1]

Livery.—The householder's crest is displayed on livery-
buttons, but his or her shield looks best on a motor-car,

FIG. 91.—The Bellenden Standard of the Earl of Buccleuch, showing his crest ensigned
with coronet, used as badge, and accompanied by minor charges from the Scots arms.
The forked ends of this standard have worn away. (See *Tartans of the Clans and
Families*, p. 28, for completed flag.)

whilst a crest or coronet on the radiator-cap looks more
dignified than any mascot. Sometimes a small banner of the
owner's arms is flown from the radiator-cap, a course now
regularly adopted on official occasions, where cars of prominent personages require to be readily identified. Such a
radiator-flag could be made of flat metal, chromium-plated,
and enamelled in colour.

The crest and badge are in Scotland considered in some
ways synonymous,[2] and it was the practice for retainers

[1] Heraldic dinner-table mats, as illustrated in Lynch-Robinson's *Intelligible
Heraldry*, are useful, and could include a series of impaled arms.

[2] J. H. Stevenson, *Heraldry in Scotland*, p. 222; Mackenzie, *Works*, ii, 628;
Nisbet, *Heraldry*, ii, iv, 18.

of a Celtic or feudal house to bear their Chief's or Chieftain's badge on a plate of silver, either fixed to their arms or hung round their necks.[1] This, of course, was for ordinary use. Municipal Officers on public occasions would have worn an embroidered scutcheon of their master's arms, back and breast, a practice long preserved in the uniform of the Town Sergeants of Aberdeen. The Edinburgh City Officers wore the City Arms on their left sleeves.

It is, however, still the custom in certain Scottish noble families for the household staff, not otherwise wearing any particular " uniform " other than the tartan, to wear buckle-crest-badges on the left breast or shoulder, a far more honourable and glamorous practice than common " house-assistants " branded with an " Institute-Badge " of no historic and noble antecedents.

Highland Dress and Ornaments.—In one respect Scotland can claim to be the country where heraldry still has freest use as a personal decoration, for almost everyone with Highland dress wears his own crested buttons—if he has a crest—and the use of the crested " cap-badge " is an invariable accompaniment of the kilt or Highland bonnet. These badges normally display the crest of the Chief, within a so-called " garter ", on which the motto is inscribed. The Chief himself surmounts his crest or badge with three little silver feathers rising out of the top, and a peer's cap-badge is " ensigned " with his coronet. The use of this so-called " garter " has been criticised as (1) an infringement of the privilege of Knights of the Garter ; (2) a breach of the Laws of Arms. Investigation shows that the long-standing Scottish practice is strictly correct. In Lyon Register the " garter " has been officially described [2] as a " belt and buckle ", and

---

[1] J. R. Planché, *The Pursuivant of Arms* (1873 ed.), p. 220 ; Mackenzie, *Works*, ii, 628.

[2] *Faculty of Advocates*, Lyon Register, 6 February 1856, vol. v, fol. 81.

Duke of Montrose

FIG. 92.

the popular Scottish cap-badge is simply a conventional form of the plate and strap with which clansmen and adherents bore their Chief's badge.[1] The use of a Chief or Chieftain's badge in this form is therefore not " usurpation of arms ", but an expression of adherence to that particular Chief or Laird. This strap and buckle crest-badge is the proper form of badge to be worn by all the family (even a Duke's younger brother and his sisters) except those who have recorded a distinct crest of their own. There is, however, no such thing as a " family " or " clan " crest. It is the property of the Chief alone, and whilst it is correct to display this in a cap-badge—with the necessary " belt and buckle " which indicates that the use is as clansman or follower—it is illegal to misappropriate the crest of one's Chief to decorate one's plate, paper or rings, such being the user's property, not his chief's property ! Sometimes a chieftain or *duine-uasal* bears a cap-badge showing his complete helmet, crest, and motto, and with his name or title on the circlet (Fig. 84).

FIG. 93.—Scots Cap Badges.

1. Peer and Chief.
2. Chieftain.
3. Clansman. (This is for *wear*, not display on plate, etc. When used other than for wear it must be accompanied by the phrase *Cirean Ceann Cinnidh*, and *also* if depicted on clan stationery, the additional words " member " of the clan Mac X".)

It is not generally realised how close is the association between Scottish heraldry and Highland dress.[2] Not only is it the form of civilian attire in which the use of heraldry has

---

[1] Cf. Mackenzie, *Works*, ii, 628 ; J. R. Planché, *The Pursuivant of Arms*, p. 220. The " great brooch " with chief or chieftainess's arms and supporters *can only be worn by the chief, his lady, and his heir.* Anyone else usurping such a brooch is liable to be fined and the brooch confiscated. To do so is also an *insult to the chief and clan.*

[2] In the form of trews, at any rate, the tartan was worn widely in Scotland— the kilt being no doubt less used in districts where riding-horses were numerous.

most prominently and uninterruptedly continued to the present time, but much important information regarding our Scottish national dress itself has been preserved from heraldic blazons such as those of Cluny-Macpherson and Skene of Skene. Engravings and carved heraldic stones such as those in Nisbet's plates (No. 77) and the stone dated 1692 at Skene House,[1] have been the means of preserving con-

FIG. 94.—Arms of Skene of Skene, from a sundial at Skene House, dated 1736. Gules, three dirks paleways argent, hefted and pommelled or, surmounted of as many wolves' heads couped, of the third. *Crest*—A dexter arm issuing from the shoulder, out of a cloud, holding forth in the hand a triumphal crown, proper. *Motto*— " Virtutis regia Merces ". *Supporters*—Dexter, a Highlandman in his proper garb, holding a skene in his right hand in a guarding posture. Sinister, another, in servile garb, his target on the left arm, and the darlach by his side.

temporary details of Highland costume, and confounding the much-canvassed statement that the *philabeg*, or little kilt, was invented by Captain Rawlinson about 1728.[2]   A hitherto unnoticed engraving of the arms of Skene of Skene from the sundial at Skene House, dated 1736, is shown in Fig. 94.   In this important example, the dexter supporter which the Lord Lyon in 1672 blazoned " A Highlander in gentleman's dress ", is shown as a man not in trews, but in kilt and plaid. The sinister supporter, blazoned " A Highlander in servile garment ", is—as in Nisbet's plates, 1694—unmistakably a

[1] W. F. Skene, *Memorials of the Family of Skene of Skene*, p. 48.
[2] Stewart, *Old and Rare Scottish Tartans*, p. 19 ; J. G. Mackay, *The Romantic Story of the Highland Garb and Tartan*, p. 67.

man in the philabeg, without any plaid at all. Although the sundial is dated 1736, the shield in this achievement is of a seventeenth-century type, so the engraver evidently worked from an earlier drawing.

Personal Ornaments.—In Scotland, the use of crested and armorial brooches is not confined to men in Highland dress, where shoulder-brooches, belt-buckles, dirks, and skean-dhu are normally embellished with the owner's crest. The women of Scotland used brooches, principally that in the middle of the breast, for fixing the tartan *arisaid*, now again coming into fashion for evening wear. They are also used for fixing a tartan sash, whilst by day Scots ladies are frequently seen with crested badge-brooches in their hats and scarves and pinning the folds of " kilt skirts ". One regrets that the day seems to be past when women wore armorial dresses, but some of the recent "jumper-suits " are as striking as a heraldic *kirtle*, and might just as well display proper heraldry as meaningless designs.

History knows no more magnificent robe than the mediaeval heraldic mantle worn by the ladies of the Middle Ages, and of which many examples survive in " memorial brasses".[1] In the reign of Victoria a ball was given at which every lady wore such a mantle, so it cannot be considered obsolete.

An unmarried lady would wear a mantle made wholly of her own arms, or a kirtle (skirt) composed of them. A married woman either wore her husband's arms on the mantle, and her own on her kirtle,[2] or else wore an impaled mantle, the dexter half of which (in this case the part covering her *right shoulder*) displayed her husband's arms, and the

[1] H. Norris, *Costume and Fashion, from Senlac to Bosworth*, pp. 322, 337; A. C. Fox-Davies, *Art of Heraldry*, p. 322 ; Instance of a male—a King wearing an armorial mantle, see B.M. Add. MSS. 25698.

[2] See " kirtle " in Plate xv (*a*) ; Nisbet, *Heraldry*, ii, 35. Another "fashion" noticed in Scotland was for married ladies to wear a kirtle of the impaled arms.

sinister half her own arms, thus the line where the two coats of arms met was down the middle of the back of the mantle.

Such a mantle is simply half or three-quarters of a circle with a circular cut for the neck. The charges may be painted or *appliqué*, but must be somewhat distorted to give the proper effect when the garment is worn, *i.e.* an animal may be on the curve where the garment is spread flat, and, incidentally, the arms will then *look* as if the husband's coat is on the sinister half. For an important dress— such as a wedding gown —few more graceful and interesting designs could be imagined than that of Margaret, Lady Camoys (1310), spangled over with numerous little shields,[1] which were presumably embroidered upon the

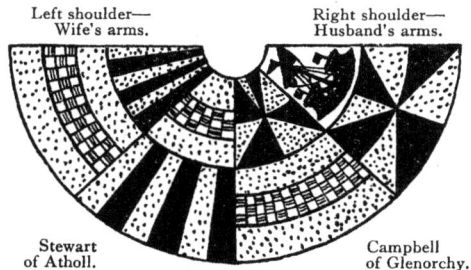

Left shoulder— Wife's arms.   Right shoulder— Husband's arms.

Stewart of Atholl.   Campbell of Glenorchy.

FIG. 95.—Armorial mantle appropriate to Lady Marjorie Stewart of Atholl, wife of Sir Colin Campbell of Glenorchy.

material. These arms would no doubt consist of the various quarterings of the family, but many suitable series could be used effectively. Dress models are also frequently shown in which monograms are embroidered. Ladies of armigerous rank should always substitute a lozenge or their badge, which not only looks more effective, but whether on dress, handbag, or elsewhere, adds individuality which a monogram lacks.

Flags and Pipe-Banners.—The house-flag as banner should display the registered arms of its owner—covering its whole surface (see p. 40). No crest, motto, or supporters, but a small " ensign " of the complete achievement may be used to indicate the whereabouts of a Chief, Laird, or Provost in a large gathering. Pipe-banners are well known from their use in Highland regiments, where they display the arms of

[1] *Art of Heraldry*, p. 34, Fig. 38.

company commanders (each of whom is expected to matriculate in Lyon Register, if not already in right of arms). The form of display varies in different regiments. In some (*e.g.* Gordon Highlanders) the whole achievement, including supporters, if any, is emblazoned on the banner, which is made the colour of the regimental "facings". In other regiments (*e.g.* the Royal Company of Archers) the older practice is maintained of emblazoning the shield-charge only over the whole banner (see p. 40). This is the more correct practice. Pipe-banners are used in civil life by most Chiefs and Lairds who have pipers, and are another ancient [1] Scottish use of heraldry which armigerous Burghs and Corporations should use for their head piper.[2] Professional pipers cannot invent and use pipe-banners to sport at dinners, etc. To do this is bad taste, usually illegal, and necessarily ridiculous.

Heraldic Design in General.—See that the shield, crest, and mantling are of a *type* consistent with the surrounding decoration. Much of the success of any heraldic scheme depends on the selection of the most appropriate style, though not necessarily of the same "period". Heraldic art passed through three important phases : (1) the Gothic, characterised by the simple lines of the shields, helmets, mantlings, and crests, as actually worn in the fourteenth and fifteenth centuries, when this style was at its best ; (2) the flamboyant style, with the twisted shields, scalloped edges, and flowing mantlings of the sixteenth and seventeenth centuries ; (3) the decorated oval shields of the eighteenth century, devoid of

---

[1] *Early Travellers in Scotland*, p. 265.

[2] A pipe-banner of *Burgh* arms can only be used regimentally when the Provost is at least an honorary officer. Otherwise it is a meaningless and contemptible "stunt" and insulting to the burgh. In all such regimental matters of original use (and in several regiments debased heraldic practices have displaced old correct ones) Lyon's rulings (being those of the Sovereign's Supreme Officer of Honour) fall to be obeyed without question by all " Officers and Gentlemen ", for in wearing of arms all nobles are thereby bound in honour as well as law.

helmets and often crests, though coronets and supporters were used when such existed.

In the first and second styles, the shield is usually *couché* when the crest is shown—and this is invariably accompanied by the helmet. *Couché* is not only the most artistic position, but also the natural one into which a real shield falls when slung upon its owner's person or hung upon a hook, and is invariably used in the stall-plates of the Knights of the Order of the Thistle.[1] The helmet and crest towers high above the shield, the true proportions being seen in splendid examples such as the arms of the Earl of Mar at Elgin (Fig. 82) and the Preston coat

FIG. 96.—Seal of Archibald Douglas, sixth Earl of Angus, 1514–1556 (16th cent. fancy style of shield).

above the doorway at Craigmillar.[2]   The puny crests and impossible helmets of the nineteenth-century draughtsmen are a form of decadence which now survives only in the workrooms of the stock-jeweller and the "heraldic stationer". Scotland, from its connection with Continental heraldic art, largely escaped these debased productions.

In arranging a scheme of heraldic display, it will often be found that whilst one shield may focus attention more than is desired, the display of three or four will bring the scheme

[1] The shield *couché et timbré* was anciently the style of armorial display of the "Tournament Nobility "—who had, moreover, to be noble both on the father's and mother's side (Nisbet, *Heraldry*, ii, iv, 3).

[2] *Details of Scottish Domestic Architecture*, pl. 48 ; MacGibbon and Pass, *Castellated and Domestic Architecture of Scotland*, i, 193.

into harmony, and gold or silver can be dulled a little, if too brilliant. No one need be afraid of " overdoing " heraldic display. Our ancestors never hesitated to display it freely, and the rich satisfaction of those schemes is largely due to the variety and interest created as the eye flits from one historic scutcheon to another, each telling its own tale and recalling different romantic memories.

Remember that heraldry is *the machinery for operating The Family*—the most important community-organisation in the world ; and Scottish heraldry is the most scientifically perfected heraldic system for that purpose, because it came under statutory-control and administration at the time when official control was slackening in other realms, where it therefore never acquired such scientific and practical perfection. To be strong, the family must *use* heraldry—as Scots do in their buckle-strapped cap-badges. Chiefs, lairds, and chieftains—and the *duine-uasal*/gentlemen of the family, should also assiduously and carefully *use* heraldry. Primarily, it maintains tradition—pride in, and loyalty to, the family, and to the chief, who represents the family. But use it correctly.

It is the machinery which makes his or her rule and representation effective. However small the chieftainly home (and many baronial towers had but three rooms), the arms should appear above the door and fireplace, and even an armorial door-knocker can serve in a temporary dwelling. In addition to the annual clan-gatherings, each branch should hold an annual branch-gathering under its own chieftain (branch-chief), or his officer, when his or her banner (or *pinsel* if not personally present) should be displayed— inside, if outside be impracticable.[1]

---

[1] The chief's *Commissioner* (of a great district), or his *Toshachdeor* of a district, or of a clan society, is the chief's appointee, his local lieutenant, or analogous to the Queen's sheriffs. He convenes the *duine-uasal* where there is no dominant " chieftain of the countrie ". The chief's *Ard-Toshachdeor* or *Toshachdeor*.

The chief's birthday, the " clan " or family Day (that on which it got its first fief, dignity, or even patent of arms), should be celebrated—and the banner flown.   The chief, chieftain, or *duine-uasal*, should use his arms on notepaper, invitation cards, marriage, and other invitations, as also on Christmas cards from chief or chieftain, which should contain portraits or prints of family seats, not caricature snow-scenes. The genealogy should be narrated along with display of the arms or banner and " portraits exposed ",[1] along with the arms or banner at christenings and marriages.   Thus is " The Family " made a living and functioning entity, whose existence, embodied in the chieftain, is ever before its members with the inspiration of tradition, heraldic colour, and sense of unity and strength, and so kept steadfastly before its children. Heraldry should therefore be used lavishly, as colour with a purpose (about which there need be no vulgar squeamishness), the symbol of the noble patriarchate, and the glory and strength of a well-knit house and clan.[2]

[1] Mackenzie, *Works*, ii, 362. It is a wife's especial duty to learn the genealogy and exploits of the house into which she has married and to impart *these*, instead of unfamilial fairy-tales, to the children.   The old Scots practice was to tell these stories on Sunday mornings, after prayers, and in the winter evenings.

[2] It is illegal and bad form for clansmen to use the chief's arms or crest on *their* notepaper, plate, etc., just as it is incorrect and illegal for such subjects to print the royal arms or crest on such.

Examples of modern Scottish armorial book-plates.

CHAPTER XIV

THE PUBLIC REGISTER OF ALL GENEALOGIES AND BIRTHBRIEVES IN SCOTLAND

JUST as Scotland is pre-eminently the land of clanship and kinship, so the Lyon Court Records are not confined to heraldry alone. Indeed Lyon's pre-heraldic duty as High Sennachie of Celtic Scotland was Judge of Genealogy,[1] to which control of Armory was added as " belonging to his sphere of duty".[2] Whilst the Lyon Register to some extent serves the purpose of preserving descent—since matriculations proceed on judgment regarding descent and representation of the matriculator—wider pedigree purposes are served by the Lord Lyon's Public Register of Genealogies.[3]

It has aptly been said that with Scotsmen " heredity is

WEMYSS, LORD BURNTISLAND. Quarterly: 1st and 4th, or, a lion rampant gules (*Wemyss*); 2nd and 3rd, argent, a lion rampant sable (*Inchmartine*); over all, a label of three points for difference.

[1] Findings in Lord Lyon Grant's judgment regarding the old Registers of Genealogies, 23 June 1942, Pub. Reg. of Genealogies, iv, 25, printed in *Proc. of Soc. of Antiquaries of Scot.*, lxxix, 127.

[2] *Juridical Review*, September 1940, p. 194, and Birthbrief preamble, p. 201.

[3] For a detailed examination to the character and contents of Birthbrieves, and comparison with foreign ones, see " Diploma of Nobility for de Landa " in *Juridical Review*, September 1940, p. 181. For the machinery whereby Birthbrieves could

a hereditary study", and in olden days most of our cities had their own " Burgh Propinquity Books",[1] but the statutory Lyon Registers have long since replaced all local ones, which in any case, to be of nobiliary effect, would require confirmation by a Birthbrief from Lyon, as was the practice regarding such local certificates abroad.[2]

In Scotland, pedigree is still a matter of moment, for nowadays, as in the past, we as a nation " take an inordinate pleasure in noble birth ",[3] even though descent has come through humble channels, for in practice the younger branches of the chiefly lines sank easily through farm and croft to the cottar house or tradesman's bench.   Still the old ties remain, the kinship acknowledged and treasured on both sides, whilst chiefs and lairds are expected to sustain tribal dignity and form a rallying point for their kin.   It is important to recollect that the King formally recognised that the Honours held by the Chief of the House of Douglas were given as a reward *to the whole surname of Douglas*,[4] not to the Chief alone. The Clan's genealogy, the exploits—civil as well as military —of the chiefs and chieftains of each house, have in Scotland ever been, as in olden time, the main subject of family conversation, and thus a source of inspiration to future generations.   It is the duty of the father to encourage the estimation of the family and sense of duty ;   it pertains especially to the mother to bring up the children from their earliest years to

be transmitted through the Foreign Office with a covering certificate of credence, see *Scottish Law Review*, October 1942, but most were presented direct to the foreign Heraldic Dept. ;   regarding Genealogy of Urrie of Pitfichie granted by Erskine of Cambo, see Nisbet's *Heraldry*, i, 255.

  [1] *Aberdeen Burgh Propinquity Book* (Extracts), Spalding Club *Miscellany*, vol. v ;   *Proc. of Soc. of Antiquaries of Scot.*, lxxxi, 115.

  [2] *Juridical Review*, Sept. 1940, p. 206.

  [3] Hume Brown, *Scotland before 1700*, p. 56.

  [4] Riddell, *Peerage Law*, p. 156.   The style and title for a peerage or baronetcy (unlike its conferment) is not a confidential matter, often involves consultation with others whose rights may be involved, has sometimes been the subject of public " proceedings " (*A.P.S. Scot.*, ii, 78), and is one on which legal advice may be required.

O

love and honour their family and its traditions, which she should learn to impart to them, along with those of her own—for each alliance brings fresh inspiration and traditions to mingle with, and build up, the history and traditions of the paternal house. In this vital duty, recourse to the family charters and to Lyon Court certificates and family manuscript histories is the parental stand-by for handing on from generation to generation the glory of *noblesse* and chiefship and the spirit of the race. Read them regularly, as also the family history, memorising important parts—and thus obtemper the fifth commandment.

There are many forms of genealogy, but each will be more attractive if decorated with the armorial bearings of the families and individuals mentioned and their respective " alliances ". Some of the most elaborate are covered with heraldry and include miniatures, as in the Seton Family Tree.[1] Parchment is the best material, and gives full scope for decorative art, but others have been embroidered or painted upon silk,[2] a somewhat perishable medium, and unsuited for fine detail ; whilst in Lesmoir Castle a Gordon pedigree was illuminated with shields on the " hood " of the hall fireplace. There was such a Seton armorial pedigree on the " boxing of the chimney at Seton ".[3]

Since a Tree cannot contain much detail, it should be supplemented by a documentary condescendence regarding *each* generation. These " condescendences ", which require to be so set out when a pedigree is submitted to Lyon Court for proof and registration, are in this form :

XI. *To prove that John Smith in Longtown was born* 20 *January 1850, died 5 March 1910, married 6 June 1894, Jean, daughter of Charles Richards of Balgley, who died 17 July*

---

[1] *Clans, Septs, and Regiments of the Scottish Highlands*, 1952 ed., pp. 117, 412 ; also inculcated by *Association de la Noblesse Française* for preserving *the Family* as an institution.   [2] *Edinburgh Heraldic Exhibition Catalogue*, 1892, pl. xlii.

[3] Nisbet, *Heraldry*, ii, iii, 36.

1915, and had two sons, Charles, afterwards of Balgley, and Robert, afterwards in Longtown.

Then follows a numbered list of each certificate, contract or document proving the foregoing facts.   If a pedigree is to be registered, such a condescendence must be annexed to the petition (see example on p. 106, *re* matriculation).

The genealogical section of the Lyon Registers deals with two distinct forms of record : (*a*) The Birthbrief ; (*b*) The Lineal Pedigree.   Either form may include social particulars incidental to family position or nobiliary status, and " exploits " of ancestors.   The former often includes several lines of ancestry, and sets forth Honours, Offices, and Tenures, and is frequently a *Diploma Stemmatis*—a Letters Patent certificate of Chiefship.

Seize-Quartiers

Much of the importance attached to quartered shields is due to a hazy association with something quite different—the " sixteen ", or " eight " quarterings known amongst Heralds as a " Proof of Nobility".   The Scotsman is of too scientific a mind to be satisfied with a lineal pedigree alone, and, like the mediaeval aristocracy, sets great store by the Birthbrief, or formal certificate regarding the nobility, not merely of his paternal father, grandfather, etc., but of *all* his four grandparents, eight great-grandparents, or sixteen great-great-grandparents, or as many of them as he can prove.   The relative shields form one of the most useful decorative series in heraldry (pp. 172-3, Plates xxx and xlii).   Many people who could not establish remote lineal pedigrees can, by grants or matriculations where necessary, secure fairly complete " branches " of high decorative value.

The " Seize-Quartiers ", or " Branches ", are simply the application of the principles and system of investigation which every farmer applies to his pedigree cattle, or racing enthusiast to his blood-stock, adapted (in an inspiring, dignified, and interesting manner) to the requirements of the human race. The Continental aristocracy, when two families are about to intermarry, *expect as a matter of course* that both parties will inform each other, *by an official certificate*, what sort of people the eight great-grandparents of the respective parties have been, and are thus in a position, through ascertaining the rank, career, and activities of each line of ancestry, to form a shrewd opinion on the prospects and desirability of the marriage, or suitability of an applicant for promotion in some foreign realm.[1]

Indeed it seems probable that much of the supremacy shown by Scotsmen in all spheres of life is due to the similar interest, long taken by all ranks in Scotland, in this important subject of "the distaff side". Vocational aptitude is at least as much a matter of inheritance as of training.

Eugenists are prone to scoff at "genealogy", meaning lineal pedigrees, and aver that nothing has been done towards scientific culture of the human race. Their critics as vehemently assert that nothing *can* be done. Both forget that much *has* been done, and that the development of the human race, like that of livestock in general, is largely the consequence of the expanding products of the "pedigree herd". Scientists may study abstruse questions regarding transmission of specific qualities, but in man or animal the best guarantee for a good social and biological inheritance is that the progeny shall have a creditable ancestry *of the type desired, in all its eight branches*. Of all forms of stirpiculture, this one is that referred to in the Bible [2] and sanctioned by the Christian Church.[3]

[1] For the contents of Birthbrieves, see *Juridical Review*, September 1940, p. 203.

[2] Genesis vi, 9. That Noah "*was perfect in his generations*" is simply the technical term for "noble in all his branches", cf. E. W. Robertson, *Scotland under her Early Kings*, ii, 310, 315.

[3] A "proof of quarterings" is essential for admission to certain fraternities.

A " Proof of Three Descents " (grandparents), the minimum requisite for " perfect nobility ", shows four quarterings (this is the old allodial *vier anen* establishing odal right, and also the " proof " for a Spanish *hidalgo*). The French *preuve* was of eight quarterings, but for some requirements at Versailles each of the eight had to be drawn back several generations.[1] In Germany and Scandinavia the proof was normally of sixteen quarterings.[2] " Four Descents " (great-grandparents) shows eight. When these are decoratively displayed the usual order [3] is :

Arms of the Father		Arms of the Mother
,, ,, Father's mother	Arms and / or	,, ,, Mother's mother
,, ,, Grandfather's mother	portrait of the subject	,, ,, Grandfather's mother
,, ,, Grandmother's mother		,, ,, Grandmother's mother

The arrangement will be best understood from Plate XLII. Sometimes the arms of the chief, the subject's wife, or remoter maternal ancestress are also inserted decoratively.

BIRTHBRIEVES

Birthbrieves are Letters Patent setting forth the descent, nobiliary status, and all such matters relating to the social, feudal, or tribal position of the petitioner as may seem useful at home or abroad, in nobiliary circles or public life, and in accrediting the applicant's position at the Court of his own or other Sovereign, or being received into foreign Orders of Chivalry, or contracting illustrious matrimony. They deal with his position as Chief or cadet in his own family and all other nobiliary matters relating to his estate, offices, family

---

[1] See *Scottish Law Review*, October 1942.
[2] E. W. Robertson, *Scotland under her early Kings*, ii, 310.
[3] Nisbet's *Heraldry*, ii, iv, 148.

history, and achievement,[1] being Letters Patent issued ministerially, though often after an inquiry, judicial or departmental. It is a writ of the Sovereign's Lieutenant in *nobilitas*, and outwith the control of any Court. It is consequently set forth as conclusive,[2] and is so received without question by " all nobles and in all places of honour ".[3]

In mediaeval Scotland, Birthbrieves were frequently obtained from local Town Councils (usually by burgesses or professional people, where the proof was less exacting than the Lord Lyon's), but these were usually for the consideration of the patriciate of foreign cities.[4] Birthbrieves were also formerly sometimes issued under the Great Seal, or even from Parliament.[5] Plate XLIII shows a Birthbrief of four branches for Dr. David Kinloch, 20 March 1596, the heraldry of which is typical of Lyon Office workmanship in the reign of Sir David Lindsay of The Mount (*secundus*). Since the seventeenth century, however, the only machinery for obtaining, recording, and confirming either a full Birthbrief, a lineal pedigree, or a proof of nobility either of four grandparents, eight great-grandparents, or sixteen great-great-

---

[1] Diploma of Nobility, *Juridical Review*, 1940, lii, 284; *ibid.*, 1938, l. 69, *Cumming*, where Lord Justice Clerk Cockburn was in 1710 and 1727 a party giving evidence before Lyon Court relating to chiefship, chieftainship, and other matters of noble status for Lyon's birthbrief—required for marriage into the princely family of Lubomirski.

[2] *Tartans of the Clans and Families in Scotland*, 1949, pp. 51-3.

[3] *Proc. of Soc. of Antiquaries of Scot.*, lxxix, 160 ; *Juridical Review*, September 1940, p. 198.

[4] *Proc. of Soc. of Antiquaries of Scot.*, lxxxi, 114.

[5] A Great Seal or a Parliamentary Birthbrief was usually the Chancery or statutory sanction for a concoction of genealogical falsehoods which would not have passed the Lord Lyon's scrutiny. (Cf. also Sir W. Fraser, *Earls of Sutherland*, i, 38.) In several of these Lyon was ordained to emblazon the arms " of the families therein mentioned "—thus evading his official criticism of the lineage (Czartoryski Birthbrief, J. M. Bulloch, *Polish Marquis of Huntly*, p. 34—Lyon Office pamphlets, xxvii, No. xiii). Moreover, a " Parliamentary Birthbrief " was not receivable in foreign noble circles, because " common burgesses ", etc., had voted on it, and a King of Arms one in supplement had to be obtained.

grandparents is a petition to the Lord Lyon for such and its registration in the Public Register of All Genealogies and Birthbrieves in Scotland. The " proof of four branches " is still required for the British Order of the Knights of St John of Jerusalem, and, as indicated by the Kinloch Birthbrief and many others, is the most popular proof in Scotland, as in Spain, though proofs of eight quarterings are almost as frequent. The charge for registration of either a lineal pedigree or a birthbrief in the Public Register of All Genealogies is an initial fee of ten guineas, and five shillings for each additional person registered.[1]   The procedure is by petition to the Lord Lyon, to which the pedigree to be judicially adjudicated, or a draft of the Birthbrief desired to be ministerially issued, is annexed along with proofs.   If the arms are, as is usual, to be displayed in a Birthbrief, reference must be made to the various matriculations in Lyon Register, or in the case of non-Scottish arms, to registrations in the College of Arms or grants from foreign Sovereigns, and the history and import or significance of the arms is usually set forth at such length as may seem useful.[2]   In Scotland, as on the Continent, it is the practice to show in each case the paternal shield, and not the lozenge, of the female ancestresses.[3] This gives the Birthbrief a more balanced effect, and displays the family heraldry more effectively.

LINEAL PEDIGREES

The Public Register of All Genealogies is also the record available for lineal pedigrees, and at the same charges.   The

---

[1] 30 and 31 Vict., cap. 17, Schedule B.

[2] A splendid illustration of a *seize-quartiers* will be found in Fox-Davies's *Art of Heraldry*, pl. 92, p. 484.   An example of a Scots Birthbrief of Four Quarterings is shown in Plates XL and XLIII, pp. 196 and 205 of this book.

[3] Cf. *Kinloch* Birthbrief of 1596 ; the *Innes of that Ilk* Birthbrief, 1698 (*Familie of Innes*, 1820 ed., Frontispiece) ; *Proc. of Soc. of Antiquaries of Scot.*, lxxix, pl. ix.

founder of an armigerous family is well advised to pay the initial ten guineas for recording a pedigree, to which descendants can thereafter be added at five shillings per head. This sum is within reach of everyone, and generation after generation can be added to such pedigrees. It has been suggested that, if necessary, testamentary instructions should be made that beneficiaries and their successors keep the official pedigree up to date.[1] A splendidly executed (but unofficial) lineal pedigree, that of Swinton of that Ilk, is shown in Plate XLII.

Pedigrees recorded as satisfactory in the Public Register of All Genealogies and Birthbrieves in Scotland, or adjudicated upon in Lyon Register as the basis for confirmations and matriculations of arms as the reinvestitures in feudal heritage, are received as sufficient evidence in succession to Baronetcies and entry on the Roll of Baronets,[2] and the matriculation as the equivalent of special service in heritage when such peers present themselves to vote at Holyroodhouse, Lyon Court's decisions consequently operating as sufficient evidence of succession unless the House of Lords acts upon a protest by two peers reported by the Lord Clerk Register. Lyon Court adjudications of genealogy are not like the modern English College of Arms Chapter registrations of pedigree,

[1] C. A. H. Franklyn, *The Bearing of Coat Armour by Ladies*, p. 123. The " Register of Successions to Arms " referred to on p. 144 of the 1st ed. of *Scots Heraldry* was no more than a calendar of claims to the character of heir. The volume (started in 1930) turned out on consideration to be of a non-effective character, in light of the principle of reinvestiture (see p. 117), and the right of an heir to make up progress of title at a reduced rate, if claiming within a year and day, pursuant to 1672, c. 47, was allowed in *Chisholm of Chisholm*, 1944, Lyon Register, xxxiii, 12 (see Plate XXIX), cf. *Ogston*, 21 March 1888, *ibid.*, x, 10. This is the true feudal principle.

[2] *Grant-Suttie, Bart.*, " If a pedigree is on record there (*in Lyon Office*) only such evidence as is not covered by it need be submitted ", Home Office Letter, 5 June 1947 ; and for Peerage Precedency Warrants (*Kinloss*, Precedency Warrant 1947), Register of Genealogies, iv, 32, Lyon Register, xxxvi, 61, 18 July 1947.

PLATE XL

Birthbrief under the Great Seal, in favour of DAVID KINLOCH, M.D., 20th March 1596.

This purports to show the four branches (i.e. grandparents) of Dr. David Kinloch, being the normal " proof of nobility " in Scotland. The pedigree is somewhat vague, but the arms appear to be work of the Lyon Court painters of Lindsay of the Mount (*secundus*); resort to a Great Seal Birthbrief may have been because Lyon would not accept the pedigree, which gives as four branches: (1) Kinloch, apparently differenced for a 3rd son; (2) Ramsay, probably for a descent from Banff ; (3) Lindsay of Edzell; (4) Earl of Erroll—which seems to suggest descent from the 8th Earl of Crawford, rather than Lindsay of Edzell as claimed in the document. The Birthbrief, however, is a good example of the style in which these were executed in sixteenth and early seventeenth century.

John de Swyntone
Henry de Swyntone
William de Swyntone
Alan de Swynton
Henry de Swynton
J'ESPERE
Alan Dominus de Swynton
Alan de Swynton
John de Swynton
Dominus Alan de Swinton
Alan de Swynton
Richard de Swynton
Hugh de Swynton
Viscount Family
Cospatric de Swinton
William
Adam
John
Ernulf de Swintun Miles
Odard
Liulf
Edulf living before the Conquest
Sir John de Swynton
Joan
Margaret Countess of Douglas and Mar
Lady Margaret Stuart
Sir John de Swynton
Lady Marjory Dunbar
Sir John de Swyntoun of that Ilk
Sir John de Swyntoune
Catherine Lauder
Elizabeth Cuninghame
Mr John Swyntoun
Marion Home
Nicholas
David
Alex'
Thomas
John Swyntoun
Katharine Lauder
George
Robert Swyntoun
Elizabeth Hay
Jean Hepburn
Alex'
George
JE PENSE

Genealogical tree of SWINTON OF THAT ILK.

Prepared in the Lyon Office by J. R. Sutherland, Hon. Heraldic Artist to the Lyon Court, and A. G. Law Samson, Herald Painter.

PLATE XLII

The Branches of the Right Worshipfull Sr Alexander
Seton. of Pitmedden Knight & Baronet, one of y^e Senators
of the Colledge of Justice

SANGUINE

SUSTENTA SIGNA

Seton of
Pitmedden

Johnston of
Elphingstons

Ogilvie of
Bamff

Douglas of
Spott

Ronyland of
Torrie

Dundas
of that Ilk

Crux Leo cor Stillans crux Cœrula celsa
Corona Miles et Armatus Bellica Signa
Ferens Sunt Pitmedden a Preclara Insignia
Gentis Partibus a Regis fida quod usque Stetit

Urquhart
of Cromartie

Home Airesse
of Spott

C. Norton Sculp^t

Seton
Lord Seton

Hamilton of
Bothwellhaugh

Edinburgh

Arms and branches of the HON. LORD PITMEDDEN.

but are *judgments of court* equivalent to the former adjudications in genealogy of the English Court of Chivalry, which likewise settled rights to honours.[1]

[1] *Halsbury's Laws of England*, xxiii, 559, n. (*a*) ; *Juridical Review*, September 1940, p. 182 ; " The English Court of Chivalry ", Scots Law Times, June 1937.

CHAPTER XV

NAME AND CHANGE OF NAME

N Scotland, it is the Lord Lyon King of Arms who has jurisdiction in matters of Name and Change of Name.[1]   In England, Royal Licences are directed to the Earl Marshal and dealt with in the Heralds' College.   In Scotland similar licences are directed to the Lord Lyon, but this is a costly process, which only gives a Royal "permission" for taking the new name, which the Courts hold to be legally unnecessary [2] except in the case of "Names of Dignity ".[3]   The name in which a person is granted arms is, however, a "name of dignity " (*i.e.* of the "dignity "

EARL OF LEVEN AND MELVILLE. Quarterly: 1st, azure, a thistle slipped proper, ensigned with an imperial crown or (*augmentation*); 2nd, gules, three crescents within a bordure argent, charged with eight roses of the first (*Melville*); 3rd, argent, a fess gules (*Melville of Raith*); 4th, argent, on a bend azure, three buckles or (*Leslie*).

[1] 1672, cap. 47 ; 30 and 31 Vict., cap. 17, Schedule B ; Green's *Encyclopaedia of the Laws of Scotland*, x, 137, *s.v.* Name and Change of Name.

[2] *Robertson-Durham*, 1900 S.C., 127 ; *Finlay*, 1870, 11 R. 910 ; *Kinloch* v. *Lourie*, 1853, 16 D. 197 (approving *Williams* v. *Bryant*, 1839, Meason & Welsby, v, 447) ; *Kettle*, 1835, 15 Shaw 262 ; *Leigh* v. *Leigh*, 1808, 15 Vesey's Reports, 92 ; *Heraldry in Scotland*, p. 364 ; *Du Boulay* v. *Du Boulay*, 1869, 2 P.C. 430.

[3] *Leigh* v. *Leigh*, 1808, 15 *Vesey's Reports*, 92 ; *Heraldry in Scotland*, p. 364.

of Gentleman [1]), and in the nature of a " title " if it comprehends a feudal designation. Hence the real ground on which Lyon takes cognisance of Names of the *noblesse*, and why changes of name are " officially recognised " and the applicant declared to be " now Known and publicly Recognised and Recorded " in the Books and Registers of the *Curia Militaris* or Court of Honour.[2] These facts reconcile the views of, *e.g.*, Fox-Davies, with those of the ordinary judges. The principle on which Lyon's exercise of the Royal Prerogative is given is thus essentially analogous to the principle on which the Court of Session recognises Changes of Name by those who fall to be of record in *that* Court, as, *qua* nobles, it is in Lyon Court.

The normal Scottish procedure in the case of the *noblesse* is, therefore, to obtain from the Lord Lyon a " Certificate regarding Change of Name ", in which his Lordship not only " officially recognises " the name assumed, but issues a Certificate which forms the necessary identification of the individual under his old name and his new one. Such a statutory Certificate is granted for 15s. and expenses (about 2 guineas where the applicants or parents are recorded in the Registers of Arms or Genealogies), and is also enrolled in the Books of Lyon Court, whence additional Extracts can be obtained. Otherwise it is normally recorded in a special section of the Register of Genealogies, the total fee in that case being some 13 guineas. The Lord Lyon's Certificate, or an Extract thereof, is thereafter produced, along with the Extract of the original Birth Certificate, which cannot itself be altered, except in fundamental error.[3]

---

[1] *Halsbury's Laws of England*, 1912 ed., xxii, 289, par. 632, per Lindsay Norroy.

[2] See *Notes & Queries*, vol. 178, p. 65, n. 5 ; *Law of Succession in Ensigns Armorial*, p. 44.

[3] In that case the Registrar-General makes any necessary alterations in obedience to a warrant from the Sheriff through the " Register of Corrected Entries ".

As in the case of a Royal Licence, Lyon's certificate is not obtainable for capricious changes of name by non-armigerous persons.[1] The grounds on which Lyon's jurisdiction can properly be invoked are Changes of Name by (1) persons in right of arms, or members of their families entitled to a courtesy of these arms ; (2) persons recorded in, or adding themselves to, pedigrees in the Public Register of Genealogies ; (3) persons succeeding to feudal property, or under settlements (the first category renders the matter one relating to tenures, and the latter presumes a formal act will be taken to effect compliance) ; (4) persons who require Lyon's certificate for naval, military, or other service reasons ; (5) where a change of name has to be authorised by a Government Department, as in entering certain professions (*e.g.* nursing), and in connection with insurance companies, and for certain foreign purposes (a University).[2] If the ground of application be (1) or (2) the ground will normally be set forth and appear from reference to the Register of Arms or Genealogies. In other cases the precise ground for invoking Lyon's jurisdiction should be set forth in the application.

Certificates granted by the Lord Lyon may refer to change of either Christian name or surname.[3] The needful procedure is a Petition, which will be in approximately the following terms :

[1] The rule, and the correct one, was (until a few years ago, when the practice was somewhat extended under a misapprehension) that Lyon's certificate was only issued to armigerous people, or, as hereinafter set forth, the 1939 Defence Regulations have again drawn attention to the procedure for other cases, a notice of change of name advertised in the *Gazette*; such a notice should describe the district, year, and number of the Birth Certificate in which the existing name was recorded.

[2] *Vigeland*, Lyon Court, 1940.

[3] *Kinloch* v. *Lowrie*, 1853, 16 Dunlop, 200; *Elphinstone of Glack*, 4 April 1928, Lyon Register, xxvii, 79; J. H. Stevenson, *Heraldry in Scotland*, p. 383.

UNTO THE RIGHT HONOURABLE
THE LORD LYON KING OF ARMS

> The Petition of JOHN ROBERT
> SMITH OF GLENSMITH in
> the County of Inverness, formerly
> John Robert White;

HUMBLY SHEWETH—

THAT he was born at 1000 Broomielaw, Glasgow, on 30 February 1872, conform to the Birth Certificate No. 5 of the 7th Registration District of Glasgow, produced herewith, and is the only son of Charles James White and his wife Elizabeth Jane, third daughter of the late Alexander Smith of Glensmith.

THAT in terms of a testamentary settlement of his maternal uncle, the late Henry Smith of Glensmith, dated 31 June 1910, and registered in the Books of Council and Session 1 March 1917, the Petitioner did, upon the death of his said uncle on 5 January 1917, succeed to the lands of Glensmith on condition that he should assume, use, constantly bear and retain the name [1] Smith of Glensmith.

THAT the Petitioner has accordingly assumed the name Smith of Glensmith in place of White, and is now commonly called and known by the name of John Robert Smith of Glensmith;

AND THAT the Petitioner is desirous of being officially recognised under said name.

> MAY IT THEREFORE please your Lordship to Authorise
> the Lyon Clerk to prepare a certificate officially
> recognising the petitioner, John Robert Smith of
> Glensmith, formerly John Robert White, under
> the name by which he is now commonly called and
> known, and to Grant Warrant for the same to be
> issued as an Extract from your Lordship's Registers.

And your Petitioner will ever pray.

> (*Signature of Petitioner or his Agent*)
> J. R. SMITH OF GLENSMITH.
> *Date*, 19*th June* 1918.

[1] A testamentary provision of this character would normally say " name and arms ", in which case the Certificates of Change of Name would be embodied in the " rematriculation " of the armorial bearings of Smith of Glensmith, and the petition would be in a form combining application for rematriculation of arms and official recognition of the change of name.

Evidence of identity requires to be produced along with the Petition (an affidavit by two credible witnesses is generally the evidence required), and an Extract of the Petitioner's Birth and Marriage Certificates should normally be lodged, but Lyon's jurisdiction is far older than such registration, and his jurisdiction, as sometimes arises when one applicant has not such certificates, can proceed on other evidence; indeed, where the applicant is already recorded in the Register of Arms or Genealogies, no Birth Certificate is asked for or considered necessary. The circumstances may be quite simple, or may be complicated. The illustration shows a case where not only the name, but a territorial designation, is assumed for testamentary reasons. In consequence of the permissive terms of 1672, cap. 47,[1] and duly recognised in 6 & 7 Geo. V, ch. 58, sec. 22, it is held that in cases where the assumer is owner of the fief from which he is " taking the name " according to feudal law, and the *basic* surname continues unaltered, the assumption or alteration of a territorial designation is regarded as an " amplification " thereof, and not as a change of the basic surname itself,[2] so a certificate is not essential on assuming or changing a designation, but such an alteration should be recorded on the margin of the matriculation, since it does vary the nobiliary title of gentility.[3] The change, or recognition, by

[1] Cf. similar view held in France, as to the interpretation of an Ordinance of 1555, *Law and Practice of Heraldry*, p. 411. This Ordinance against changes of name in France was held not to affect the right to assume names from fiefs, nor changes of name made under family settlements; de la Rocque, *Traité de la Noblesse*, p. 329; also cf. K. Fedden, *Manor Life*, p. 208; *Association de la Noblesse Française*, May 1952, *re* survivance of *noblesse de terre* in South France until the Revolution (since when pre-1789 use must be proved).

[2] *Encyclopaedia of Laws of Scotland*, *s.v.* Name and Change of Name, par. 309; G. Morant, *Annuaire de la Noblesse Française*, 1933, pp. 180, 210.

[3] *Bernard of Dunsinnan and Buttergask*, 23 April 1901, Lyon Register, xv, 26; *Watson of Ayton*, 22 June 1898, *ibid.*, xi, 98; *Anderson of Buckton*, 27 May 1895, *ibid.*, ix, 19.

Lyon Courts will then be included in the annual return made to the Lord Chamberlain and in the *Edinburgh Gazette*.

Territorial Designations.—These " titles ", so common in Scotland, are not only part of the feudal system, but also one form of the Celtic *bun sloinn,* or genealogical second surname,[1] by which the various branches of a clan, or house, are distinguished, and the " designation " is (like a peerage title) legally regarded as *part of the name itself,* when " ordinarily used " as such, and the parties " adject the designation " to their signatures in terms of the Statute 1672, cap. 47.[2] They are used not merely by the head of the family, but also by the heir and daughters of the house,[3] but seldom by younger sons. These designations may be used apart from the ownership of the lands from which they are derived.[4] This, and the legal character[5] of such " titles ", was actually established at the instance of the Crown in a series of cases after the Jacobite risings, in order to establish Attainders, the Lord Advocate successfully maintaining that such (*e.g.*

FIG. 97.—Archery Medal of Alexander Macleod, younger, of Muiravonside. Quarterly: 1st and 4th, azure, a castle argent, gated and windowed gules; 2nd, gules three legs armed proper, flexed and conjoined triangularly at the upper end of the thigh, garnished and spurred or; 3rd, azure, a deer's head cabossed or; over all a label of three points for difference. *Crest,* a lion's head erased gules.

---

[1] David Stewart of Garth, *Highlanders of Scotland*, p. 26, and App. xxxv.

[2] *Encyclopaedia of the Laws of Scotland*, vol. x, par. 300.

[3] *Maclean of Ardgour*, Fort William Sheriff Court, 28 November 1930; Perth Sheriff Court, 20 January 1931 (Actions for Correction of Registers).

[4] *Cameron of Lochiel*, 1749, Morrison's *Dictionary of Decisions of the Court of Session*, p. 4161; *MacNiel of Barra*, 27 May 1915, Lyon Register, xxii, 60. For the German practice, see J. Woodward, *Heraldry, British and Foreign*, i, 408.

[5] *Moir of Leckie*, Morrison's *Dictionary*, 15538 (see p. 88); *Crichton of Castlemayns, ibid.*

" Cameron of Lochiel ", etc.) were " ordinary names " and not " descriptions of property ". Accordingly the right to acquire from lands, and to continue to bear, and to register these designations *as part of the name* in registrations of births, etc., has continued, and—upon an attempt to suppress it in 1927—anew established,[1] and, when appointees supply the correct particulars, they continue to be employed in British Crown appointments,[2] as was invariably the case in old Scottish practice. They have been recognised by Committees for Privileges as " titles "; the " *title of Barone of Spynie* " in a Crown Charter was held a territorial and not a peerage dignity,[3] and the use of them, where so desired, has never ceased in the Great Seal Register.[4] Similarly, in the Parliamentary " Return of Landowners ", 1873–4, the Scottish " Owner's Name " column differed from those for England and Ireland by including the designations. These are never assumed from burgage or lotted feus, and " Esq.", being less than " laird ", should not be added.[5] The court assumes that a person has a

[1] *Encyclopaedia*, vol. x, par. 301 ; *Maclean of Ardgour*, Fort William and Perth Sheriff Courts, *supra*. Where the family is not that of an owner (or representative) of a fief (or of arms " of that description "), Lyon's certificate may be required to vouch authenticity and admissibility. They duly appeared as part of the name in National Registration Cards, 1939, *e.g.* S.W.H.X. 49/1, 2, 3, 6 ; and, where an assumption on succession and matriculation took place, such cards were amended after reference to Lyon ; *Mrs Borthwick of Borthwick*, Reg. Gen. ref. J.W./NR/ERR/S.C.A., 20/3/1945, following on matriculation, 26 July 1944, Lyon Register, xxxv, 14.

[2] Major-General Sir J. L. G. *Burnett of Leys, Bart.*, gazetted C.B. 1 January 1932, *Edinburgh Gazette*, p. 9 ; Major Sir Basil Hamilton Hebden *Niven-Spence of Uyea*, Knight, M.D., F.R.C.P. (as Lord-Lieutenant of Shetland, 25 June 1952, *Edinburgh Gazette*, p. 442).

[3] J. Riddell, *Peerage Law*, p. 635 ; cf. *Maclean of Ardgour*, Register of Genealogies, iv, 26 ; *Proc. of Soc. of Antiquities of Scot.*, lxxix, 113.

[4] *E.g. Rose of Kilravock*, 1889, No. 122 ; *Laing, younger of Crook*, 1892, No. 211 ; *Munro of Foulis*, 1899, No. 163 ; *Dalrymple of Newhailes*, 1913, No. 28 ; *Burnett of Leys*, 1918, No. 200 ; *Burn-Clerk-Rattray of Craighall*, 1929, No. 20, vol. cclxx, f. 66 ; *Spence of Uyea*, 1952.

[5] Green's *Encyclopaedia*, vol. xii, pars. 28, 31, and see p. 203, n. 5, *supra*,

PLATE XLIII

house for legal citation at any territorial place if he use the style thereof.[1] A territorial title was so indispensable in Scotland that landless Lord Lyons were ordained to be "callit writtin and intitulat", *e.g.* Sir William Stewart *of Luthrie*, Knight.[2] So long as a person is owner of a fief he, theoretically, under Scoto-feudal law's elasticity (being entitled at any time to add or subtract any of his estate-names), not invariably uses the whole ; but with increasing precision of "forms" and records, variations in practice tend to create "questions" amongst inexpert officials—and confuse laymen. If not the actual estate-owner, wife, or heir, then as a simple name the whole must (as anyway such styles *should*) be regularly used—as the chieftains' wives and daughters of our historic houses do in any case. English officials who readily accept French *surnoms terriens* such as "Champion de Crespigny, Baronet", will often attempt to discourage or evade use of any "Scotch" name or style, but those who use theirs *regularly* (and so come under the English decision in *Du Boulay*) avoid bother in Anglic circles and enjoy their Scots legal rights unquestioned.[3] Their use is no "longer" than many peer-signatures, and they are of importance in Continental society (where the analogous *surnoms terriens* are always used by those entitled to them), and in many ways of practical as well as of historical and social value in Britain.

Inheritance of Names.—Nobiliary names recorded in Courts of Arms are inherited along with the relative arms, much like a peerage title. Such are the "name or title" in which the arms are "on record" in Lyon Regis-

---

[1] Morrison, *Dictionary of Decisions of the Court of Session*, p. 3750.

[2] Privy Seal, xxxvii, 44.

[3] *Clans, Septs, and Regiments of the Scottish Highlands*, 1952, p. 409. The subsistence of the chieftainly titles is one of the keys on which the survival of the Scottish social organisation depends—hence efforts to suppress them, to which weak or anglicised lairds sometimes submit. The French *noblesse* have, even in a Republic, been more tenacious of family and name-rights.

P

ter.[1] The idea that non-armigerous people inherit a surname is of recent origin. A surname is legally a description or identification of the individual. Normally it falls to the parent, as guardian of the child, to " take unto it " a surname with which it is to start life. Usually he confers his own surname upon his children, but, save as regards titles of dignity, freedom of selection is unrestricted,[2] and Lord Advocate Sir George Mackenzie recognised that different children in the same family may be given different surnames.[3] Normally a departure from the father's surname takes place only according to the requirements of some entail or legacy, or succession to the representation of some territorial or Celtic house. On the other hand, by entail or contract, it is possible to oblige specific individuals to refrain from bearing any particular name, a condition imposed by *Macdonell of Glengarry* when he sold his ancient inheritance,[4] purchasers of which were astricted not to use the words " of Glengarry " as part of their name.

Celtic Patronymics.—Mediaeval Highland patronymics were essentially descriptive, and in the seventeenth century Macallister of Loupe was described as *Hector McGorry vich Eachin vich Allister vich Ian Dhu.* Abbreviations of this system led to patronymics such as *McIain Stewartach* (Stewart of Appin).

The chief of a clan was, however, known at home in the

[1] The Lord Advocate successfully maintained : *Cameron of Lochiel,* " attainted by that name, behoved, if he had got a pardon, to have been pardoned by the same ; people lose their rights by forfeiture but not their ordinary names ; and these designations do not necessarily imply either the property or the right of apparency, to the estates from which they are taken " (Morrison, *Dictionary,* 4161, line 28). In Cluny-Macpherson's case (*ibid.,* line 2), it was stated—" it is not the custom of Scotland to design a man ' of ' a place for his residence "—another difference from English usage. (See *Clans, Septs, and Regiments of the Scottish Highlands,* 1952 ed., pp. 402-405, for some further details.)

[2] Green's *Encyclopaedia, s.v.* Name and Change of Name, par. 304, *e.g.* in Scotland a child cannot have the prefix " Lord " or " Sir " in its forename registered, unless the authority for such is demonstrated to the Registrar.

[3] Mackenzie, *Works,* ii, 490.   [4] Green's *Encyclopaedia,* vol. x, par. 302.

duthus simply as " Maclachlan " or " Macdonald ". The celebrated Gaelic Charter by the Lord of the Isles, 1408, commences,[1] " I, *Macdonald*, grant and give—", but both love of clan country, and the practical inconvenience that a patronymic title such as " Macleod " or " Macdonald " was open to confusion outwith the clan's own district, speedily led to the use of territorial descriptions,[2] even by *Macdonald of the Isles* himself, or a reduplication such as " Macgregor of Macgregor " (usual where the reduplication is *patronymical*) or the well-known Scottish style " of that Ilk " (usual where the reduplication is *territorial*), *e.g.* " Arbuthnott of that Ilk ". Many chiefs combine a patronymic with a territorial designation, *e.g.* " Macdougall of Macdougall and Dunollie ". The reason for this was that in the Lowlands, " Macdougall of Dunollie " would not convey the idea of " Chief " amongst lairds designated " of that Ilk ", whilst such names as " Macdougall of Macdougall " alone are sometimes inconvenient, as they specify no locality—*e.g.* " Mackintosh of Mackintosh, Captain and Chief of Clan Chattan ", was held an *insufficient* designation in an action concerning landed property![3] The title *Laird of Mackintosh* is perfectly correct, and duly used by Lyon (10 September 1672) and Parliament, but it then [4] relates to no *landed* estate, but to the Clan or Family of Mackintosh as an incorporeal heritable subject.[5] The difficulty would have been avoided had he incorporated the old territorial style " Mackintosh of Mackintosh and of Dunauchtan ", analogous to the style used, for

---

[1] *Scottish National MSS.*, p. 59.

[2] The older style of *Macdonald* was, however, *Donald of Donald* (cf. *Scottish National MSS.*), *i.e.* " Macdonald of Macdonald ", and whilst the Lordship of the Isles was annexed to the Crown, a territorial barony of *Macdonald* in Skye was erected in 1727 (1950 Scots Law Times, Lyon Court, p. 8).

[3] *Mackintosh* v. *Mackintosh*, 9 June 1835, S.C., 13, Shaw, 884.

[4] " The Mackintosh Estate " has since become a landed description, cf. Lyon Court, 9 April 1947, Lyon Register, xxxvi, 40 (1950 Scots Law Times; Lyon Court, p. 2). [5] Innes of Learney, *Tartans of the Clans and Families*, 1948, p. 62.

example, in a House of Lords Appeal by *Sir Evan John Murray Macgregor of Macgregor and Balquhidder, Baronet.*[1] Since the designation is regarded as part of the name, affixes such as " Baronet ", " Knight ", " C.V.O. ", etc., *follow the designation* in formal Scots Deeds and Crown Charters.[2] The prefix " The ", used by chiefs of the whole Name or Clan, is really of Lowland origin, a fifteenth-century custom in which Lowland chiefs adopted such a style as " Le Lindsay ", but owing to the Scotsman's deep attachment to land, this soon gave way to the characteristically Scottish territorial or quasi-territorial system of " territorial designation ". Nevertheless, the prefix " The " has become of practical importance in a wider world, as it at once identifies a Chief of a Name or Clan as such, in circumstances where his status would not otherwise be apparent, and it has Royal and official sanction.[3]

A chief, Highland or Lowland, is also officially described as " Laird of "—*e.g. The Laird of Maclachlan* ; *The Laird of Lochiel* ; and if also a feudal Baron, as " *The Laird and Baron of Cromarty* " (inscription on portrait of Sir Thomas Urquhart of Cromarty), whilst on the Continent, and in any formal deed for use abroad, Lairds *in baroniam* are styled *Baron of Cambo, Baron of Balquhain,* etc., and as the social equivalents of the *chiefs* of Baronial Houses in Baronages of Continental realms. Our authorities emphasise that no false modesty should restrain them from asserting their rank and titles amongst Continental Barons.[4]

[1] *Macgregor* v. *Brown,* 1838, 3 S. & McL., 84 ; Register of Genealogies, iii, 2.

[2] *E.g. Burnett of Leys, Bart., Edinburgh Gazette,* 1932, p. 9 ; *Burn-Clerk-Rattray of Craighall-Rattray,* C.B., Great Seal, 1929, No. 20.

[3] The Mackintosh, 9 April 1947, Lyon Register, xxxvi, 40, and Lyon's Note.

[4] *E.g.* Public Register of Genealogies, i, 1 ; *ibid.* iii, 8, 20 ; Lyon Register, *Baron of Esslemont,* xxxi, 20 ; *Baron of Comer,* xxxiii, 12 ; *Baron of Ardgour,* Public Register of Genealogies, iv, 26 ; *Baron of Auchinhove,* Lyon Register, xxxiv, 64 ; *Baron of Niddrie-Marischall, ibid.,* xxxv, 31. Royal letters are similarly addressed, *e.g. Baron of Kilravock,* see *ibid.,* xxv, 8. The titles of Baron and Baroness (*Ban-Baran* in Gaelic) were colloquially most used about the High-

Married Women.—In Scotland it was not until the nineteenth century that wives adopted their husbands' surnames upon marriage. The custom came from England, and although no doubt convenient in ordinary life, is still not legally essential in Scotland, and is most confusing to the subsequent genealogical inquirer. In Scots documents a married woman is still described by both her surnames, *e.g.* Mrs Margaret McCulloch or Armstrong (to which her husband's " designation ", if any, will be added). There is, however, no reason why the man should not assume his wife's name on marriage,[1] and in most old Scots entails he is required to do so. If the representation of the Family has devolved on his heiress wife he must do so if he is to enjoy the armorial " Courtesy of Scotland ", just as the husband of a Scots peeress in her own right became peer by courtesy.[2] Although Scotswomen thus to a great extent preserve their own names,[3] they always assume their husband's " titles ", whether peerage, territorial (see Fig. 87), or chiefly designations, and likewise use these titles in the prescribed manner in their signatures.[4] Feudal rank is legally communicated to the wife, and a Laird's wife is *legally* " the Lady Lour ". In rural Scotland, at any rate, this correct address (invariably

land line, *e.g.* Scott's *Baron of Bradwardine* in *Waverley* (*Proc. of Soc. of Antiquaries of Scot.*, lxxix, 157).

[1] *Dalyell of the Binns* (formerly *Loch*), 1 March 1938, Lyon Register, xxxiii, 8 ; *Maclachlan of Maclachlan* (formerly *Rome*), 3 December 1948, *Scotsman* advert., Lyon Register, xxxv, 72.

[2] *Balfour of Burleigh* decision 1869 ; *Notes & Queries*, 22 November 1940, for *Lundin of Lundin*, Lyon Register, i, 180.

[3] Mrs Matheson of Achany (wife of Lionel Trower), 5 April 1933, Lyon Register, xxx, 53, is an instance of a wife bearing a name and designation of her own.

[4] Statute 1672, cap. 47 ; Acts viii, 95 ; see also Plate XLIII. *E.g.* the ladies of Sir Michael Malcolm of Balbedie and Sir Ian Malcolm of Poltalloch are not " Lady (Michael) Malcolm " and " Lady (Ian) Malcolm ", an unauthorised practice of recent origin. Under Scots *law*, these ladies are distinguishable as *Lady Malcolm of Balbedie* and *Lady Malcolm of Poltalloch*. Moreover, whilst in England the wife of " John Smith " is apparently legally described as " Mrs John

used in the old Scottish Law Reports) is still in use.[1] Official rank, however, confers neither rank nor title on the other spouse,[2] except where this has been specially conferred on wives by Royal Warrant,[3] and the recently invented title [4] of " Lady Provost " could not be allowed in any State documents or judicial proceedings.[5]

A widow or divorcing wife, with custody of children, cannot change their names so as to take them out of her husband's family (which it is her duty faithfully to maintain), saving changes for normal and expedient collateral or ancestral representational reason, officially recognised by Lyon. The same *e converso* applies to husbands of heiress-chiefs.

Smith ", in Scotland this is not so. *Ella Richards*, wife of The Mackintosh, was never " Mrs Alfred D. Mackintosh ", but was either *Madam Mackintosh of Mackintosh, Madam Ella Mackintosh of Mackintosh*, or in full-length description *Madam Ella Richards or Mackintosh of Mackintosh*, and of course briefly *The Lady Mackintosh*, whereby The Mackintosh's wife should always be addressed.

[1] The Lady Warthill, cf. H. Beaton, *Back o' Bennachie*, p. 104. The writer's mother was known amongst the people of Deeside as, and styled, *Lady Learney*, and that of the Captain of Dunstaffnage as *Lady Dunstaffnage* (cf. " The Lady Bargarran " at p. 227 *infra*).

[2] Lord Advocate Sir G. Mackenzie, *Works*, ii, 553; Nisbet, *Heraldry*, iv, 278.

[3] Wives of Lords of Session, 3 February 1905. The wives of such as were Lairds were (and are) of course *Lady* . . . (not " Hon." however), and it was not until they aped English " Society ", which scouted the Scots judges as " Paper Lords " and declined to accord them their titles, that their wives became termed " Mrs ". Lord Polton, for instance, was " Mr Calderwood " to Londoners. The older judges declined to kowtow to English prejudice and maintained the feudal rights of their spouses, *e.g.* Lord Auchinleck, when asked, on his second marriage, if his wife would be called Lady Auchinleck or " Mrs Boswell " after the new fashion, acidly retorted, " I'm ower auld tae start keeping mistresses noo."

[4] It is sometimes now alleged that the Secretary for Scotland either conferred or approved this title in 1925. He, however, did nothing so unconstitutional. He avoided taking the only action by which the title would be rendered valid, viz. recommending that a Royal Warrant be issued, such as that which conferred the title " Hon. Lady " on wives of landless Lords of Session. The actual " title " used by a Provost's consort appears to have been " The Provost's Lady of Elgin " (*Boharm Parish Registers*, 5 June 1734). Hence it may be deduced that the correct style of the consort of the Lord Provost of the capital should be " The Lord Provost's Lady of Edinburgh ". This seems quite a lawful description.

[5] *Encyclopaedia of the Laws of Scotland, s.v.* Name, vol. x, par. 297.

CHAPTER XVI

THE ROYAL ARMS AND NATIONAL FLAG

Highest and midmost was descried   Wherein proud Scotland's royal shield
The Royal Banner floating wide,   The ruddy lion ramped in gold.

HERE is much confusion in the public mind regarding the nature and use of Royal Arms. A modern official term, " Personal flag of the Sovereign ", some years ago led one overseas statesman to describe the Royal Arms as " the domestic symbol of the Royal House ", which is precisely what the Royal Arms are not.

Royal Arms are technically described as " Ensigns of Public Authority ", and are governed by different rules from other arms. They are not hereditary, but pass by " succession, election or conquest " along with the *sovereignty* of the dominions which they represent.[1] The Duke of Rothesay bears the Royal Arms with a plain label for difference, in consequence of his relation to the Throne, as heir, but younger children of the Sovereign inherit no right in the Royal Arms until a differenced version of them has been assigned by Royal Warrant, and that differenced version

EARLDOM OF ATHOLL. Paly of six or and sable.

[1] Nisbet, *System of Heraldry*, ii, iii, 89.

211

is then not the actual Royal Arms, for " differenced arms are different arms ".[1]

From the time of the accession of the House of Hanover until 1948, warrants for differencing the Royal Arms were

passed only to Garter, and even when a Prince received a Scottish dukedom, some version of the English arms was assigned. On older precedent, when a Royal Prince received for his principal dignity a Scottish title, a differenced version of the Scottish form of the Royal Arms would—as in the case of the Duke of Albany and York,[2] 1672 (in addition to any existing arms[3] and in virtue of a Warrant directed to

FIG. 98.—The Royal Arms of Great Britain, as used in Scotland.

the Lord Lyon)—be matriculated for such Prince in Lyon Register, and thereafter descend to his successive heirs.[4] On the creation of the Royal Dukedom of Edinburgh at the marriage of H.R.H. Princess Elizabeth, however, King George VI issued a separate Warrant directed to Lyon ordaining the Duke's arms therein " depainted " to be " extended " (blazoned) by the Lord Lyon and matriculated in Lyon Register according to the Law of Scotland.[5]

[1] 1920, S.C. 764, per Lord Sands at 801, but subject to specialities.
[2] Lyon Register, i, 26; *Lennox, ibid.*, xviii, 70.   [3] See p. 84.
[4] *Encyclopaedia of the Laws of Scotland, s.v.* Precedence, pars. 22-24.
[5] Lyon Register, 11 May 1948, xxxvi, 136; Precedence Warrant, 22 December 1952.

PLATE XLIV

The Great Seal for use in Scotland—as depicted on the reverse of the seal, prepared on the accession of Edward VII, and used for subsequent reigns. Designed at the sight of the Lord Lyon, in Lyon Office, by J. R. Sutherland, assistant Herald Painter, and engraved in Edinburgh by Alexr. Kirkwood and Sons.

Had the post-Union Great Seals for Scotland not been designed in Lyon Office (it being part of the Lord Lyon's functions in relation to the Royal arms to see this done) it seems unlikely that the Scottish quartering would have survived. (*Cf. Heraldry in Scotland*, p. 400.)

PLATE XLV

The Royal Arms of Great Britain, achievement as officially used in Scotland.

Quarterly, 1st and 4th, the Royal Arms of Scotland; 2nd, the Royal Arms of England; 3rd, the Royal Arms of Ireland; around the shield is the collar of The Most Ancient and Most Noble Order of the Thistle.

Crest—On an Imperial crown proper, a lion sejeant gules, armed and langned azure, holding in dexter paw a sword and in his sinister paw a sceptre, both proper, and in an escrol over the same this motto, " In Defens ".

Supporters—On a compartment, with this motto, " Nemo Me Impune Lacessit ", are set, dexter, the unicorn, crowned, and, sinister, the lion gardant, the former sustaining a banner emblazoned azure a saltire argent, the latter argent a cross gules.

" The ruddy lion ramping in his field of tressured gold "
has been the Royal Arms, or " Ensigns of Dominion and
Sovereignty " of the Kings of Scotland, since the days of

FIG. 99.—Royal Arms of Scotland; 16th century achievement
drawn in the reign of James V.

Alexander II, and probably even of William the Lion; that
is to say, it indicates the authority of the Scottish Government, vested in the King of Scots as *pater patriae*. Since
the Union of the Crowns, it has been quartered with the arms
of England and Ireland, but north of the Border the tressured
lion always occupies the first and fourth quarters of the shield.
In addition to this quartered version of the Royal Arms, the

tressured lion still retains its individual status as a sovereign coat of arms, and there are still many occasions on which both shield and crest are officially employed. Our Kings have carefully preserved the sacred character of the emblem of Scottish sovereignty, and at the institution of the Public Register of All Arms and Bearings in 1672, Charles II, who (along with his brother, the Duke of Albany and York) set his subjects a good example by obtempering the Statute himself, "gave in" not only the quartered Royal shield,[1] but also the Tressured Lion Rampant with its Unicorn Supporters and Lion Crest, which therefore stands recorded in Lyon Register as the exclusive property of the Sovereign.[2] About the close of the nineteenth century ignorant

FIG. 100.—Banner of the King of Scots.

---

[1] Lyon Register, i, 18.

[2] Lyon Register, i, 14. The banner in the Royal achievement is here expressly registered as "A banner, charged with the Royal Armes of Scotland", which are on the same page blazoned, Or, a lion rampant within a double tressure flory counterflory gules. The sinister banner is merely blazoned, Azure, a St Andrew's Cross argent. These descriptions, recorded by the Crown in 1672, carefully guard against the principle subsequently determined in *Stewart-Mackenzie* v. *Fraser-Mackenzie*, that "exterior ornaments" may be registered for more than one party whilst arms cannot. The lion is thus deliberately blazoned in terms which fix it individually upon the Crown, whilst the description of the St Andrew's flag is significantly in terms which do not conflict with the registration thereof in name of the Nation on p. 20 of the Public Register.

tradesmen began selling cheap and usually hideously proportioned versions of the Scottish Royal Banner under the trade
description of " Scotch Standard ".[1] No subject would have
dreamt of displaying such a flag in the Middle Ages, and so
late as George IV's visit in 1822, contemporary drawings
show that no such flag was used in decorative schemes,
though there is nothing in the Law of Arms to prevent any
coat of arms being used as a unit in a decorative scheme,[2]
so long as it is attributed *to its proper legal owner*, and is not
" brought into contempt ", or authority suggested,[3] and the
owner does not interfere.[4] When the Royal Lion is flown as a
flag, or in place of the Scottish National Flag, St Andrew's
Cross, a statutory offence is committed against the ordinary

[1] A " Standard " is a long, narrow, tapering flag, upon which the badge is the
principle feature (see p. 43) and the Royal Standard was 11 yards long.

[2] The Police Circulars of 1907, Nos. 512 and 520, legally refer *only* to use of
this nature. See Hansard, 4th ser., vol. 178, p. 544 ; *Scots Year-Book* for 1928–9,
p. 55 ; Lyon Office Circular, 19 June 1933 ; and Hansard, 6 July 1933. By
Royal Warrant, 3 September 1934, permission is granted for H.M.'s *loyal* subjects
to display the flag *as a mark of loyalty to the Sovereign*. This is, in legal technique,
decorative ebullition and does not cover *other* uses. (Cf. Nisbet, *Heraldry*, ii,
iii, 69.) The warrant actually contravened the Decl. of Rights, 1695.

[3] *Royal Warrantholders* v. *Alexander*, Lyon Court, 21 March 1933. There
is no distinction between using arms on a shield or on a flag—" a banner charged
with " is the technical description, and cf. St. John Hope at p. 40, n. 5, *supra*, and
Nisbet's *Heraldry*, i, i, " of use ", " also upon banners and pennons from whence
they (*armorial bearings*) are called armorial ensigns ". The position of the
1834 Warrant is that the Crown, not being mentioned in the " whosoever shall
use " clause of 1672, cap. 47, is in regard to its *own* arms entitled by Warrant to
constitute an extended latitude (so long as it does not alienate) its Ensigns of Public
Authority—here for a supposed regal purpose of fostering ebullitions of " loyalty " ;
whereas an armigerous subject could not grant, or any subject's permittee exercise,
such a latitude regarding subject's-arms without infringment of the " use " clause.

Display of a banner as a house-flag, or otherwise as (*e.g.* a carried company-flag)
a mark of identification (which is the *normal* and *assumed* purpose of displaying a
banner), is the antithesis of display as a " mark of loyalty ", which imports the
display will be clearly related to the regal-owner and not in any manner where,
in the Law of Arms, identity or Lieutenancy would be inferrable.

[4] That is as regards *appropriate* display. This does not apply to irregular or
unnatural " use ", nor to use of arms for " wear " or to any unwarrantable display
legally inferring " use ". (Cf. Coronation Decorations rule, 27 April 1952.)

Parliamentary Law of Scotland,[1] as well as a piece of heraldic bad taste. The Scottish Lord-Lieutenants in their official capacity, and a few Great Officers who are *ex officio* the Queen's Lieutenants,[2] are entitled to " display the Queen's Banner ", and it is in this capacity [3] that the Secretary of State, as Lord Keeper of the Great Seal of Scotland, is entitled to fly the Tressured Lion over the Scottish Office in Whitehall.

The Lieutenants, on whom, in commissions, this right of displaying the King's Banner was conferred by the clause *vexillum Nostrum gerendi*, treated the flag with the utmost solemnity. When at sunrise the tressured lion was hoisted before the Lord-Lieutenant's pavilion, it was greeted by a salute of trumpets,[4] and such a salute it was, in 1645, that first warned Argyll that Montrose, the King's Lieutenant, had crossed the hills and descended upon Inverlochy.

Usurpation of the Royal Arms or Banner still legally renders the offender liable to the capital penalty,[5] and momentous consequences can still arise out of irregular display of the Royal Flag.[6]

[1] 1672, cap. 47 ; Acts, viii, 95.

[2] *I.e.* the Regent, if any ; the Lord High Commissioner ; the Lord President of the Council, *i.e.* the Lord High Chancellor or Keeper of the Great Seal ; the Lord Wardens of the Marches ; the Lord Lyon King of Arms ; and other lieutenants specially appointed (Denmiln MSS. Nat. Lib. 34-11-7).

[3] Similarly it was as " Guardian of the Realm " that Sir William Wallace used this flag in 1297, and he expressly describes it as *vexillum regium*, " the flag of the Sovereignty " (*Scots Peerage*, iii, 304).

[4] At Highland Gatherings the tressured lion flag is similarly hoisted with fanfare when the Lord-Lieutenant of the county attends. The local chief's *own* banner is likewise hoisted with a fanfare and bagpipe *failte*, when such chief comes on the gathering-ground.

[5] Ordinance, 28 February 1558–9, *Liber Curiarum* of Lord Lyon Forman of Luthrie ; Lord Advocate Mackenzie, *Works*, ii, 583.

[6] Sir Frederick Ponsonby, *Sidelights on Queen Victoria*, cap. i, " The Fatal Gun ".

THE SCOTTISH NATIONAL
FLAG

The Scottish National
Flag and Arms, so defined
by Act of Parliament,[1] are
Azure, a saltire argent, and
this is recorded in Lyon
Register,[2] pursuant to 1672,
cap. 47, as the " Armes or
Badge " proper and peculiar
to the Kingdom of Scotland.
This national badge, " the
Silver Cross to Scotland
dear ", is traditionally said
to have been instituted by
Achaius, King of the Picts
(really Angus II, who
actually did introduce the
veneration of St Andrew).
The Cross of St Andrew is
the flag which any Scotsman
is entitled to fly, or wear as
a badge,[3] as evidence of his
national identity or patriot-

[1] Acts, vol. vi, pt. ii, p. 817.
[2] Lyon Register, i, 20.
[3] Statute of 1388, Acts, i, 555;
1672, cap. 47; *Historical Account of
the Royal Visit*, 1822, p. 90.

FIG. 101.—The Scottish National Flag,
St Andrew's Cross, supported by a
Scottish soldier wearing the St Andrew's
(Scottish National) badge.

ism.[1] This is also the proper flag to fly on Scottish churches, and corresponds to St George's Cross in England, to the Red Dragon in Wales, and St Patrick's Cross in Ireland.[2]

THE SCOTTISH NATIONAL BADGE

Just as a Sovereign kingdom requires both Ensigns of Dominion and Sovereignty (viz. the Tressured Lion), and a National Flag (viz. St Andrew's Cross), so it is usually considered necessary to have a National *Badge* for wear in bonnets or as a brooch or jewel. The Scottish National Badge is a *Thistle* proper, as that of England a Rose, Ireland the Shamrock, and Wales either a Daffodil or a Leek.

This badge may be worn by any Scotsman, and when any of these badges are used in an official capacity, they are ensigned with the Crown. The *Crowned Thistle or*, and *a Rose gules, crowned or*, are Royal badges. [3]

OTHER ROYAL ARMS CONNECTED WITH SCOTLAND

The arms of *Nova Scotia* [4] are *Argent, a saltire Azure, an inescutcheon of the Royal Arms of Scotland*. These are presumably the " Ensigns of Dominion " of the Government of Nova Scotia, and no doubt the St Andrew's Cross, on a white flag with a blue saltire, was intended to be the National Flag of the Province.

The arms of the Kingdom of the Isle of Man, *Gules, three armed legs, flexed, conjoined proper*, are still quartered

---

[1] Scotland's Sovereign Banner, *Scots Year-Book*, 1928–9, p. 55 ; W. Macmillan *Scottish Symbols* ; W. Macmillan and J. A. Stewart, *The Story of the Scottish Flag*.

[2] The " Ensigns of Dominion and Sovereignty " of All Ireland are Azure, a harp or, stringed argent.

[3] Lyon Register, i, 20.   [4] *Ibid.*, i, 485.

Royal Thistle ⁘
⁘ Badge

Royal Saltire ❖
❖ Badge

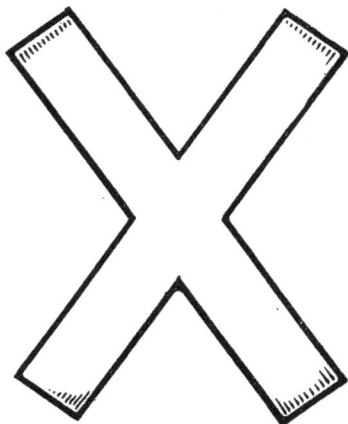

Saltire Badge:
❖ of the Scots

Thistle Floral:
❖ Badge

FIG. 102.—Scottish Badges.

Nos. 1 and 2 are the Royal Badges, Nos. 3 and 4 (the saltire and thistle proper) the badges provided for indicating Scottish identity.

by the Duke of Atholl,[1] who represents the " King of Man ". This island—still an independent State—was formerly under the suzerainty of the King of Scots.   Its arms are also quartered by Macleod of Macleod.

Royal Arms in Public Decoration. — People are frequently puzzled to find the Royal Arms prominently displayed in churches, and in country houses (the chief messuage of a feudal barony is technically a " public place "), where they usually appear above one mantelpiece and in some prominent position on the outer walls to indicate a Crown vassal, and above or opposite the pulpit or upon the spires of churches. The reason for this display is that every national church was, in the Middle Ages, required to display the arms of the Sovereign State within which it was situated—maybe to counterbalance tacitly the claims of spiritual sovereignty made by the Roman See.[2]   The *flag* to be flown on a church displays, however, the badge of the nation's patron saint—in Scotland, of course, the Cross of St Andrew.

FIG. 103.—Arms of Nova Scotia, as carved on the Scottish National War Memorial.

[1] Fig. 16 (*a*), p. 49.
[2] Mackenzie, *Works*, ii, 577, sec. 17.

PLATE XLVI

Extract of Matriculation and Confirmation of Arms and Chiefship to Duncan Alexander Mackintosh of Clan Chattan, as 31st Hereditary Chief of Clan Chattan. 9th April 1947, *Lyon Register*, xxxvi. 36. See 1950 *Scots Law Times*, p. 5; Lyon Court Reports.

Domestic Architecture.—It was the ordinary rule to display the arms of the feudal superior *above* the arms of the actual owner [1] over the principal gate or doorway and over the most important fireplace (see p. 171), consequently the Royal Arms are frequently found decorating the Castles of the Scots Baronage. This use of the Royal Arms is strictly correct, but only competent where the owner of the building holds his land as a Crown vassal—even these, no doubt as a precaution against a charge of " usurpation ", not infrequently labelled the Royal Shield, *arma regis* (arms of the King), as, for example, on one of the carved bosses of the vaulted hall (*circa* 1593) at Towie-Barclay Castle in Aberdeenshire.

"Royal" Institutions.—Certain institutions which have obtained permission from the Crown to use the word " Royal " in their title, immediately assume that they have authority to display either a crown or the whole Royal Arms. This belief is erroneous, and bodies such as the Royal High School, Royal Burgess Golfing Society, and even the Royal Company of Archers, have been compelled to take out individual coats of arms.[2] Nor has one Royal institution in Scotland yet been given *permission* to display a *crown*.[3] If arms other than the Silver Cross of St Andrew, the Union Jack, or the St George's Cross of England are to be used on the badge, it must be the individual registered coat of arms of the institution concerned. The Royal Arms indicate the Crown and its public authority, and no body which is not part of the national machinery of government, or a Royal tradesman " By Appointment ", has any right to display the Royal Arms, and the offence of doing so is dealt with either

---

[1] Bartolus a Saxaferrato, see *Heraldry in Scotland*, p. 26 ; Ferne, *Glorie of Generositie*, p. 268.

[2] Lyon Register, xxiv, 71 ; *ibid.*, xxix, 7 ; *ibid.*, xviii, 24, 5 March 1905.

[3] The Royal Automobile Club and Royal Scottish Automobile Club badges are excellent examples of the correct use of the national device in effective individual styles, but the latter had recently to be stopped *starting* a crown !

Q

through the Royal Warrantholders' Association,[1] or the Procurator-Fiscal of the Lyon Court, the penalty actually

FIG. 104.—The Sovereign Achievement (Royal Arms) of Scotland
(Lyon Reg., i, p. 14).

imposed (under the Statutes of 1672 and 1867) being £8 6s. 8d. and expenses for each offence, and confiscation [2] of articles whereon the arms have been depicted.

[1] *Warrantholders* v. *Alexander & Co.*, 21 March 1933 (*Scotsman*, 22 March).

[2] In Lyon Court, 1592, cap. 125, cf. Interdict in Court of Session, *Warrantholders* v. *Robb*, 1 March 1935, through not delivering to the lay-complainer dies, etc., which they should have asked as essential to make the decree effective; unlike the Procurator-Fiscal (for the Crown) the *Warrantholders per se* may not have seemed entitled to " delivery ".

CHAPTER XVII

CORPORATION HERALDRY

ROM the earliest times heraldry has been used not only by individuals but by corporate bodies, and of recent years this branch of the science has attained much greater importance, especially in Scotland, where corporations appreciate the statutory and common law security enjoyed by armorial bearings in Scotland, for there would be little use possessing a coat of arms if it could not be protected from misappropriation. Even before the foundation of the Lyon Register, the Lord Lyon had jurisdiction over corporate arms.[1] When the Public Register of All Arms and Bearings was instituted, a special division was set apart for the arms of corporations, and in 1680 the Royal Burgh of *Jedburgh* was compelled not only to register arms, but to discontinue a shield which it had invented in 1650.[2] All the Burghs were enjoined to obey the Statutes,[3] and most of those which then had arms did so.

LORD FORRESTER OF CORSTORPHINE.

---

[1] *City of Aberdeen*, 1637, *Spalding Club Miscellany*, v, 151.
[2] *Jedburgh* Burgh Records, 13 March 1680, and Lyon Register, i, 459.
[3] J. D. Marwick, *Records of Convention of Royal Burghs*, ii, 635, 665.

Of course there were several who neglected to obey the Statute. In 1732, the *City of Edinburgh* [1] itself was prosecuted, and registered its arms; and in 1909 *Dunfermline* [2]

FIG. 105.—THE ROYAL BURGH OF ELIE AND EARLSFERRY. Quarterly: 1st and 4th, gules, on the waves of the sea in base undy argent and azure, an ancient one-masted ship in full sail or, flying the Scottish pennon, and the mainsail charged with (the arms of *Macduff, Earl of Fife*) a lion rampant of the field, armed and langued of the third; 2nd and 3rd, vert, an ancient one-masted ship in full sail, oars in action, or, flying the Scottish pennon, and on the mainsail the arms of *Scott of Grangemuir*, viz., or, on a bend azure, between two crescents of the field, a mullet argent. A bordure engrailed gules. *Motto*—" Unitas alit Comitatem, 1589 and 1598 ".

obtempered the law after the Lord Advocate had instructed prosecution of the Town Council. The arms of Scottish burghs are ensigned with a " burghal coronet "—a mural crown proper.[3] During the years 1916–30 practically every corporate body in Scotland, municipal or commercial, known to be using arms, was, on instructions of H.M. Treasury, compelled to obtemper the law.[4] Numerous insurance and commercial firms have also recorded arms voluntarily; others have been obliged to conform. The *Northern Assurance Co. Ltd.*, having a double domicile, was obliged to rematriculate in Lyon Register arms which it had been granted in England; [5]

[1] Lyon Register, i, 455.

[2] 12 May 1909, Lyon Register, xx, 35.

[3] Application for a non-burghal circlet for " honest " touns is under consideration and may be a crown vallery in some specific tincture, whilst such a crown Vert, its points alternated with garbs Or, has been granted for a County Council circlet, *Kirkcudbright*, 1952 (Lyon Register, xxxviii, 139).

[4] See p. 82 above. In some cases the investigation of claims to ancient arms took considerable time to adjust, *e.g. Forfar's* claim was not settled until 31 May 1948, Lyon Register, xxxvi, 138.

[5] 27 May 1930, *ibid.*, xxix, 20.

and amongst numerous other recent examples, the *Clyde &*
Mersey Investment Trust,[1] and the *Royal (Dick) Veterinary*
College,[2] which had " assumed unto themselves " bogus
arms, were obliged to obtemper the law.[3]

Some arms recently granted to Scottish corporate bodies
are fine examples of heraldic design. Amongst such may be
included that of the
General Accident, Fire
& Life Assurance Co.
Ltd.,[4] based on those of
the City of Perth,[5] and
the crest suitably alludes
to the arms of the Earl
of Airlie, one of the
Directors.

Armorial Trade-
marks.[6]—In the Middle
Ages, merchants were

FIG. 106.—Union Bank of Scotland (Lyon Reg.,
xxxvi, p. 68).

forbidden to use armorial bearings as trade-marks, but
firms which have been unable to obtain Royal Warrants or
other " distinguished patronage " attempt to hoodwink their
customers by the use of heraldic trade-marks, for which the
laxness of English heraldic law has given opportunity.

In Scotland the law is different, and the registration of
unwarrantable heraldic trade-marks in defraud of the
Treasury and to the confusion of the public has now been
stopped, as the Registrar submits such applications to the
Lord Lyon. Whilst the use of such heraldic trade-marks is

[1] 15 February 1930, *ibid.*, xxix, 2; *Rintoul*, 26 May 1948, *ibid.*, xxxvii, 4;
Ballantyne, xxxviii, 49.
[2] 12 January 1913, *ibid.*, xxix, 59.
[3] Marquess of Bute, *Arms of Royal and Parliamentary Burghs*, p. 208,
contained many illegal arms now stopped, superseded, or matriculated.
[4] Lyon Register, xxix, 64.   [5] *Ibid.*, i, 455.
[6] *Encyclopaedia of the Laws of Scotland*, *s.v.* Heraldry, par. 1400.

Q 2

deprecated in Scotland, the *owner* of a Scots coat of arms duly recorded in Lyon Register is entitled to use *his* arms in that way if he wishes, and register it as his trade-mark. Continental nobles make a lavish use of their arms in labelling the wines and other products of their estates, and one accordingly finds even the crowned escutcheon of such magnates as *Prince Windischgrätz* on wine-labels from his Hungarian estates. If, however, the " arms " are not actually *his own* property, it is a statutory offence under 1672, cap. 47, either to use or to put the device forward for registration under the Trade-marks Acts.[1] In such cases registration is now refused, or, if actually made, can be cancelled ; [2] *e.g.* A. & A. Crawford, whose application to register the Earl of Crawford's arms as a trade-mark was refused,[3] and their subsequent use of these arms was stopped by Lyon Court. The firm then petitioned for and obtained a coat of arms of its own.[4] If the " armorial trade-mark " is thereafter to be transferred, the right to the arms in it must also be conveyed [5] by resignation *in favorem*,[6] and transfer is subject to Lyon's confirmation, otherwise chaos would arise regarding such " property ".

An erroneous impression seems often to exist, that a device is not a " coat of arms " unless it appears on a shield. " Many people have thought to evade the authority of the Crown and the taxation imposed by the Revenue by using heraldic designs without depicting them on a shield." Arms, however, can be " depicted on a banner, a parallelogram, a

[1] Trade-marks Act, 1905, sec. 11 ; *Warrantholders* v. *Alexander & Co.*, 21 March 1933, Lyon Court (*Scotsman*, 22 March).

[2] Trade-marks Act, 1905, sec. 41. *Tullis Russell & Co.*, 1947, cancellation of the assumed trade-mark enforced before a grant of arms was considered, Lyon Register, xxxvi, 31. [3] Trade-marks Application, No. 29830.

[4] Lyon Register, xxix, 3. See also *Rintoul*, 27 April 1948, Lyon Register, xxxvii, 4, and 1951 Scots Law Times (Lyon Court Reports), p. 12.

[5] See *Scottish Notes & Queries*, 1933, p. 188.

[6] Cf. *Scott of Synton*, Lyon Register, ii, 189 ; *Grant of Auchernack, ibid.*, i, 505.

square, a circle or an oval ", or any of the numerous fancy forms of cartouche,[1] and have been so displayed from the earliest days of the science. In Scotland, whether a device is, or is not, a *coat of arms* is simply a question of legal fact in which the Lord Lyon is Judge of first instance, and many firms have been compelled to abandon devices which constituted a breach of the Law. Putting a device on a shield almost always makes a " coat of arms "—even if a bad one !

In Scotland, as in the wine-growing districts of France and Spain, Lairds have used their arms as marks for the produce of their estates—a proper feudal use, and a practical ground for the protection of Armory.[2]

Club Badges, etc.—Queries are often received as to what form of badge may be used by Sports Clubs and other Associations under the patronage of some local magnate or Council. Obviously the arms of the patron or superior cannot be appropriated, and it is a statutory offence for him to " grant permission ", or otherwise condone the assumption of his own arms, in defraud of the Treasury fees which would be exigible if the Association itself applied to Lyon for a grant.

If armorial bearings are to be used at all, the Club must petition for a grant of arms,[3] costing £59, when some version of the superior's arms, suitably differenced, is usually assigned.

---

[1] *Art of Heraldry*, p. 36.

[2] An early and celebrated instance is that of Christian Shaw of Bargarran, heretrix of that house, who advertised in 1725, " The Lady Bargarran and her daughters having attained to a great perfection in making . . . thread . . . to prevent people being imposed upon by other thread which may be sold under the name of Bargarran thread, the papers in which the Lady Bargarran and her daughters . . . do put up their thread shall . . . have thereupon the above coat of arms (*Azure, three covered cups Or*). Those who wish the said thread may write to *The Lady Bargarran, at Bargarran.*" (Chambers, *Domestic Annals*, i, 511.) This also illustrates the correct form of addressing a Laird's wife.

[3] *Queen's Park Football Club*, Glasgow, 28 December 1929, Lyon Register, xxviii, 72 ; *Scottish Bowling Association*, 13 December 1953, *ibid.*, xxxix, 124.

A cheaper and more satisfactory plan for smaller Associations which do not wish to apply for arms is to devise a non-heraldic badge. For this purpose the simplest and most historically correct course is to make the basis of the badge a round disc of the superior's livery colours (these are normally the colours of his wreath), parted per pale, and across this to display his motto, or *cri de guerre*, upon a scroll. The name of the Institution should then appear on a circlet or strap and buckle.[1] Such a livery badge will infringe no statutes, involve no licence duty, and yet be usually consistent with the rules of badges and liveries.

Where a municipal corporation is in right of armorial bearings, these may, since 1929, be used as the badge of all schools under control of that corporation's Education Authority. Where any particular school or other corporation department desires a distinctive device, a differenced version of the corporation arms may be matriculated in name of such school or department.[2] Similarly, masonic lodges dependent on Grand Lodge of Scotland [3] matriculate differenced versions of the arms of Grand Lodge itself.

When two armigerous corporations are amalgamated, the combined corporation is regarded as " heir " of both, and may, by rematriculation, obtain a quarterly achievement of both the former armorial bearings.[4]

[1] In England, the " garter " is of course not admissible, but that restriction does not apply to the "belt and buckle" in Scotland, unless the motto appropriate to any Order of Chivalry were inscribed upon it.

[2] *Portobello High School*, 21 January 1933, Lyon Register, xxx, 46; *Elgin Academy*, 31 March 1933, *ibid.*, xxx, 53.

[3] *Grand Lodge of Scotland*, Lyon Register, xxvii, 62; and cadets, *Provincial Grand Lodge of Argyll and the Isles*, 21 February 1929, *ibid.*, xxviii, 21; *Lodge Prince of Wales*, 18 May 1931, *ibid.*, xxix, 76.

[4] *North of Scotland and Town and County Bank*, 20 May 1908, Lyon Register, xix, 74 (amalgamating the *North of Scotland Bank*, Lyon Register, vi, 73, and the *Town and County Bank*, Lyon Register, vi, 89); *Royal Burgh of Elie and Earlsferry*, 1930, *ibid.*, xxix, 32.

CHAPTER XVIII

ARMORIAL BEARINGS AS AN INVESTMENT

LTHOUGH arms are in the nature of Honours, since they have been held by our law courts to be a piece of " undoubted property ",[1] and " a question of property which may be vindicated and protected ",[2] there is no reason why that property should not have a financial value. Even a peerage-dignity in the Middle Ages, *e.g.* a territorial earldom or, in its later English form, the comital grant of the " third penny of the Shire ", had an acknowledged cash value, so why not a coat of arms ? In the case of the individual, as well as in some of the older and greater corporations, the principal value of ensigns armorial is no doubt genealogical and historical, but, like any other " estate "—and certainly in connection with one—the arms of the Laird or Lady can have a business value in connection with fruit and other estate-produce, just as the feudal arms of Continental magnates

KEITH, EARL MARISCHAL. Argent, on a chief gules, three pallets or.

[1] Per Lord Robertson in *Macdonell* v. *Macdonald*, 1826, 4 Shaw & Dunlop, 371.
[2] Per Lord Justice-Clerk in *Stewart-Mackenzie* v. *Fraser-Mackenzie*, 1920 S.C., 764 at p. 791.

appear on the wine-bottle labels of " Châteaux " clarets, made upon their estates. Corporate heraldry has also advanced by leaps and bounds, and in the case of many trading corporations and public schools armorial bearings have not only a definite utility value, but in many cases actually *earn for their owner a regular annual income*, like those of the vineyard-owning feudal magnates, so that the initial registration fee proves not an outlay but a remunerative investment. This is due to Scottish armorial bearings being protected by law, and the mercantile community has quickly appreciated that it is a sound reason for enforcing that protection. The Procurator-Fiscal will, on behalf of H.M. Treasury, prohibit the use of unregistered arms, or the attribution of registered arms to other than the registered owner. No infringement of the Crown's prerogative takes place merely by depicting a coat of arms for its obvious purpose of designating its registered owner (*e.g.* in a *relevant* book illustration, record, or memorial—so long as that owner acquiesces. The arms, however, being the exclusive [1] *property* of that owner, he is entitled to say when or where, and whether, his property shall be displayed at all. He can, if necessary, interdict a person from making free with his ensigns armorial, even if no damage should result. If, however, a person displays the ensigns armorial of another, thereby " hindering a man in the use of what is his own ", or even by " wearing a mark of honour which belongs to another ", both Mackenzie of Rosehaugh,[2] Lord Advocate, and Erskine [3] lay down that a " real injury " is committed under the Common Law of Scotland. Erskine points out that whilst real injuries of this nature,[4] including ordinary slander, are no longer in Scotland regarded as a crime at

---

[1] Save as set forth on p. 227, and cf. pp. 232-3. [2] *Works*, ii, 170.
[3] *Principles of the Law of Scotland*, bk. iv, tit. 4, sec. 45.
[4] Where not amounting to *crimen falsi, i.e.* forgery.

Common Law,[1] they still infer *liability for damages in a civil action*.[2]   In a number of cases, steps have been taken, through the Lyon Office, to stop abuse or injury of this very nature, and proceedings could, if necessary, be taken either in Lyon Court or before any Judge Ordinary.[3]   Such complaints most usually arise as follows :

A school or corporation having obtained a registered coat of arms, at a cost of £59 or so, grants to some firm, upon a commission basis, the exclusive right of making and vending garments, caps, blazers, etc., depicting the corporation's arms, for the use of its members.   From this source, the owner of the arms obtains a steady revenue.   Sometimes another firm attempts to manufacture in opposition—free of commission—or to undersell, when the owner of the arms suffers not merely a technical legal " injury ", but actual financial loss.   In every case of complaint, steps have been successfully taken to stop this form of interfering with an armigerous owner's " use " of his heraldic property.

Another time-honoured commercial employment of personal arms is in the well-known Inn Sign and relative hotel names, such as " Kilmarnock Arms ".   This originated in the banner of a noble being hung outside the inn which he patronised in town, but presently these signs were found in almost every country village where the local hostelry maintained by the feudal magnate displayed his arms, which served as a guarantee of the standing and respectability of the establishment.   Consequently, " mine host " increases

---

[1] The use of " unwarrantable arms " is, however, both a common law and a statutory offence (see p. 82) and punishable under that category ; *Macrae's Trustees* v. *Lord Lyon King of Arms*, 4 June 1926 ; 1927 Scots Law Times, p. 285; *Fiscal of Lyon Court* v. *Scottish Watchmakers' and Jewellers' Association*, 18 January 1954.

[2] Erskine's *Principle of the Law of Scotland* (21st ed.), pp. 752, 754.

[3] *Privy Council*, 2nd ser., vi, 392, but where any question involving right to the arms arises, the Lyon Court alone has jurisdiction (*Macdonell* v. *Macdonald*, 1826, 4 Shaw & Dunlop, p. 371) and can " replegiate " all heraldic cases.

his business, and the Laird obtains a better rent for his hostelry (see *The Coat of Arms*, July 1952).

Chiefs and Chieftains have now become careful about the display of their arms and crests—the machinery for leading their clans and families. Like schools, they insist on contracts with specific firms, a nominal commission (which is devoted to the expenses of efficient exercise of chiefship) and their interests are watched by the *Standing Council of Scottish Chiefs*, 18 Duke Street, Edinburgh.

Where the strap and buckle badge is shown on note-paper of Clan Societies, or clansfolk's wearing apparel, the words *Cirean Ceann Cinnidh* are required to appear to prevent assertions that it is " the clan's badge " and so on.[1]

Similarly, though no financial consideration arises, the permission to display the Royal Arms, " By Appointment ", is a valuable privilege, and just as fashionable firms display foreign, royal, or princely achievements, there is neither a legal nor a social impropriety if a peer or magnate elects to confer upon a tradesman the privilege of displaying his arms, " By Appointment ", implying genuine patronage of his establishment, and that no question arises of a *right* being created to use of the patron's arms.[2]

The " owner " of a private company has been allowed to issue a " redeemable " conveyance of a version of his arms (to be differenced by Lyon) and on this a defeasible grant was made to the private company.[3] The purpose of this patent was to enable the operator of a private company to enjoy through it the same use of arms as foreign princely wine-growers do. The " redeemable " clause illustrates the

[1] Innes of Learney, *Clans, Septs, and Regiments of the Scottish Highlands*, 1952 ed., p. 488 ; *i.e.* other than the strap and buckle *brooch*.

[2] The magnate may exact such remunerative terms as he pleases from the firm for the " privilege " of receiving his Appointment.

[3] *Rintoul*, 22 November 1948, Lyon Register, xxxvii, 41 ; 1950, Scots Law Times, p. 12.

applicability to arms of such provisions in older armorial deeds.[1]

It is, of course, a statutory offence to authorise anyone to use *your* arms as *their* arms, when they ought to have applied for a grant of their own. Several Scottish magnates who have carelessly given " permission to use " their arms have had this brought to their notice in recent years, and were glad to withdraw the permission before proceedings were instituted by the Fiscal for conspiring to defraud H.M. Treasury of £59 or thereby.

Since, in several of the appeals to the Higher Courts, the Bench, though unanimously admitting the competency of the proceedings, has sometimes expressed the notion that the Laws of Arms have " little to do with the serious realities of life ",[2] it has seemed as necessary as it is desirable to point out that this form of " undoubted property " has, or can have, that *cash value* which at once inspires the sympathetic attention of any British tribunal. In the last such case which came before the Higher Courts,[3] when the subject at issue was essentially the liability for fees due to H.M. Treasury, there was—both from Bench and Bar—a significant and complete absence of these banal allusions to " the barren honours of Heraldry ".[4]

[1] *Myreton of Cambo*, conveyance of arms, *Scottish Notes & Queries*, 1935, p. 187 ; cf. *Earldom of Lauderdale, Scots Peerage*, v, 304.

[2] The magnate may exact such remunerative terms as he pleases for the " privilege " of receiving his Appointment; and to use the privilege without the words " by appointment " or " under patronage ", or to attempt to register the arms depicted under the *privilege*, is fraudulent and renders the perpetrator liable to both penalty and damages.

[3] Per Lord Sumner, at p. 52, *Stewart-Mackenzie* v. *Fraser-Mackenzie*, 1922 S.C. (H.L.), 52.

[4] *Macrae's Trustees* v. *Lord Lyon King of Arms*, 14 June 1926 ; 1927 Scots Law Times, p. 285.

CHAPTER XIX

GUIDE TO FURTHER STUDY OF
SCOTTISH HERALDRY

SINCLAIR, EARL OF CAITHNESS. Quarterly: 1st (*Orkney*); 2nd and 3rd (*Sperra - Nithsdale*) ; 4th (*Caithness*): over all a cross engrailed, quarterly argent and gules (*Sinclair*).

HEN the development of Scottish Heraldry, as a branch of the Civil Law, was being cultivated in the fifteenth and early sixteenth centuries, Lord Lyon Sir William Cumming of Inverallochy based his judicial proceedings upon the works of Bartolus a Saxaferrato, of which a special transcript was made for Cumming's use.[1] These authors expressed the contemporary international Law of Arms, as accepted in the countries which drew their jurisprudence from the Roman Law, and apart from Gilbert of the Haye's translation of Bartolus made in 1456, two centuries passed before an individual Scottish writer treated of the Laws of Heraldry, as developed in the Case-law of Lyon Court and the legislation by which the Civil Law of Arms was amplified in Scotland. Of our

[1] British Museum, Harleian MSS. 6149; also Nat. Lib. MSS. 31-6-5; *Heraldry in Scotland*, p. 25. *The Boke of St. Alban's* was also received.

ancient institutional writers, there are only two : [1] the celebrated Sir George Mackenzie of Rosehaugh, whose *Science
of Heraldry*, published in 1680, was written prior to 1672,[2]
and Alexander Nisbet, who compiled the compendious
System of Heraldry in two volumes. The latter is still the
most detailed work on Scottish Heraldry, and a mine of
information, whilst Sir George Mackenzie of Rosehaugh's
Science of Heraldry has been declared authoritative.[3] Nisbet,
though more detailed, is less clear and objective than
Mackenzie. Both these works are indispensable to the
serious student.

George Seton's *Law and Practice of Heraldry in Scotland*
has now been replaced for practical purposes by the beautiful
Heraldry in Scotland of J. H. Stevenson, Marchmont
Herald (1914). Much more, however, has been discovered
since 1914, and fresh " case-law " accumulated from decisions
in Lyon Court or on appeal to the Court of Session and
House of Lords. Later information regarding the law and
practice of Scottish Heraldry has been embodied in this
book itself, and in more legal aspect will also be found
(though now in several respects superseded by later research
and decision) in the new edition of Green's *Encyclopaedia
of the Laws of Scotland*, under the headings : Heraldry,
Lyon King of Arms, Name and Change of Name, Precedence, where the jurisdiction and practice of the Court of
the Lord Lyon is explained in some detail, with references
to the latest judicial decisions, also in *Sources and Literature*

---

[1] The Lord Lyon stopped publication of heraldic books calculated to circulate
bogus arms, *e.g.* suppression 16 March 1772 of proposed new edition of Nisbet's
Heraldry (*Heraldry in Relation to Scots History and Art*, p. 108). This was
eventually issued in 1816 and criticisms of part iii fully warrant the step taken by
Lyon in 1772 (Ross and Grant, *Nisbet's Heraldic Plates*, xxxix-xlv).

[2] It is most easily accessible in Mackenzie's *Complete Works*, ii, 574.

[3] Lord Justice Clerk in *Maclean of Ardgour* v. *Maclean*, 1941 S.C., except, of
course, in so far as any statements made as before 1672 are affected by 1672, cap.
47, etc., or subsequent Acts of Parliament or Ordinances of Lyon Court.

of the Law of Scotland (Stair Society), *s.v.* HERALDRY and PEERAGE LAW.

The following list of works will be useful to those who wish to make a deeper study of Scottish Heraldry :

ANCIENT AUTHORITIES (still of frequent value)

Mackenzie of Rosehaugh, Sir George, *Science of Herauldrie*, 1680. (*Complete Works*, ii, 574.)

Nisbet, Alexander, *System of Heraldry*, 1816 edition.

Haye, G., *Buke of Lawes of Armys* (Scot. Text edition), p. 277.

GENERAL AUTHORITIES (often incorrect as to Scottish details)

Copinger, W. A., *Heraldry Simplified*, 1910.

Fox-Davies, A. C., *Right to Bear Arms*, 1900; *The Art of Heraldry*, 1904; *Heraldry Explained*, 1908; *Complete Guide to Heraldry*, 1920.

Hope, Sir W. St John, *Heraldry for Craftsmen and Designers*.

Norris, Herbert, *Costume and Fashion, from Senlac to Bosworth*.

Wheeler Holohan, T., *Boutell's Heraldry*, 1931 edition.

Wagner, A. R. (Richmond Herald), *Heralds and Heraldry*, 1939.

MODERN SCOTTISH AUTHORITIES

Encyclopaedia of the Laws of Scotland (1929–32), *s.v.* Heraldry, Lyon King of Arms, Name and Change of Name, Peerage, Precedence.

Grant (Lord Lyon), Sir F. J., *Manual of Heraldry*, 1924; *Memorial Catalogue of the Heraldic Exhibition* (Edinburgh, 1891).

Innes of Learney (Lord Lyon), Sir T., Diploma of Nobility, etc., *Juridical Review*, September 1940, p. 181 ; *Summary of Argument for Miss Mac-lean of Ardgour*, 1938 (limited print, 1945); *Law of Succession in Ensigns Armorial* (Green & Son).[1]

Paul (Lord Lyon), Sir J. Balfour, *Heraldry in Relation to Scottish History and Art* (Edinburgh, 1899).

Robes of the Feudal Baronage of Scotland in *Proc. of Soc. of Antiquaries of Scot.*, vol. 79, p. 111, and *Huntly Processional Roll*, *ibid.*, vol. 77, p. 154.

Seton, G., *Law and Practice of Heraldry*, 1863.

Stevenson (Marchmont Herald), J. H., *Heraldry in Scotland*, 1914.

[1] A number of important articles on the Scottish Law of Arms by Albany Herald, which appeared in *Notes & Queries*, 1939–41, are conveniently indexed by G. T. Cope in *Aslib*, 1948, p. 108.

Moncreiffe of Easter Moncreiffe (Kintyre Pursuivant), I., and Pottinger, D., *Simple Heraldry*, 1952.

SCOTTISH COATS OF ARMS

Fox-Davies, A. C., *Armorial Families* (7th edition, 1929–31).
Lindsay of The Mount (Lord Lyon), Sir David, *Heraldic MSS.*, 1542 (published 1822 and 1878).
Paul (Lord Lyon), Sir J. Balfour, *An Ordinary of Arms in the Lyon Register*, 1903.
Stoddart, R. R., *Scottish Arms*, 1878.
Woodward, J. W., and Burnett, S., *Heraldry, British and Foreign*, 1892.

SCOTTISH FAMILY HISTORY (and Genealogist's Guide)

Innes of Learney (Lord Lyon), Sir T., *Tartans of the Clans and Families of Scotland* (5th ed., 1949). The Introduction is a very detailed exposition of the family and clan organisation in Scotland.
Innes of Learney and Frank Adam, *Clans, Septs, and Regiments of the Scottish Highlands*, 1952 ed. This contains much information on clan and family ceremonial and custom.
M'Kechnie, H., *Pursuit of Pedigree* (ex. *Juridical Review*).
Paul, Sir J. Balfour, *The Scots Peerage*.
Stuart, Margaret, *Scottish Family History*, 1930, a bibliography of family histories and guide to writing such histories.
A History of the Court of the Lord Lyon and biographical account of the successive Lord Lyons is also in preparation; this will add considerably to the information at present available regarding that historic office and the administration of Heraldry in Scotland.

The reader will now have learnt not only the origin, theory, and practice of our Scottish Heraldry, but the services it affords, the manner in which it is used, and the reasons for which it exists. If he would delve deeper into this fascinating study, he has been shown the way to do so effectively. Heraldry is no abstruse or incomprehensible science, but the means through which the history of successive

R

ages and generations is fascinatingly and forcibly linked together. Dates and inscriptions weary the eye and may fade from the memory, but a coat of arms once seen is easily remembered. Once associated with person, place, or event, it is indeed never forgotten. In the glowing pageantry of emblazoned Armory, the annals of Scotland, of its clans, its houses, and its surnames, are written in characters which inspire the mind and thrill the eye, but which above all proclaim our native pride, and the kindly ties of Scottish clanship and kinship.

Scottish Royal Arms
(Elgin Cathedral)

APPENDIX

Acts of Parliament and Council relating to
Administration of Armorial Bearings
1592, c. 125 ; fol. edit. c. 29 (Jac. VI)

Concerning the Office of Lyoun King-of-Armes and his brether Herauldis

Oure Souerane Lord and Estaitis of this present parliament, Considdering the greit abuse that hes bene amongis the leigis of this realme in thair bearing of armes, vsurpand to thame selffis sic armes as belangis nocht vnto thame, sua that it can nocht be distinguischit be thair armes quha ar gentlemen of blude be thair antecessouris, Nor zit may it be decernit quhat gentlemen ar discendit of noble stok [1] and linage, ffor remeid quhairof his hienes, with aduise of the saidis estaitis, hes geuin and grantit, and be this present act gevis and grantis full power and commissioun, to lyoun king-of-armes and his brether herauldis, To visite the haill armes of noblemen, baronis, and gentlemen [2] borne and vsit [3] within this realme, and to distinguische and discerne thame with congruent differences, and thairefter to matriculat tham in thair buikis and Registeris, And to put inhibitioun to all the commoun sort of people nocht worthie be the law of armes to beir ony signes armoriallis, That nane of thame presume to tak vpoun hand to beare or vse ony armes, in tyme cuming, vpoun ony thair insicht or houshald geir, vnder the pane of the escheating [4] of the guidis and geir, sa oft as thay salbe fund

---

[1] Arms are in law evidence of " noble stok " and of " noble linage ", and the Act is *inter alia* to ensure that arms shall continue to be insignia indicating this.

[2] The " gentlemen " may be corporate *personae*, as evidenced by the *contemporanea expositio* and *charge* under the Act given to the Burghs (see p. 223).

[3] " Vsit " was given technical and full import in *MacRae's Trustees* v. *Lord Lyon*, 1927 (see pp. 13, 79), including power to erase and cast down unwarrant arms.

[4] The " escheating " is here (cf. Erskine's *Principles of the Law of Scotland*, II-V, 23) not the (only two) technical " escheats " but is used in the sense of " confiscation ", and a penalty is imposed only when the Fiscal moves for confiscation (*Warrantholders* v. *Alexander*, 1933).

239

contravenand this present act, quhaireuir the same armes salbe found grawin and paintit, to our souerane lordis vse ; And lykwayis vnder the pane of ane hundreth pundis to the vse of the said lyoun [1] and his brether herauldis. And failzeing of payment thairof, That thay be incarcerat in the narrest prissone, Thairin to remane, vpoun thair awin chargis, during the plesour of the said Lyoun.

Item, Because charges of treason hes not bene execute and used, with sik solemnity and Officiares of Armes, as the weichtiness thereof requires : It is statute and ordained that Our Soveraine Lordis Thesaurer, and utheris directers of sik letters, deliver them in time cumming, to be execut be the ordinar Herauldes and Pursevantes, bearand coattes of armes, or Masers, to be used be thame, as of before ; and gif ony execution, under the paine of treason sall be execut utherwaies, declaris the execution to be null, and of nane availe.

Item, In consideration of the great abuse of Messengers and of Officiares of Armes within this Realme, quhilkis for the maist part ar not qualified for using of the said office, being admitted be extraordinar and importune suites, be quhais abuse the Liegis of this Realme ar heavily troubled and oppressed : Therefore it is statute and ordained, that the said King of Armes, be advise of the Lordis of Councell and Session, deprive and discharge all sik Officiares and Messengres of Armes, as he sall finde unworthy of the office, And take sicker soverty of the remanent, for observation of their Injunctiones in time cumming : With power to the said King of Armes, with advise of the saids Lords, to enjoyne further necessar injunctiones to the saids messengers, for keeping of gude ordour in their offices : discharging him in the meantime to admit ony maa officiares hereafter, quhil the haill messengers, presently bearing armes, be reduced be death or deprivation, to the number conteined in the Acte of Parliament, maid anent the confused number of officiares of armes.

Item, Because the jurisdiction of the Lyon King-of-Armes is not able to execute dew punishment upon all [2] persones that sall happen

---

[1] Under 30 & 31 Vict., cap. 17, sec. 11, these penalties are payable to H.M. Exchequer.

[2] Until modern times enforcement of jurisdiction (even of the Court of Session and Privy Council) was a lengthy and costly matter in remote areas. Here, and in matters not of great financial value, the local magistracy was invoked to facilitate cheap and effective enforcement.

to offend in the office of Armes : Therefore our Soveraine Lord, with advise of his three Estaites in Parliament, ordainis and commandis all civil Magistrats, as they sall be required be the King of Armes, or ony utheris in his name, to concur with him, to see the acts maid in his favours of his office put to dew execution in their jurisdictions : As alswa to concur with him, to the punishment and incarceration of all sik persons as sall usurp the bearing of his Majestie's Armes after dew deprivation, under the pain of rebellion, and putting of the disobeyers to his Hienesse horne ; with certification to them,[1] and they failzie, being required, letters sall be direct simpliciter to put them to the horne.[2]

1672, c. 21 ; fol. edit. c. 47 (Car. II)

Concerning the Priviledges of the Office of Lyon King-at-Armes

Our Soveraigne Lord Considering that, albeit by the 125 Act of the 12 Parliament, holdin by his Maiesties grandfather in the yeir 1592, the usurpation of Armes by any of his Maiesties leidges without the authority of the Lyon King-of-Armes is expresly discharged ; And that, in order therto, Power and Commission is granted to the Lyon King-of-Armes, or his Deputes, to visite the whole Armes of Noblemen, Barrons, and Gentlemen, and to matriculate the same in their Registers, and to fine in One Hundreth pounds all others who shall unjustlie usurp Armes ; As also to Escheit all such goods and geir as shall have unwarrantable Armes ingraven on them : Yet, amongst the many irregularities [3] of these late times, very many

---

[1] This is a general certification to the " magistrates " that if, on being " required ", they fail to " concur " for the ready enforcement of the Lord Lyon's decrees, the defaulting *magistrates* will be liable to horning.

[2] Letters of Horning, on seven days' charge to pass on the Lord Lyon's decrees, are provided by another Act, 1669, cap. 95.

[3] This Act more definitely classifies certain abuses " of these late times " : (*a*) the assuming of arms by those with *no* right ; (*b*) the bearing of arms *without a proper difference*, indicating position within the family ; (*c*) " cheiff " is related to the " family " in the next clause, and the whole Act is based on the Realm—organised on a *familial* basis in which the great and numerous families (in Gaelic *clans*) and their Hereditary representative (*called* " chief ") were the operative units in both civil life and military defence.

have assumed to themselvis Armes, who should bear none, and many
of these who may in law bear, have assumed to themselvis the Armes
of their cheiff, without distinctions, or Armes which were not caried
by them or their predicessors: Therfore His Maiestie, with advice
and consent of his Estates of Parliament, Ratifies and Approves the
forsaid Act of Parliament; And for the more vigorous [1] prosecution
thereof, Doth hereby statute and ordain that lettirs of publication of
this present Act be direct to be execute at the mercat-cross of the
heid Burghs of the Shires, Stewartries, Bailliaries of Royaltie and
Regallitie, and Royall Burrowghs, chargeing all and sundry Prelates,
Noblemen, Barons, and Gentlemen, who make vse of any Armes or
Signes armoriall, within the space of one yeir aftir the said publication, to bring or send ane account of what Armes or Signes armoriall
they are accustomed to vse; and [2] whither they be descendants of
any familie the Armes of which familie they bear, and of what
Brother of the ffamilie they are descended; With Testificats [3] from
persones of Honour, Noblemen, or Gentlemen of qualitie, anent the
verity of their having and vseing those Armes, and of their descent
as afoirsaid, to be delivered either to the Clerk of the Jurisdiction
where the persones duells, or to the Lyon Clerk at his office in
Edinburgh, at the option of the party, vpon their receipts [4] *gratis*
without paying anything therefore; Which Receipt shall be a
sufficient exoneration to them from being obleidged to produce
again, to the effect that the Lyon King-of-Armes may [5] distinguish
the saids Armes with congruent differences, and may matriculat the
same in his Bookes and Registers, and may give Armes to vertuous
and well-deserving Persones, and Extracts of all Armes, expressing
the blasoning of the Arms, vndir his hand and seall of office; For
which shall be payed to the Lyon the soume [6] of Tuentie merkes by

---

[1] These are for more effective enforcement of 1592, c. 125.

[2] They are to specify: (*a*) if they are "descendants" of the family; (*b*) specifically of what brother (*i.e.* son other than the inheritor of the chiefship) they are
descendants.

[3] Testificats are made an admissible form of proof and that from the chief of
the name or of a branch here carries considerable weight (cf. *Heraldry in Scotland*,
p. 84, No. 1).

[4] For the importance of these in the working of the Act see p. 78.

[5] The Lord Lyon *may* (not *shall*). What people *give in* is one thing; what
they were to *get matriculated* quite another. Unless the right was of "verity"
they might get nothing.

[6] Superseded by Schedules of Fees and 30 & 31 Vict., c. 17, Scg. B.

every Prelat and Nobleman, and Ten merks be every Knight and Baron, and Five merkes by every other persone bearing Armes, and noe more : And his Maiestie hereby Dispensses with any penalties that may arise be this or any preceiding Act for bearing Armes befor the Proclamation to be issued herevpon : And it is Statute and Ordained, with consent forsaid, that the said Register shall be respected as the true and unrepeallable rule of all Armes and Bearings in Scotland, to remain with the Lyons office as a publict Register of the Kingdome, and to be transmitted to his Successors in all tyme comeing : And that whosoevir shall vse any other Armes any manner of way aftir the expireing of year and day from the date of the Proclamation to be issued herevpon, in maner forsaid, shall [1] pay One Hundred pounds money *toties quoties* to the Lyon, and shall likewayes escheat to his Maiestie all the moveable Goods and Geir vpon which the saids Armes are engraven or otherwise represented : And his Maiestie, with consent forsaid, Declaires that it is onlie allowed for Noblemen and Bishopes to subscrive by their titles ; and that all others shall subscrive their Christned names, or the initiall letter therof with there sirnames, and may, if they please, adject the designations [2] of their lands, prefixing the word " Of " to the saids designations : [3] And the Lyon King-at-Armes and his Brethren are required to be carefull of informeing themselvis of the contraveiners heirof, and that they acquaint his Maiesties Councill therwith, who are hereby impowered to punish them as persones disobedient to, and contraveiners of the Law : It is likewise hereby Declared that the Lyon and his Brethren Heraulds are judges in all such causes concerning the Malversation of Messingers in their office, and are to enjoy all other priviledges belonging to their office, which are secured to them by the lawes of this kingdome, and according to former practice.

[1] Cf. footnotes 4 and 5 on 1592, c. 125.
[2] Other forms of signature being *disallowed*, are obviously null and ineffective subscriptions.
[3] This did not (as some imagine) *originate* territorial and feudal titles as designations (which are indeed here recognised as *existent*—as indeed they had been for centuries). It only prescribes the relative form of signature.

Register of the Privy Council of Scotland, 2nd Series, Vol. III, p. 594

Act in favour of the Lyon King-of-Arms against painters, goldsmiths, and others, who issue coats of arms to persons not privileged to wear them

Forsameekle as the Lords of Secreit Counsell ar informed that diverse painters and goldsmiths, gravers, cutters and others artisans takes upon thame without anie lawfull warrand or auctorite to grave, paint, cutt and give armes to all rankes of persons promiscuouslie at thair pleasure, and oft tymes to suche persons as ar not priviledged be the law of armes or be warrand frome his Majestie to weare coate armour or cognoissance of gentrie,[1] and thir painters at the funeralls of noblemen,[2] barons and gentlemen, usurpes upon thame libertie to draw thair armes and cognoissances in suche forme and order as they please, sometymes giving to persons of base birth and qualitie the armes of noblemen in haill or in part, and sometymes giving to noblemen under the degree and rankes of marquieses and dukes and to knights some part of the armes onlie dew to marqueises and dukes, so as thir ignorant painters, following the directioun of these who imployes thame at thair funeralls, and without anie knowledge in themeselffes what is right or wrong, drawes thair armes accordinglie, quhairby the nobilitie and gentrie of good ranke and qualities ar verie farre wronged and persons ignoble be directioun of thir ignorant painters assumes to thameselffes the armes in haill or in part of noblemen and barons of qualitie; quhilk abuse is most disgracefull to this kingdome and caryes with it ane foule imputatioun, as if there wer nather order nor rankes of persons within the same. And thairfoir the Lords of Secreit Counsell, following his Majesteis directioun and command in this mater, hes recommendit and recommends[3] to the Lyoun King of Armes and to his care and diligence the reformatioun of this abuse throughout the haill parts of this kingdome; and for the better executioun heirof[4] ordains and com-

---

[1] Arms are recognised by the Council as insignia of social status ("gentrie" being used in the sense of *nobilitas minor*).

[2] The word "nobleman" is used in the restricted seventeenth-century sense of "peer" (*i.e.* the higher section of *nobilitas major*), but in 1592, c. 125, "noble" is correctly applied to the whole *nobilitas*.

[3] The term "recommend" recognises that the powers were already in Lyon.

[4] The Act is for the *more effective* execution of the laws and suppression of the abuses.

mands the haill painters within this kingdome to exhibite to the said
Lyoun King of Armes all thair bookes of armes, genealogeis, papers
and others draughts concerning this purpose to be seene and con-
sidderit be him, to the intent that after his perusall thairof and
notice of the samine made to the Lords of his Majesteis Privie
Counsell,[1] he may rectifie suche abuses and errours as is thairin and
destroy and cancell suche bookes and papers as sall be found be
him to be erroneous ; Commanding and inhibiting heirby all painters
within this kingdome that nane of thame presoome at anie tyme
heerafter to paint or give coate of armes, standard, pennoun [2] or
escutcheouns to anie noblemen or gentlemen or to anie others of
whatsomever qualitie, and that they meddle not with interments nor
funeralls, without the speciall consent and advice of the said Lyoun
herauld or his depute [3] had and obteanned to that effect, under all
highest pane, charge, cryme and- offence that they by thair diss-
obedience may incurre in this behalffe. And siclyke ordains and
commands all goldsmiths, gravers and cutters to exhibite thair saids
bookes, draughts and papers to the said Lyoun to be seene, reformed
and rectified be him ; and ordains that no goldsmiths, gravers nor
cutters within burgh sall have anie books of armes, papers or
draughts tuicheing this purpose bot onelie the deacoun of the craft,
who sall have ane perfyte booke of armes allowed and approvin be
the Lyoun, and all the rest of the craft sall follow the armes and
draught allowed and approvin be the Lyoun in the deacons booke as
said is : Discharging heirby all painters, gravers, cutters and
goldsmiths and others artisans of all painting, drawing, cutting or
carving anie armes bot according [4] . . .

[1] The notice is to ensure that the matter *has* been dealt with.

[2] The standards and pennons (of course " Ensigns Armorial ") are likewise
expressly subject to the " special consent " of Lyon or his depute and *not* left to
the devising of the armiger.

[3] The " advice " of Lyon or his depute is here the considered " advising "
judgment implied in the term " decern " in 1592, c. 125 (cf. J. H. Stevenson,
Heraldry in Scotland, pp. 436-7), and is applied to the " arms " as well as the
particular *additamenta* whereby they are in various heraldic " ensigns " displayed.
And all these uses are, if contrary to Lyon's authorisation, actings incurring
penalties.

[4] Concluding general prohibition of any attributing of arms except according
to the " Law and Order of Arms "—which is determinable in Lyon Court—or
order by Lyon if not already covered.

S

NOTE.—The course to be taken by goldsmiths and jewellers and die-sinkers is clear and simple :

(1) Ask the customer : *Is this your crest coat of arms?*
(2) *From which King of Arms is it held?* (If of older date than customer's great-great-grandfather, then, unless he is holder of an ancestral estate, suggest he should " make up progress of title ".
(3) If customer cannot answer questions (1) and (2), then suggest he read *Scots Heraldry*, or the Heraldic Chapter in *Clans, Septs and Regiments of the Scottish Highlands*.

The foregoing (which does not so strictly apply to strap and buckle badges—which are worn by followers and clansfolk, and *not as their crest*) will clarify the position as regards most customers, and prevent waste of time and money.

Remit to study a heraldic text-book will also save much waste of everybody's time, and there is little need for either party to apply to Lyon Office, and incur a series of search-fees, unless and until the customer knows (*a*) the nature of arms or crest, (*b*) what he *really* wants or is claiming.

INDEX

www.ingramcontent.com/pod-product-compliance
Lightning Source LLC
Chambersburg PA
CBHW060143280326
41932CB00012B/1611